CW00540673

Stanhopes
A closer view

A History & Handbook for
Collectors of Microphotographic Novelties

Resumés des chapitres en français

Stanhopes
A closer view
by Jean Scott

Published by: Greenlight Publishing,
The Publishing House,
119 Newland Street, Witham,
Essex CM8 1WF
United Kingdom
Tel: +44 (0)1376 521900
Fax: +44 (0)1376 521901.
email: info@greenlightpublishing.co.uk

Distributed by: K and J Scott
Highburton Collections,
42 Frankland Crescent, Poole,
Dorset BH14 9PX
United Kingdom
Tel/Fax: +44 (0)1202 747674
email: jean@stanhopes.info
www.stanhopes.info

Printed by: Buxton Press, Buxton, Derbyshire

Photographs by: Ken Scott and others as acknowledged

Translations by: Alain Soroko and Jacqueline Geoghegan

ISBN 1 8977 38 099

© Jean Scott 2002

All rights reserved. No part of this publication may be reproduced,
stored in a retrieval system, or transmitted in any form by any
means, electronic, mechanical photocopying, recording or
otherwise, without the prior permission of Greenlight Publishing.

Contents

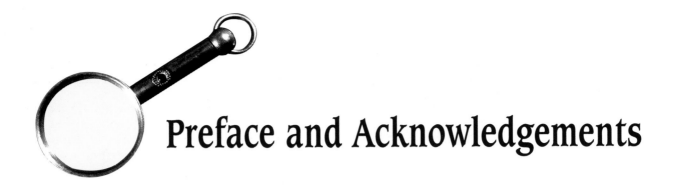

Preface and Acknowledgements

Acorns and oak trees come to mind regarding the scope of this book. However did a booklet about Stanhopes in sewing tools expand into a handbook covering most aspects of Stanhope collecting? What prompted an interest in nineteenth century microphotographs, when modern automatic cameras test the limits of my own photographic skill? Why, oh why, did an Englishwoman with a fragile grasp of the French language become immersed in a topic of research where almost the entire scenario took place across the Channel?

Gallic friends find this strange behaviour perfectly natural, convinced that I have been gripped by a *grande passion* for one of their compatriots. Why else would I insist on a pilgrimage to the birthplace of one René Prudent Patrice Dagron, handle his effects with such reverence or study his piercing gaze in fading photographs? A romantic thought, and admittedly I do harbour the greatest admiration for this handsome, but long-departed Frenchman. However, sadly for French national pride I must confess that I have been overwhelmed by a stronger force than *l'amour*: a passion for research! Other devotees will recognise the familiar feeling of deep satisfaction in finally tracing a primary source of information, the pleasure of confirming an elusive date and a gradual realisation of the true facts emerging from the veils of speculation and supposition.

I cannot remember specifically choosing to research the history of Stanhopes. At first I merely sought the answers to a few questions, after which I uncovered a little more information. Before I realised it, I was far along the trail and thoroughly addicted. I finally recognised my goal when, having followed up all the usual and known sources, I realised in frustration that I had failed to learn anything new. I became aware that many fellow collectors were asking similar questions, but the same material was being recirculated amongst us, inevitably undergoing change and alteration in the process. Frédéric Luther's book, "Microfilm: A History from 1839-1900", was published in 1959, and most articles written about Stanhopes since then have drawn heavily on this one source. In recent years many Stanhope novelties have been discovered, and more people are collecting them. Yet nobody has been able to reveal where and how the actual Stanhope lens was made before the image was applied in Paris, or what happened to the microphotographic industry after René Dagron's death in 1900.

I later wondered at my temerity in starting this project, for there are many collectors with more impressive collections than mine, and others have a lifetime of expertise in handling nineteenth century cameras or understanding early photographic processes. I did have two distinct advantages, however: some of our dearest friends live in France, and I have a husband who speaks and reads French with ease and enjoyment. To these were added my own growing enthusiasm and a series of unexpected but heartwarming coincidences, eventually leading me to new and invaluable archive material. The amount and quality of this information convinced me that if I succeeded in completing my research, it must be made available to anyone else who shares my fascination for Stanhopes, for the sharing of knowledge among collectors is fundamental to their understanding and enjoyment of any collectable.

First and foremost, this book is a tribute to the Dagron family of Paris and the Reymond family from the Gex region. The great-grandfather of Georges Dagron established the microphotographic industry in Paris in 1859, and the father of Roland Reymond finally ceased the commercial manufacture of Stanhope lenses in Gex in 1972. Both families are justly proud of the achievements of their forefathers, and have carefully preserved documents, photographs and artefacts recording their hard work and dedication to the industry. The Dagrons and the Reymonds both demonstrated a warmth and generosity of spirit, and without their willing and enthusiastic co-operation I would have been unable to achieve the scope of this book. Their documentation has enabled me to chart the progress of the Stanhope industry in France from start to finish.

Georges and Marie-Thérèse Dagron spread before me their wealth of historic evidence, and endured my endless questions with patience and gentle good humour. The genealogical history of the Dagrons and related families provided the answers to several puzzles, and surviving correspondence between the descendants of René and Caroline Dagron clarified many other details. Early glass photographic plates with portraits of René Dagron, his family and the Ambassador of Siam are fragile reminders of his status as "Photographer to the Emperor", long before he achieved fame as the microphotographer responsible for the success of the "Pigeon Post" during the Siege of Paris. To be able to examine the prototypes of his microphotographic glass "jewels" and dual-lens "Kinéscopes", to view them through his own hand magnifier and to study the detailed images from a box full of miniature monoculars he had thought important enough to preserve for posterity were unexpected and moving experiences. Such material provided the inspiration to expand this book from a collector's directory to a historical reference guide. Without some knowledge of René Dagron himself, a description of historical events affecting the course of his life or further evidence of his inventive mind, collectors would have remained unaware of the full extent of his contribution to the existence of the Stanhope industry in France. I am indebted to Georges Dagron for allowing me free access to his family treasures, many of which have been reproduced in this book and attributed to the "Dagron Family Archives". I am sure that all descendants of René Prudent Patrice Dagron will share a justifiable pride in this account of *"L'Inventeur"*.

Preface

I also appreciated the immediate friendliness and warmth of welcome from Roland and Danièle Reymond, touched with sadness that I met the family too late to meet Roland's father, Roger Reymond. Although the original Stanhope factory building has now been sold and the larger equipment dispersed, Roland Reymond has been able to preserve the hand tools and meticulous invoice and order books of his grandfather and father. Specimens demonstrating the different stages in the cutting and polishing processes of the Stanhope lens were shown and explained to me, and I treasure the examples he gave to me. As a young man, Roland Reymond learned how to make Stanhope lenses himself, and I share his regret that the industry has come to an end with little recognition of its original importance in the Gex region. I was delighted to receive his personal account of the method, materials and equipment used to produce Stanhope lenses, on which I have been able to base an entire chapter. This irrefutable primary source answered many queries that have perplexed Stanhope collectors, and I trust Roland's account will focus attention on a unique industry that was already fading into the mists of time and memory. Emmanuel Reymond's excellent photographs of his grandfather's workshop, and others to illustrate stages in the manufacture of Stanhope lenses, are an important record of the past, and I acknowledge his generosity in permitting me to use some of them in this book.

The Scotts and the Sorokos of Paris have enjoyed a profound *entente cordiale* for many years, and each member has made some contribution to the appearance of this book. Special thanks are due to Alain, patient translator of the chapter summaries. His sense of humour has often enhanced our visits to the *Marché aux Puces*, and we have enjoyed many lively debates concerning minor details of French history in the late nineteenth century. Marie-Christine, Alexandre, Thomas and Marine have allowed us to benefit from their vast store of Parisian lore, accrued from the experience of many generations. They have enabled me to trace the footsteps of René Dagron in the beautiful city where different generations acclaimed, then forgot, his fascinating novelties and inventions.

Our long time and cherished friends, Ann and Andy Veenhoff, the folks who live on the hill in Bièvres, deserve particular thanks for their foresight in choosing to live in the same village as the *Musée Français de la Photographie*. This local source initiated my search for Stanhope material in France, fuelling casual interest into dedicated research. In 1998, a meeting with the helpful curator, M. Bonzon, led to the discovery of a Stanhope enthusiast, M. Georges Pérot. His own research and notes about methods have helped to prevent a significant loss of historical detail about the French Stanhope industry. Meanwhile, Ann and Andy never failed to provide a haven of peace and tranquillity during hastily arranged visits for more research in their adopted country.

Another happy coincidence that enabled me to complete this book with an accurate account of the Stanhope industry in Gex was the location of my sister, Suzanne Pasche, who lives in Geneva, Switzerland, a short distance from the French border. A visit to the Gex region with her friend Vivianne Moser produced exciting results, culminating in an introduction for me to the Reymond family. The two intrepid research assistants were helped in their quest by M. Guichard, archivist at the *Mairie de Gex*, and by the kind auspices of M. Pierre Emery, family friend of the Reymonds. Another Swiss friend, Mme. Ines Keller, is thanked for her kind contribution regarding the later history of the French Imperial Family.

Inevitably, the greater part of my research took place in France, and I cannot fault the patience and efficiency of those who helped me in various official organisations. The staff at the *Institut National de la Propriété Industrielle* (the French patents office) in Paris helped me to search for the earliest microphotographic patents, and showed me examples of some of the original documents. Our visit to the *Bibliothèque Nationale de France* was also a profitable experience, during which I obtained a photocopy of the first and rarest book produced by René Dagron in 1862.

The *Musée Nicéphore Niépce* at Chalon-sur-Saône preserves a wonderful collection of Dagron cameras and an exciting amount of microphotographic memorabilia. M. François Cheval, Conservateur and Chef du Musée, was a generous and munificent host, while M. Gérard Bonnier and M. Christian Passeri spared time they could little afford to ensure that everything relevant was put at our disposal. Despite a busy programme, M. Passeri has conscientiously answered my queries on several occasions since then. I am extremely grateful for all the information and help available to me at the *Musée Nicéphore Niépce*, and am glad to acknowledge its contribution to this book for the appropriate illustrations.

Another memorable visit was to the International Museum of Photography, at George Eastman House, Rochester, New York, when the kind welcome from Joseph R. Struble, Assistant Curator, and Mark Osterman, Photographic Process Historian, made us feel privileged visitors. For the first time I was able to examine a Dagron camera, while Mark's explanations of the wet and dry collodion processes helped me to understand Dagron's success with the "Pigeon Post". Joe also provided the information which lead us to making contact with René Dagron's great-grandson, thereby enriching this book with the wonderful material preserved by Georges Dagron. Becky Simmons in the Library was quick and efficient at extracting a vast amount of documentation for us in the shortest possible time. Next time we plan to actually tour the museum itself!

Strong support for my project was provided by Douglas Jull, Chairman of the Stanhope Collectors' Club. We have both been delighted by the success of the society we founded together in 1999, and enjoy contact with members around the world. Through our club magazine, "The Peeper", we endeavour to keep members informed of interesting facts about specialist categories, record members' discoveries and warn of fraudulent activities concerning Stanhopes. Doug has been generous in lending items from his own superb collection, encouraging in his advice and enthusiastic in learning the results of my research. Many other members of the Stanhope Collectors' Club have also responded with enthusiasm to my proposed book, with additional support from friends and fellow collectors around the world. Packets began to arrive in the post containing prized novelties to be photographed, together with boxes of transparencies, selections of microphotographs and copies of useful articles. Some of my illustrations are courtesy of generous collectors who have done all they could to share the pieces they love, and I acknowledge their kind contributions, in the hope that none will be forgotten and all can share the results.

In Britain, Jo Ball, Rita Heath, Jeanne Kottler, Mike Lishman, Roy Pilling, Gillian Stannard, Phyllis Savage and Peter

Preface

Townsend have all lent items for photography, and I'm sure they will agree that a shared treasure gives twice the pleasure! A book of this type also builds on the discoveries of individual collectors, and many new avenues of research have been suggested by articles or programme presentations from friends and fellow Stanhope enthusiasts. Information about specific topics has been garnered from the following: David and Gillian Bates of Woodsetton Designworks, Jane Bowen of the Mauchline Ware Collectors' Club, John Harvey, Diane Hodges, Mike Kessler, Tom Lawson, Stephen Leonard, Bobbi London, Shirley Manaley, Norma Spicer and Anne and Terence Taylor. Molly Pearce, fount of knowledge concerning Queen Victoria and her numerous offspring and relations, has helped to identify many "royal" images. As well as the provision of valuable research information, I acknowledge Roy Pilling's meticulously detailed inventory of his collection, which has provided the model for my own recording. The sharp eyes of Jonathan Howe led to the discovery of images on dual lenses, which instigated my research into the *Kinéscope* and associated "persistence of vision" novelties, while Natalie Scott was an obliging and photogenic model.

Yet another happy coincidence lead to a meeting with Ashley Lawrence. He is a dedicated postal historian and an authority on *ballons montés* letters, and has been kind enough to check the accuracy of my chapter concerning the Franco-Prussian War and the Siege of Paris. The colourful illustrations from his own collection of memorabilia from this period were generously offered and gratefully accepted. I also thank him for proofreading my manuscript.

Reproductions of a portrait of Charles, 3rd Earl Stanhope, and a calotype of Sir David Brewster are by courtesy of The National Portrait Gallery, London. Drs. B. Bracegirdle and J. McCormick readily gave permission to reproduce the self-portrait of John Benjamin Dancer from their superb book: "The Microscopic Photographs of J. B. Dancer". This is a most appropriate illustration of the inventor of microphotography, for it was enlarged from an original but very rare glass slide collected by Dr. Bracegirdle. I thank them both for such a kind gesture.

Information and illustrations of Sunbury House, refuge to Dagron's wife and family during the Siege of Paris, were provided by the enthusiastic members of the Sunbury and Shepperton Local History Society, and I am happy to recognise the fruits of their research. Mr. Nigel Beale, Chairman of J. E. Beale plc, kindly furnished me with early prints of "The Fancy Fair" in Bournemouth and a photograph of the founder, his great-grandfather, John Elmes Beale. It has given me the greatest pleasure to prove a link between the Paris Stanhope industry and my own birthplace.

Mike Kessler, Bobbi London and Stephen Leonard, Stanhope Collectors' Club members from the U.S.A., have been most generous in their efforts to share special pieces from their own collections with a wider audience. Mike sent the major part of his collection on slide transparencies for me to study, and was patient with my many requests for further information and exact measurements. Bobbi has been interested and supportive about this project for many months, never failing to answer a request for information or elucidation. Her own article about "Miss Jewel", the Stanhope doll, is a model of historical accuracy and provided several new leads for me to follow up. Other American collectors who made contributions to this book include Christina Bertrand and Virginia Neill, both of whom sent

commemorative pieces for photography. Diana and Gary Kwader, and George Sparacio provided further information and support from across the Big Pond.

Thanks are extended to The Department of International Communication of The Business School at Bournemouth University, particularly to Jacqueline Geoghegan for proof reading and advising on the final text of the French summaries and to Hélène Lewis for inspiring Ken to maintain and improve his French.

Many collectors are frustrated by the very nature of the Stanhopes they collect. Originally the hidden images were often displayed in secrecy, but today people want to share their prized microphotographs, despite the hazards of passing them around for general perusal. Many Stanhope collectors yearn for the possibility of a pictorial record of the images in their novelties, but only a few photographic experts around the world possess the skill to make this a reality. As this book took shape, I realised that photographs of the novelties themselves were not enough. I was determined that illustrations would include reproductions of the Stanhope images. Milan Zahorcak had photographed the microphotographic images from the London and Kessler Collections, using a camera and microscope combination. His results were among the first to be published, and his contribution to the art and to this book is acknowledged with pleasure. The quality of the microphotographs produced by Terence Taylor has set standards that are difficult to match, as are those produced by Charles Horton without a microscope. I am pleased to include acknowledged samples of their work.

I began to investigate professional help to produce the numbers of views I anticipated, but although several photographic experts were interested, it seemed that they knew little more than we did about how to enlarge and reproduce microphotographic images from Stanhopes. I could afford neither the time nor the expense of waiting for others to experiment in photographing the images from my Stanhopes, so my husband Ken decided to tackle the project himself. He had already photographed my own Stanhope novelties in colour to illustrate the text, and in this book every uncredited photograph was taken by him, mainly using items from my own collection. Now Ken began the learning process of using a camera on a microscope, for thanks to Holton Machinery, his employer, we were able to borrow a microscope each weekend. Several different methods and types of film were tried and discarded before any success was achieved. Special thanks are owed to Phil Thomas and Larz Ignberg, as well as to Chris Hammond of Leeds University, for their advice enabling Ken to surmount each photographic obstacle as it occurred.

Microphotographs mounted on flat glass slides, such as those produced by J.B. Dancer, can be photographed with relative ease, but those on Stanhopes are mounted at the end of a glass cylinder about 8mm in length, which must stand on end to be photographed. In addition, the camera cannot imitate the eye by easily focussing through the magnifying lens, but can focus more easily on the reverse image from the plane surface at the opposite end. Ken became quite adept at reading the back-to-front captions, and I acquired a reputation in local photographic stores for my strange requests to "reverse the negatives before printing, please"! Here I must include my grateful thanks to the helpful staff of the photographic departments at Boots, The Square, and Jessops, Gervis Place, both of Bournemouth, Dorset.

There were many disappointments, for the eye is often forgiving where the camera is not. Scratched lenses or crazed image glasses obliterated many promising pictures, while others were impossible to photograph because the glass cylinder was badly positioned in the novelty. It was particularly difficult to reproduce images from lenses inserted in deep holes (e.g. in Cornish granite barrel charms), as insufficient light penetrated for successful photography. A similar problem was encountered with Stanhopes in novelties made of dark materials, such as bog oak, jet and wood. Nevertheless, passable images began to accumulate.

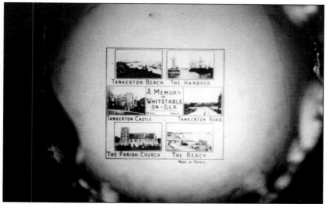

i. A topographical image from a bog oak pig charm, c. 1890. The rough edge of the circular image glass is visible in this photograph.

ii. The same image, cropped but enlarged.

In the photographs, at the magnification chosen for clarity, most images were bounded by the circular edges of the image glass. When considering how much of the original photographs to include as illustrations in this book, we chose to eliminate almost everything beyond the image frame, and then enlarge the picture itself. We also decided to use computer enhancement where necessary and possible. Others may not approve, but we preferred to aim for

the nearest possible image to that seen with the naked eye. What all readers should remember whenever they study one of these illustrations, is that each one is an enlargement of a microphotograph only 1 millimetre square: that is, the size of the head of a dressmaker's pin. The magnification can be as much as 100 times or more. Those who are more familiar with the most modern photographic and computer techniques may produce superior results to our attempts; we will be happy if we can stimulate others to improve and build on our foundations.

In the interests of consistency and scale, I needed to make a decision concerning which units of measurement to use throughout the book. I chose to apply metric measurements as used by the manufacturers of Stanhopes. Collectors should familiarise themselves with these units, for due to the great differences in sizes of various Stanhope novelties, it has been impossible to establish a general rule of enlargement for the photographs. Possibly the smallest item in my own collection is a tiny silver heart-shaped bracelet charm, hallmarked for 1895, which measures 8mm in width, 9mm in length and is only 4mm thick. For illustration purposes, this item needs to be considerably enlarged.

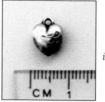

iii. Silver bracelet charm, actual size.

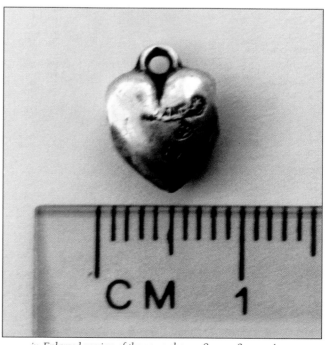

iv. Enlarged version of the same charm: 8mm x 9mm x 4mm

Preface

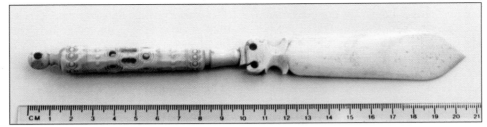

v. Bone letter opener, c. 1880: 20.3cm in length.

By contrast many larger objects, such as penholders and letter openers, are more suitably dimensioned in centimetres. The illustrations of such items need to be reduced in size.

Whether enlarged or reduced, the true size of each novelty is recorded in the caption, unless "actual size" is specified. Incidentally, even centimetres are inappropriate for one item in my collection: a vast wooden rosary, with a Stanhope of Mont St. Michel in the crucifix. The chain of beads linked by metal loops measures 2.25 metres in length i.e. 225 centimetres, or 2250 millimetres! Such outsize rosaries are still produced in several Mediterranean countries as souvenirs of visits to a religious shrine, and are brought back to be hung on the wall of the family home.

vi. Outsize wooden rosary, showing the crucifix contrasted with a bone crucifix of standard size.

A final comment concerns the value of Stanhope souvenirs in the nineteenth century. In 1862 the cost of Dagron's "photographic cylinders" in London was one shilling, then equivalent to 1.25 French francs or 50 U.S. cents. In 1864 the price of a single Stanhope lens on which a specially ordered microphotograph had been mounted was 5 French francs. However, three years later itinerant hawkers at the *1867 Exposition Universelle* were selling complete novelties for as little as 50 centimes (0.5 francs). This would have been the approximate price of transport from the Paris suburbs to the exhibition site. However, although the majority of Stanhope items acquired a reputation as cheap "throwaway" souvenirs, a considerable number were quite expensive, and have remained so. At one end of the scale were the mass-produced bone binoculars, penholders and crucifixes, with prices well within the reach of all but the most poverty-stricken. At the other were the early gold watch fobs and jewellery, followed later by well-designed Stanhope items, such as small metal mechanical pencils. These were produced in smaller numbers and sold at higher prices. The original differences in availability and cost are reflected in the wide range of values of Stanhope novelties in the modern antiques trade.

I reserve particular thanks for Alan Golbourn of Greenlight Publishing, who has graduated from novice to authority on Stanhopes within the space of a few months! He has listened to and advised me from our first meeting, and I have appreciated his constant encouragement and determination to help me achieve the best result. Matt Lawrence has been knowledgeable and meticulous in building up a comprehensive and valuable database of contacts in the world of Stanhope collecting, and its use in promoting this book. He also redesigned all my diagrams at a late stage, when my own efforts proved unsatisfactory.

I have left the best until last, though. In addition to the many weary hours of photography, Ken has made such a major contribution to this book that it would have been a poor effort without his help and support. His knowledge of French has smoothed the path for me on many occasions, in telephone conversations, letters, translations and explanations. He has proofread my manuscript, found the answers to numerous queries and produced most of the illustrations for this book by photographing the novelties and the microphotographs they contained. Many hours were spent enlarging and enhancing the latter, providing collectors with a large selection of images for comparison with their own examples. He has also accepted with equanimity my long-term relationship with René Dagron, which in recent months has developed into a positive obsession! Throughout our marriage he has always supported my projects and helped me to reach my goals, no matter how far-fetched they seemed. This time he has enabled me to realise a dream. So, with love for his endless encouragement, I dedicate this book to Ken, the real and living object of my devotion, with an assurance that the regime of convenience foods is at an end, and a promise that he will never again run out of clean socks!

I hope my thanks have been all-inclusive, but should I have been ill mannered enough to forget anyone who has helped in any way towards the completion of this book, I hope they will blame but forgive only me.

Jean Scott, February 2002.

Why the "Stanhope"?

Many collectors of small antiques will remember their delight and amazement when they first became aware that some articles contain a hidden extra: a "peep" or "Stanhope". Those who know what to look for can be spotted at antiques fairs and markets, standing motionless with uplifted elbow and squinting ferociously at a small object held close to one eye. They gaze fixedly towards the light, then a satisfied exclamation and a smile of pleasure indicate that the secret has been revealed.

1. The Stanhope collector's familiar pose!

An uninitiated but curious observer, deciding upon a closer inspection of the item, will discover a small circular glass "bead" set into one side or camouflaged among the decoration, with another on the reverse. In fact, these "beads" are the opposite ends of a single rod-shaped magnifying lens. When this is held upwards and focused towards a light source, it reveals a miniature black and white photograph, like a tiny window through which one can gaze entranced at people and places of long ago.

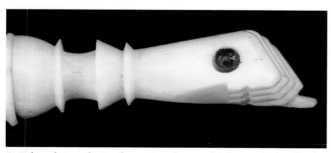

2. Enlarged view of a Stanhope microphotographic lens in the handle of a bone needle case, c. 1870. (Actual diameter of "glass bead": 2mm)

Meanwhile, the dealer looks on benignly, knowing well that a higher price can be asked for any collectable containing a Stanhope. Those in good condition, with dated or unusual views, are much sought after and can augment the price of some otherwise unpretentious object from the past, whilst competition from specialist Stanhope collectors further inflates the value.

Qu'est-ce que le Stanhope ?

Certains petits objets de collection contiennent une surprise cachée: un "Stanhope". C'est une lentille grossissante miniature dans laquelle une photographie microscopique peut être visualisée. Beaucoup de ces objets "bijoux photomicroscopiques" datent de plus de cent ans, et ont été vendus en grandes quantités comme souvenirs en Europe et aux Etats-Unis. Aujourd'hui il est difficile d'en trouver et ils coûtent cher .

Lord Charles Stanhope (1753-1816) inventa une lentille cylindrique grossissante avec deux surfaces de courbure inégale. Une version ultérieure offrit une surface bombée à une extrémité et une surface plate à l'autre. Cinquante ans après, son invention fut associée à une microphotographie pour produire un objet que l'on appelle depuis 1860 environ un "Stanhope". Lord Stanhope aurait été étonné de voir son invention noble et scientifique utilisée pour produire des articles de souvenir bon marché.

During the latter part of the nineteenth century, a great number of inexpensive souvenir articles containing Stanhopes was widely available in Britain, most European countries and the U.S.A., yet today they are relatively scarce. It is true that the material, design and function of many everyday objects or souvenirs of that era rendered them unsuitable for the insertion of such a lens, but others were produced in tens of thousands. Given their early popularity, why should a collector need to search so diligently for such items today?

The reasons are easily explained. The majority of Stanhope souvenirs were so readily available and commonplace that few purchasers felt the need to cherish and preserve them for a future generation. Many were lost because of their small size, and others were discarded when their

Why the "Stanhope"?

images were no longer topical. Also, and perhaps of more interest to a collector, in many cases the location of the microphotographic picture in some novelties became forgotten, remaining undetected for decades. Close observation of likely collectables has resulted in the discovery of many delightful examples in recent years, but there is still an element of "treasure hunting" when searching for Stanhopes which is lacking in other antiques quests. Many have been found in Victorian "toys", a term suggesting children's playthings, but often applied to adult novelties. These were any decorative or utilitarian objects that incorporated an element of surprise and amusement. Those containing Stanhopes certainly fulfil this requirement, and collections of many different categories of small antiques would be incomplete without a selection of these unusual and fascinating items.

For many years the internationally acceptable name for this type of miniature viewer with a microphotographic image has been "Stanhope". The term commemorates one of the many inventions of Charles, third Earl Stanhope (1753 – 1816). Lord Stanhope was an eminent eighteenth century English politician, a brilliant experimental scientist and a practical inventor. Although several of his inventions contributed to the growth of the machine age in Britain during the Industrial Revolution, Lord Stanhope was none the less a supporter of the rights of the common man.

At this time the microscope was one of the foremost scientific instruments, revealing much that had been previously veiled from human eyesight by reason of minute size. One of Lord Stanhope's inventions was a quality hand-magnifying lens of unusual design: a double-convex lens, having two surfaces of unequal curvatures. These were

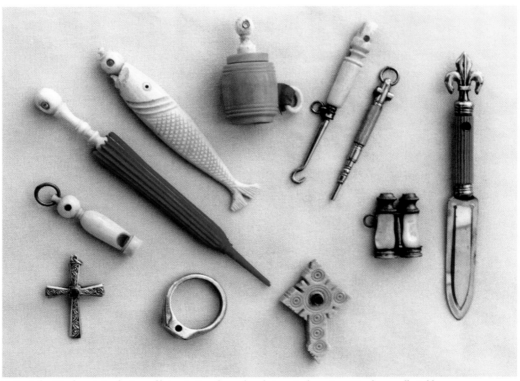

3. Spot the Stanhope! A selection of late nineteenth- and early twentieth-century Stanhope collectables.

Although Stanhope novelties are beginning to command high prices at auction, their true value is not financial, but lies in the photographic discoveries and dedication of their inventors, and in the historical details they portray. To discover and understand their origin encourages a proper appreciation of these small treasures.

The "peep" made its appearance in the mid-nineteenth century, yet it was inspired by a series of scientific discoveries spanning the previous fifty years. It was achieved by combining two important inventions: the microphotograph and the tiny rod-shaped lens through which to view it. The lens had been perfected several decades before the earliest microphotographs originated, but there were to be many years of experiment and discovery in photography before the two became united. As often happened, a popular and very commercial Victorian "toy" was the by-product of other more important inventions.

separated from each other by a considerable thickness of glass, and the distance between them was calculated so that when the more convex lens was turned towards the eye, minute objects placed on the opposite curved surface appeared within the focus of the lens. This hand viewer enabled amateur enthusiasts to study the natural world around them without resorting to the microscope and the preparation of glass slides. Later, the rod-shaped lens was adapted to incorporate a single curved surface at one end, with a plane surface at the other, which made it even easier to view small items. The "Stanhope lens" was said to be particularly useful for observing the scales on butterfly wings, which readily adhered to the flat surface of the glass.

Half a century later this lens resurfaced across the English Channel to assume a leading position in the world of cheap mass-produced souvenirs. Although "Stanhope" originally referred only to the type of lens, the term is now used for the entire unit, including the microphotographic image itself. No doubt Lord Stanhope would have been astonished and intrigued at the way in which one of his noble inventions was adapted in a popular novelty.

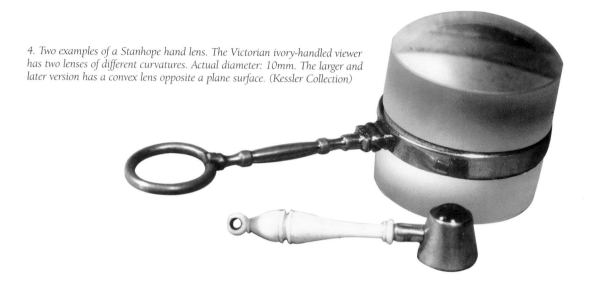

4. Two examples of a Stanhope hand lens. The Victorian ivory-handled viewer has two lenses of different curvatures. Actual diameter: 10mm. The larger and later version has a convex lens opposite a plane surface. (Kessler Collection)

5. Charles, 3rd Earl Stanhope, (1753-1816). This portrait in oils was exhibited by John Opie in 1803, possibly to celebrate the eminent scientist's fiftieth year. (By courtesy of the National Portrait Gallery, London.)

2 J. B. Dancer, Inventor of Microphotography

The invention of microphotography was a significant stage in the evolution of photography. Much has been written about this field of scientific discovery, but a short account of early experiments in capturing a photographic image will bring into focus the major contribution of John Benjamin Dancer, the inventor of microphotography.

The first permanent photograph using a camera was achieved in 1827 by Joseph Nicéphore Niépce of France. Later he entered into partnership with Louis Jacques Mandé Daguerre to improve the method. Niépce died before this was complete, and it was not until 1839 that Daguerre was ready to reveal to the world his "daguerreotype" process. This involved several hazardous chemical operations, all of which were usually performed by the photographer himself. A silver-coated copper plate was sensitised to light by the fumes of iodine vapour. The plate was placed in the camera and exposed to light for the photograph for several minutes. Finally, the effect of toxic fumes from a bath of heated mercury produced a positive image on the surface of the metal plate. In Britain, William Henry Fox-Talbot invented the "calotype" process the following year. His method was the first to make possible the repeated production of identical positive prints on paper of an image from a single negative plate.

John Benjamin Dancer (1812-1887) inherited his father's successful optical business in Liverpool. He became a designer and manufacturer of optical and other scientific instruments, and having mastered the new photographic processes, began to make and sell daguerreotype cameras. He also experimented with combining the techniques of photography and microscopy by installing a microscope lens in a camera. As early as the end of 1839, J. B. Dancer succeeded in producing a miniature photo-

6. Enlargement of a microphotograph from glass slide No. 33: "J. B. Dancer F.R.A.S. The Originator of Micro-Photography". (By courtesy of B. Bracegirdle and J. B. McCormick, authors of "The Microscopic Photographs of J .B. Dancer")

graph, the earliest microphotograph on record. The object, a document twenty inches long, had been reduced 160 times by the lens until the image measured only one-eighth of an inch in length. When the picture was mounted on a glass slide and viewed through a microscope to a magnification of 20x, the document was legible. Dancer was not completely satisfied with this achievement, for the quality of the image was impaired by the opaque background of the daguerreotype.

In 1841 Dancer moved his business to Manchester, where he introduced photography to that city. He made many influential friends in the scientific world, supplying them with high quality microscopes and other instruments, specifically designed for their experiments. He continued to make microphotographs on daguerreotype plates, but at this stage considered them novelties of no commercial value, apart from demonstrating the techniques and high quality of his camera and microscope lenses.

For several years photographic scientists experimented to find an alternative to the metal plate. The most successful was Frederick Scott Archer, also of Manchester. In 1850 he produced a very fine grain image on a glass plate coated with collodion emulsion and sensitised by immersion in silver nitrate. The best results were produced when the photographic plates were exposed while the film of collodion was still wet and sticky. J. B. Dancer found that the "wet plate" collodion process enabled him to develop many new ideas, such as photographic slides for the popular "magic lantern", and the first twin-lens stereoscopic camera. Eventually the finer detail possible with this process encouraged him to aim for higher quality microphotographs. In February 1852 Dancer achieved the first "wet plate" microphotograph, mounting the resulting collodion film with the positive image on a standard microscope slide.

J. B. Dancer : l'inventeur de la microphotographie

John Benjamin Dancer (1812-1887) était un fabricant britannique d'instruments optiques et scientifiques. Il s'était intéressé à la photographie et commença à fabriquer des appareils photographiques. Ses premières expériences lui permirent de produire la première microphotographie, en utilisant le procédé du daguerréotype. Après le développement de la technique du collodion humide il réussit à obtenir une microphotographie sur film de collodion en 1852. Celui-ci fut monté sur une lamelle et visualisé à l'aide d'un microscope.

Sir James Brewster (1781-1866) encouragea la promotion des lamelles photomicroscopiques de Dancer pendant un voyage en Europe en 1856-7. Il imagina d'utiliser des pierres semi-précieuses adaptées et montées dans des pièces de bijouterie pour visualiser des microphotographies. De tels assemblages devinrent très à la mode. Il exposa des lamelles de Dancer à Paris, et un grand nombre de photographes commencèrent alors à expérimenter la réduction d'images.

Dancer montra le "Micrograph" à l'Exposition Universelle de Londres en 1862. C'était un petit ensemble d'objectifs de poche avec une douzaine de lamelles micrographiques rondes. En 1880 Dancer devint aveugle, et bien que ses deux filles aient continué le commerce pendant quelques années, ce fut la fin d'une ère pour les lamelles photomicroscopiques. Elles étaient considérées trop fragiles et trop grandes, et avaient été éclipsées depuis de nombreuses années par les efforts d'un Français, René Dagron.

During his early experiments, whenever Dancer produced a good quality microphotograph, he mounted it on a microscope slide, signed the glass with a diamond and presented it to one of his scientific friends. In April 1853 he made a further kind gesture. William Sturgeon, famous in the mid-Victorian era for his experiments and discoveries in the field of electricity, had died in Manchester in 1850. His friends had commissioned a marble wall tablet for Kirkby Lonsdale Church, recording his achievements. J. B. Dancer was asked to photograph the tablet, which he did using a negative of standard size. He then decided to copy the image as a microphotograph, and reduced the inscription consisting of 755 letters within a frame of 2mm. He mounted several of these miniature photographs on glass microscope slides, and presented them to Sturgeon's

friends. They were surprised and touched to receive these unusual memorials, and much interest was aroused locally by their display and distribution.

In 1854 the term "microphotograph" for highly reduced photographs was used in print for the first time. George Shadbolt, editor of "The Photographic Journal", used a similar method to J. B. Dancer and applied the term "microphotographs" to some examples he had produced for sale to a London manufacturer of microscopes. As a result, it was several years before Dancer achieved public recognition as the first person to produce microphotographic slides. George Shadbolt mistakenly believed he had produced the earliest example and took all the credit for this for many years. Eventually the existence of Dancer's 1853 slide of Sturgeon's memorial stone would furnish the necessary proof to acknowledge him officially as "the inventor of microphotography".

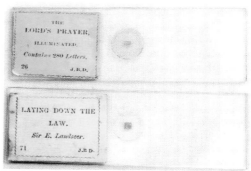

7. Slides produced by J. B. Dancer.
The microphotograph is within the circle: diameter 10mm.

8. Microphotograph image from J. B. Dancer Slide No. 26:
"The Lord's Prayer, Illuminated", which contains a total of 280 letters.

Although Dancer had originally used his microphotographic slides to promote the excellence of his microscope lenses and cameras, their popularity made him realise that they had a commercial application in their own right. Despite the time-consuming method of fabrication, he started to produce them in considerable quantities. The slides bore green, yellow or white labels with the title of the image. The majority of them were numbered, and generally included his initials "J.B.D." They revealed views of famous places, royal portraits, eminent Victorians and assorted text material, such as quotations from the Bible, memorial

J. B. Dancer

tablets, poems and bank notes. Dancer began to supply them to dealers locally and further afield, and eventually his slides were sold in the novelty shops of London. His photographic curiosities had found a lucrative market, and soon many Victorian homes began to display a microscope and series of slides on different subjects to view as a parlour entertainment.

One of the friends to receive a gift of slide-mounted microphotographs from J. B. Dancer was Sir David Brewster (1781-1866), a well-known Scottish physicist. The slides fuelled Brewster's own enthusiasm for microphotography, and he became a great admirer of their inventor. Towards the end of 1856, Brewster embarked on extended European travels and took with him examples of Dancer's expertise. He was determined to further his friend's interests and to gain for him international recognition for his contribution to photographic progress. Brewster realised

10. A calotype of Sir David Brewster (1781-1866), photographed by David Octavius Hill and Robert Adamson in 1843. (By courtesy of the National Portrait Gallery, London.)

9. Microphotographic image from J. B. Dancer Slide No. 71: "Laying Down the Law", from a painting by Sir Edwin Landseer .

that microscopes were not always readily available to view the slides, and decided to take with him a powerful hand magnifier. He himself had designed a suitable instrument in 1820, which had become known as the "Coddington Lens". A deep groove was ground around the central circumference of a complete sphere of glass. This was filled with "opaque matter" and the resulting lens gave a wide field of view. A Mr. Coddington of Cambridge had ordered a hand magnifier to be made for him to Brewster's specifications, and the optician referred to it as the "Coddington Magnifier", mistakenly assuming that his customer had been the inventor.

Brewster spent the winter months in the warmth of Italy, and displayed Dancer's slides everywhere. He later wrote that "Mr. Dancer's photographs were exhibited...to the Pope and Cardinal Antonelli at Rome, and at Florence to the young Grand Duke and Grand Duchess of Tuscany, the Marquis of Normandy, Professor Amici and others". The enthusiastic and well-connected traveller also visited a distinguished jeweller, Signor Fortunato Castellani, and as Brewster viewed the cut and polished stones he was inspired with a novel idea. He suggested to Castellani "the

idea of constructing brooches containing precious stones, so that the photographs might be placed within them, and magnified by one of the precious stones, or by colourless topaz or quartz formed into a lens". The jeweller concurred, and his interpretation was well received, rapidly developing into a new fashion trend.

Sir David Brewster reached Paris late in the spring of 1857 and Dancer's microphotographs caused much excitement amongst French photographers. Parisian jewellers were similarly inspired by Brewster's idea for microphotographic jewellery, but any items they produced were individual and expensive. Brewster returned to England, his enthusiasm for Dancer's achievements undiminished. He wrote an article for the eighth edition of "The Encyclopaedia Britannica" (Volume 14), published in October 1857. He stated: "Among the wonders of microscopic photography are the fine microscopic portraits taken by Mr. Dancer of Manchester, and copies of monumental descriptions so minute, that the figures in one, and the letters in the other, are invisible to the eye. A family group of seven complete portraits occupies a space the size of the head of a pin, so that ten thousand single portraits could be included in a square inch."

Microphotography was becoming the sensation of the era, and Sir David Brewster suggested several other possibilities concerning its use apart from jewellery or entertainment. He wrote: "Microscopic copies of despatches and valuable papers and plans might be transmitted by post, and secrets might be placed in spaces not larger than a full stop or a small blot of ink." None of these suggestions conveyed any financial reward to Dancer, the inventor of microphotography, but Sir David Brewster's articles were responsible for gaining much deserved recognition for his friend.

At the 1862 International Exhibition in London Dancer introduced a variation in format of his microphotographic slides. J. B. Dancer materials and equipment were exhibited in "Class 14", and among these was "The Micrograph". This was a neat little pocket set containing a dozen microphotographs in a rectangular case. This time they were mounted on glass slide discs only 1.7cm in diameter, fitting into two rows of plush-lined slots. With them was a small viewing lens through which the discs could be viewed. The case also included an instruction sheet for using the Micrograph.

By 1871 the business of J. B. Dancer employed eight men and about four apprentices. The 1873 trade catalogue for microphotographic slides from his Manchester premises offered 277 different titles at one shilling each, or ten shillings and sixpence per dozen. Inevitably, Dancer's idea was copied by several competitors, each of whom produced different commercial series of slides. These included Edmund Wheeler and W. Watson & Son, both microphotographic slide manufacturers in London, and several others identified on the slide labels only by their initials. Microphotographic slides from European manufacturers have also been discovered: J. D. Möller of Prussia and J. J. Zaalberg van Zeist of Amsterdam.

lantern", and established the "American Stereoscopic Company". They also began to produce microscopic photographs mounted on glass slides, and in their 1861 catalogue thirty-three different examples were offered for sale. These included "Portraits and Views taken from Nature", and well-known events and personalities from the American Civil War. Printed documents were also available, such as "The Lord's Prayer" and "The Declaration of Independence". The latter was "surrounded with the Portraits of the Presidents and the Coats of Arms of the Thirteen Original States", and contained 7850 letters. The catalogue noted that "every sentence in this memorable document, every signature and every portrait is revealed distinct and clear". This particular slide cost $1.00, but the other specimens, being "less difficult to produce", were priced at 75cents each. Following William Langenheim's death in 1874, the business and photographic equipment, including lenses for microscopic photographs, were sold.

J. B. Dancer continued to manufacture microphotographic slides, but some years before his death in 1887, his eyesight began to fail; he was no longer able to guarantee personally the quality of his microscopes. The optical side of the family business began to deteriorate, leaving just the income from photographic commissions. Dancer had passed on his photographic expertise to his daughters, Elizabeth Eleanor and Catherine, who continued making microphotographic slides while he was incapacitated, and for several years after his death. In 1896 they sold any remaining microphotographic negatives and the process instructions to Richard Suter, a London microscope dealer and specialist mounter of slides. In 1900 he advertised 512 different titles of microphotographic slides from the J. B. Dancer stock, although some of these have yet to be found by collectors. Previous competitors no longer seemed to be in business, for the advertisement stated "Mr. R. Suter is now the only preparer of Micro-Photographs." At the start of the twentieth century, these fragile souvenir microphotographs mounted on glass were no longer considered practical or financially viable. Indeed, a different format had overtaken their popularity many years before. Like that of the long-dead Lord Stanhope, J. B. Dancer's contribution to the invention of "peeps" had been eclipsed by the efforts of another. It was a Frenchman who had combined the two British inventions into a single innovative unit.

11. "The Micrograph", produced by J. B. Dancer in 1862.
Actual diameter of circular glass slide: 1.7cm (Kessler Collection)

Meanwhile, on the opposite side of the Atlantic, the Langenheim brothers were enjoying success in a similar field. William and Frederick Langenheim were German immigrants who had established a photography business in Philadelphia, Pennsylvania, in 1842. They tried out the photographic processes originating from Europe, and experimented to achieve better results themselves. The Langenheim Brothers were particularly successful in developing slides of excellent quality for the "magic

3 René Dagron and Mass-produced Microphotography

Almost one hundred miles west of Paris, on the fringes of the Forest of Perseigne in the Sarthe region, can be found the twin villages of Aillières-Beauvoir. In Napoleonic times it was recorded that Beauvoir existed independently, although it numbered less than three hundred inhabitants and only sixty-four *feux* or hearths. The Dagron family had lived in the surrounding area for generations, as farm labourers, innkeepers and wardens of the forest. On 17th March 1819 René Louis Dagron, the local tax collector and landowner, arrived at the Town Hall to register the birth that morning of his new son. Witnesses were prominent worthies from the surrounding villages: M. Prudent Bourderon, the magistrate from La Fresnaye, M. René Pierre Morel, a farmer and relation from Louzes, and M. Bouton, the Mayor of Beauvoir. The infant was baptised with the names of Prudent Patrice René, although it was to be the last that became familiar in the photographic world. He was the fourth child born to René Louis and Cathérine Louise Dagron, and eventually the family was blessed with seven children.

12. The birthplace of René Dagron, (1819-1900). Detail from "A New Map of the North-west Part of France Divided Into Its Departments, with the Most Frequented Routes to Paris", produced by R. Laurie and J. Whittle in 1802 and published in 1807.

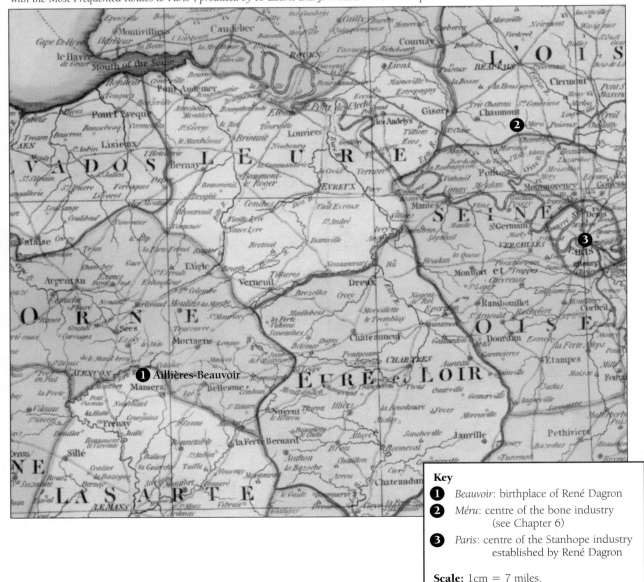

Key
❶ *Beauvoir*: birthplace of René Dagron
❷ *Méru*: centre of the bone industry (see Chapter 6)
❸ *Paris*: centre of the Stanhope industry established by René Dagron

Scale: 1cm = 7 miles.

The Dagron home was situated in the centre of Beauvoir, and beyond it the track led gently uphill, soon to be swallowed in the depths of the quiet beech forest. The house was stone built, with deep-set windows and a steeply sloping roof of terracotta tiles. It still stands today, although the walls have been smoothly resurfaced, and grey tiles have replaced the faded and sunken roof. Modern square windows allow light to penetrate the spacious loft where the Dagron children slept almost two centuries ago.

13. *The birthplace of René Prudent Patrice Dagron at Beauvoir (now Aillières-Beauvoir), in the Department of la Sarthe.*

Life could be hard in this rural community, and most families cultivated the soil, tended the cider orchards or were engaged in forestry. However, René Louis Dagron's status enabled the family to enjoy some degree of comfort. Remaining examples of his elegant handwriting are evidence of his own good education, and his children must have received the same attention. Certainly his fourth child was able to develop an enquiring mind, leading to a lifelong fascination for physics and chemistry. Perhaps with too many siblings to share the family inheritance at Beauvoir, René Dagron decided that his fortune lay beyond the boundaries of his birthplace. In time-honoured fashion, at the age of seventeen years, he left the village and travelled to Paris to make his way in the world. Little is known about his early years in Paris, although one can guess that the young man was amazed by the frenetic pace and clamour of central Paris after the tranquillity of the Sarthe countryside. Dagron found work during the day, reportedly with a coal-merchant, but persevered with his studies in the evening.

On 1st October 1846 René Dagron married eighteen-year-old Angela Caroline Lendy, known as Caroline. It was an excellent match for René, the country tax-collector's son, for his young wife was very well-connected on her father's side. Her grandfather had been a Swiss Guard in the service of the Pope, and her father, Captain Armand Lendy, had an illustrious military career. His rapid promotions caused the family to travel extensively, and Caroline had been born in southern France at the foot of the Pyrenees. Family documents include Captain Lendy's appointment by King Charles X as *Chevalier de l'Ordre royal de la Légion d'Honneur*. Certainly any wealth and influence

appears to have originated from Caroline's family, which may have been the reason for her strong position in the Dagron family. No photographs exist of the wedding, but there is a single portrait of René Dagron taken a few years later that reveals the confident and handsome man-about-town who had captured Caroline's heart.

In 1849 René Louis Dagron wrote from Aillières to send New Year's greetings to the family. He addressed his daughter-in-law in the most affectionate terms, and described his delight at the birth of his new grand-daughter, Pauline Angèle; advanced age had prevented him from travelling to Paris to see her. In a postscript he asked a single question about his son: *"Que fait Dagron?"* ("What is Dagron up to?") At this time the young family was living at *22 rue Poissonnière*, the first of several addresses within the same small area of central Paris where the Dagron family took up residence. It is known only that René Dagron was thirty years of age by this time, and from the manner of the envelope address, employed at the same place where they lived. Four years later they were living at *121 rue Montmartre*, and during 1855-56 he was selling *pâtes alimentaires et tapioca des îles* (pasta and tapioca) at *191 rue du Vieux Columbier*. It is not known when René Dagron first became interested in photography, but at some time during

14. *An early photographic portrait of René Dagron, c. 1849 (Dagron Family Archives.)*

René Dagron

these years he worked for a Parisian photographer. Gradually he began to master all the complicated chemical processes involved in achieving permanent photographic images. Possibly Caroline's family had been unimpressed by her husband's lack of commercial success previously, but eventually it was his photographic expertise which was to change the situation.

Shortly before 1859 Dagron was able to establish his own photographic business at *66 rue Neuve des Petits-Champs*, on the corner of *rue d'Antin*. This address was close to the *Place Vendôme*, in a bustling area of shops and other small businesses. It was within easy distance of the beautiful *Jardin des Tuileries* and near many of the most imposing examples of architecture toured by visitors to Paris. Dagron hoped to prosper by taking photographic portraits of prominent Parisians and foreign visitors, but a large part of his business included the wholesale production of *cartes de visite*, the latest fashionable accessory throughout Europe. These were small photographic portraits, distributed and collected by friends and acquaintances, and popular with everyone, including Queen Victoria herself. By this time Caroline Dagron had given birth to her fourth child, and Pauline had been joined by two sisters and a young brother, Fernand René.

After Sir David Brewster had exhibited J. B. Dancer's microphotographic slides in Paris, several French photographers began to experiment with the new process. By 1859, the *Salon de Photographie* in Paris featured displays of microphotographs by Nachet, Wagner and Bernard, and their work was praised as *"la merveille de l'exposition"*. All examples still needed to be viewed through a microscope or powerful hand viewer. René Dagron's name was not included amongst those who exhibited their microphotographs on this occasion, but in view of later events it is certain that he was aware of the new photographic process and had mastered it himself.

By the time Dagron had reached his fortieth year, he had still achieved only moderate success as a portrait photographer. However, he had become certain that microphotography pointed the way to future prosperity, and sought to utilise this invention in some type of novelty business. The boulevards of central Paris were crowded with tourists, and the fashionable salons and international exhibitions were thronged with visitors. Dagron was aware of the thriving trade in cheap souvenirs, and wondered if one of these could be combined with a microphotograph. Unlike other photographers with similar commercial ideas, it was the viewing method that occupied Dagron's thoughts, rather than the microphotograph itself. Dancer's fragile glass slides holding the images needed careful handling and required substantial viewing equipment. Quality jewellers had already copied Brewster's suggestion for photographic jewellery, using magnifying lenses ground from precious stones, but these were too costly for the extensive market anticipated by Dagron. He planned to combine an "all-in-one" microphotograph and magnifying viewer in a single unit of extremely small scale and very low cost. At this time he had additional workshop premises a few streets away at *rue des Bons Enfants*, and it was here that his invention was designed and perfected.

It is unlikely that the idea for Dagron's first microphotographic novelty occurred overnight, but a story reported in *The Constitutionel* a few years later describes a possible inspiration for his invention. It seems that an unidentified but important person was madly in love with a beautiful

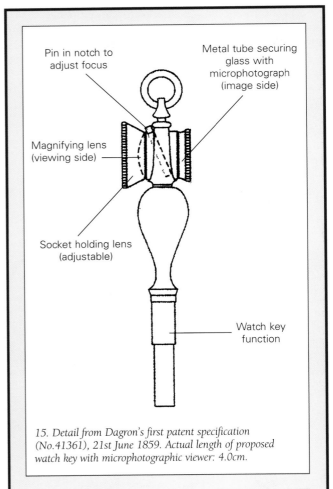

15. Detail from Dagron's first patent specification (No.41361), 21st June 1859. Actual length of proposed watch key with microphotographic viewer: 4.0cm.

16. An early Stanhope watch key novelty produced by "Dagron & Cie", c.1862. The image is "The Lord's Prayer". (Kessler Collection) Actual Length: 3.3cm.

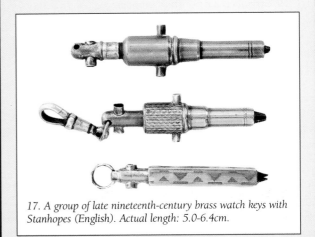

17. A group of late nineteenth-century brass watch keys with Stanhopes (English). Actual length: 5.0-6.4cm.

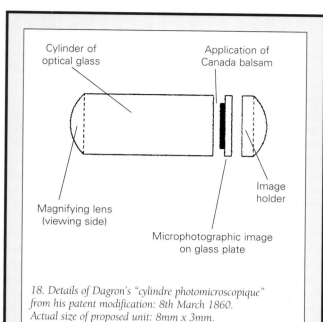

18. *Details of Dagron's "cylindre photomicroscopique" from his patent modification: 8th March 1860. Actual size of proposed unit: 8mm x 3mm.*

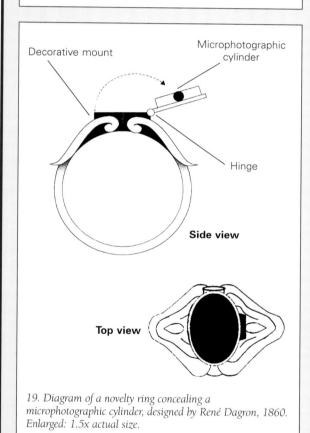

19. *Diagram of a novelty ring concealing a microphotographic cylinder, designed by René Dagron, 1860. Enlarged: 1.5x actual size.*

20. *An early gold watch fob produced by Dagron & Cie, c. 1860. It contains an erotic image entitled "Le Grenier". Actual size: 9mm x 4mm. (Jull Collection)*

lady. She spurned his advances in favour of another, and he was left with only her portrait. The lovelorn gentleman visited René Dagron and asked him to reduce the photograph of his lost love as small as possible, and place it in a ring mount so that he could always wear it. Having fulfilled his commission, Dagron was excited by the idea of "secret miniature photographs". He began to design other suitable mounts for microphotographs, whereby the image could be kept hidden until the owner chose to reveal it. Dagron remained closeted in his workshop for almost a year, and became a source of lively conjecture amongst the neighbours. Was he making counterfeit money, perhaps? Whatever the truth of this story, René Dagron's first novelty mount was incorporated in an object carried on the person of a large proportion of the male population at that time: the key that hung from a gentleman's watch chain, in order to keep his pocket watch wound regularly.

Most watch keys were quite small, measuring only 3-4 cm in length, and were produced in large numbers at minimal cost. They were made inconspicuous by their very familiarity, making them ideal holders for secret pictures. As for microphotographs, the subject matter was infinitely adaptable. Portraits of family members, royalty and personalities of the time, commemorative images of historical events and universal exhibitions, copies of great works of art and pictorial souvenirs of visits to cities, seaside resorts and religious shrines: all could be retained on a miniature image, to be admired in secret or revealed at will. Perhaps René Dagron had found a winning formula for financial success at last.

He lost no time in applying for a fifteen-year patent for his tiny invention, hoping to be protected from imitators wanting a share of the lucrative souvenir market. On 21st June 1859, represented by M. Ricordeau from the legal firm of Armengaud, who specialised in applications for inventions in France and abroad, René Dagron applied for his first patent, No. 41361. This described *"un microscope bijou à effets stéréoscopiques et propre aux observations microscopiques d'imageries, insectes, fleurs, etc."* ("A novelty stereoscopic microscope for viewing miniature pictures, insects, flowers, etc.) His patent drawings show a *"microscope nain"* (a "dwarf" or miniature microscope) mounted in a watch key, which he suggested could also be incorporated into "any other ornament or small portable article of general use".

Dagron's first patent specification described a more complicated mechanism for viewing the image than the process for which he eventually became famous. The magnifying lens was held in a socket surrounded by a ring, and fixed at one end of a metal tube. The ring could be turned to adjust the focus of the lens. There was also a small pin screwed into an inclined notch in the tube, providing a further means of obtaining a clear image. This was situated at the opposite end of the tube, and surprisingly Dagron suggested that a direct positive or a photographic image on paper were equally suitable. He requested exclusive rights to market novelties made to his design, including any variations in shape, size, decoration and material. He commented that his miniature microscopes could be inserted in lorgnettes, fans and rings, thereby widening his market to include female customers.

Dagron's patent was granted on 29th July 1859 and it must be assumed that he lost no time in manufacturing and marketing his novelty watch keys. Nevertheless, he continued to modify the process, and on 8th March 1860 he applied for additional patent coverage for a simpler

René Dagron

method. This time he described a small cylinder of glass, with the ends ground as convex lenses. The cylinder was composed of two sections of unequal length. The longer part was the magnifying component and the shorter part held the microphotographic image, which was glued to its inner surface. The two sections were joined together by optical adhesive.

The glass cylinder could also be encased in metal for additional protection, which would enable the lens to be incorporated into a much wider selection of fobs, charms and trinkets. In fact, the specification also included a design for a novelty ring in which the central ornament was "made to open on a hinge, and the miniature microscope fixed inside the lid of the hinged part". This patent modification was granted on 7th May 1860.

René Dagron et la microphotographie à grande échelle

Patrice Prudent René Dagron est né dans le hameau de Beauvoir dans la Sarthe le 17 mars 1819. La famille comptait sept enfants, et à l'âge de 17 ans René quitta son foyer pour se rendre à Paris. Il occupa diverses professions avant de trouver son métier quand il commença à travailler chez un photographe. En 1846 il épousa Caroline Lendy, et établit un studio photographique au 66, rue Neuve des Petits-Champs.

Après avoir connu le nouveau procédé de microphotographie, il chercha à éliminer le besoin d'utiliser un microscope pour visualiser les images miniatures. Ainsi, il combina l'objectif de Lord Stanhope à la microphotographie de J.B.Dancer dans une unité miniature simple, qu'il appela un cylindre photomicroscopique. Il déposa son premier brevet le 21 juin 1859 pour un appareil incorporant un microscope miniature dans une clé de montre. Les modifications postérieures inclurent une bague et des lentilles à double image de telle sorte que l'observation puisse se faire indifféremment par les deux extrémités.

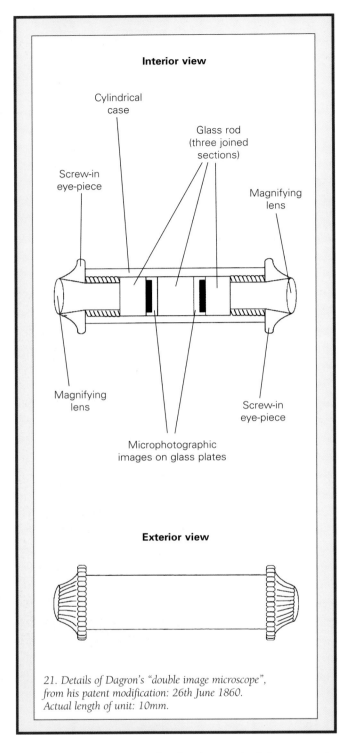

21. Details of Dagron's "double image microscope", from his patent modification: 26th June 1860. Actual length of unit: 10mm.

Dagron's inventive mind had been working on further improvements to the process, and he had already perfected a more complicated design: the "double image microscope". This permitted a different image to be viewed at either end. The instrument consisted of a cylindrical frame, into which an eyepiece with a magnifying lens could be screwed at each end. In the centre of the tube was a glass rod holding the two images apart from each other. Dagron applied for the patent on 26th June 1860 and explained in the specification: "the image only occupies the centre of the glass, to which it is made fast, so that the visual rays extend around the first image in order to give light to the second image." He was granted yet another fifteen-year patent on 21st August 1860.

Meanwhile, Dagron's legal advisors had been wisely applying for overseas patents. On 28th March 1860 the specification in English stated that "Aené (sic) Prudent Patrice Dagron of Paris, in the French Empire, Photographer", applied for letters patent for "An Improved Microscope to be used for Exhibiting Photographic Views and Productions". He included not only the designs for a watch key and a ring, but also for a double-ended microscope, which at that time he had not even applied for in France. He also suggested his invention could be used in "a key, a pencil case, or be worn on the finger as a ring, a pen or pencil holder or on any article of office, library or general use". The image could be "a calendar or almanack (sic), or other commercial or domestic reference as desired". English Patent No. 801 was granted on 27th September 1861.

22. A greatly magnified hand-written caption from "Le Grenier" microphotographic image, c.1860. (Jull Collection).

The majority of Dagron's early microphotographs were captioned in the distinctive hand-written style now known as "French script". They also included substantial advertising captions. Microphotography was still in its infancy and Dagron wanted to ensure that his name more than any other became associated with the miniature novelties he was launching on the souvenir market.

An early and rare caption is an abbreviated form of *"Reproduction microscopique"* and *"Dagron et Companie Breveté Paris"*: his business name and location, and an implied warning that his process was patented. Later captions omitted the word "microscopique" as the public became more familiar with the miniature photographs.

23. René and Caroline Dagron with four of their children, c.1859.
(Dagron Family Archives)

Caroline Dagron's older brother, Captain Auguste Frédéric Lendy, had married an English wife, Sophia Bulley. In 1855 he had leased Sunbury House at Sunbury-on-Thames, and founded the "Sunbury House Practical Artillery Institution" there. The two families kept in contact, and no doubt the Dagrons had heard about forthcoming plans for a second International Exhibition in London. By applying for English patents as soon as possible, René Dagron was trying to ensure that he stayed ahead of his competitors at home and abroad.

Protected, as he thought, by his fifteen-year patents,

Dagron began to manufacture microphotographic novelties in considerable numbers. These consisted of rings, watch keys and watch charms, such as miniature telescopes, monoculars and binoculars. Some were made in gold or silver, but for those who could only afford the cheapest novelty, turned bone was used in imitation of ivory. Penholders, letter openers and needle cases were added to the list of items produced with microphotographic views, and different images were being introduced regularly. The time had come to reach a wider market.

4 Expanding the Market

René Dagron was keen to promote his *bijoux photomicroscopiques* and bring them to the attention of the populace. He began to court the Press by using methods that would seem quite naïve today, yet they resulted in a series of articles which certainly caught the interest of the Parisian public. The first was a story, which has yet to be proved.

An article appeared in *The Constitutionel* on 23rd November 1860, which described how a most unusual ring had been found in the Champs-Élysées area and handed in to the local police station. This ring was said to be extremely valuable, as the mount included a "royal crown in diamonds and rubies and the initials 'V.A.' also in diamonds." However, beneath the mount was a hidden secret: a double-image miniature microscope, through which could be seen the portraits of Prince Albert and the Prince of Wales, with their names below the portraits. The police had already received a report of a similar item stolen from a casket of jewellery being sent by train from Paris to London.

The following day the Chief of Police received a novel claim to the recovered property. René Dagron brought with him another ring, in which the microscopic viewer revealed the text of two letters. One was written by Dagron himself, and the other was a letter from "le comte Ruland", secretary to Prince Albert. Dagron explained that the jewelled ring in the possession of the police had been included in a box of eleven items of jewellery he had despatched to Her Majesty, the Queen of England, on 17th November via *le chemin de fer du Nord*. This item had been stolen en route, to re-surface in central Paris. The Count's letter disclosed that when he showed Dagron's *bijoux photomicroscopiques* to Queen Victoria, Prince Albert and the Prince of Wales they were most pleased, and wished to keep them all. It is unlikely that Dagron could afford to present this amount of jewellery to the British Royal Family as a gift; it is more probable that the items were sent "on approval", with payment expected later.

A follow-up article appeared in *The Constitutionel* on 23rd December 1860, which reported that Dagron had sent a replacement ring to Queen Victoria, containing a different double image. This time, Windsor Castle could be seen in one view, and ten members of the Royal Family were combined in the other.

The newspaper also reported that another example of Dagron's small double-image cylinders showed a portrait of Napoleon lll at one end, and one of the Empress Eugénie

24. Composite image from a bone monocular: "La Famille Royale d'Angleterre". The inclusion of Prince Albert with Queen Victoria and their children dates this microphotograph before his death in late 1861. It was almost certainly produced by Dagron & Cie. (Jull Collection.)

at the other. Other publications began to print articles about Dagron's invention, and following such good publicity, his microphotographic trinkets became the marvel of the day. A steady stream of customers began to arrive at his studio in the *rue Neuve des Petits-Champs* to avail themselves of his latest novelties.

25. A lady's ring set with seed pearls and garnets, concealing a microphotographic cylinder, c. 1861. Although this contains a Dagron image, the design of the ring resembles Héricé's patent more than Dagron's own specification diagram. (Dagron Family Archives)

Dagron's success was the envy of his many competitors, and several of these made patent applications for their own variations of magnifying viewers for microphotographs. The first was Louis Eugène Adolphe Martinache, a Parisian optician and jeweller, who applied for Patent No. 49123 for a miniature viewer on 4th April 1861. His specification described a cylindrical tube of any suitable material, with separate glass ends. At one end, a circle of clear glass held the microphotograph, while a convex lens at the other end magnified the image. The tube could be made of metal, ivory, wood, cardboard or glass, and could be incorporated into gold, silver or rolled gold jewellery. (His design drawing shows it attached to a cravat pin.) The patent was granted on 15th June 1861, but he had already applied for additional coverage on 7th May for a simpler design. Dagron took Martinache to court to protect his own patent and maintain a monopoly of the trade, but lost the case. The dispute was settled in July when Dagron bought the Martinache process, but he was forced to pay a high price. This is an indication of the great commercial value placed on the microphotography business at that time.

On 8th May 1861 Jules Jean Héricé, also a Parisian jeweller, requested a patent for a monocular of rather complicated construction. It had a moveable eyepiece, permitting a precise focus. He also included a design for a novelty ring. Unlike Dagron's design, which was hidden horizontally beneath a hinged lid, Héricé concealed his microphotographic tube vertically behind the decoration. This tube could be incorporated in toys, bracelets and pins, and could be made in any material: gold, silver, brass and ivory, or decorated with engraving or enamelling.

Patent No.49624 was granted to Héricé on 17th July 1861, but already he had been inspired to insert miniature viewers in other luxury items: fans, canes, parasol and umbrella handles and hairbrushes. He continued to modify his designs, and the following year he patented a more useful monocular design. Using a bayonet fitting, the end opposite the eyepiece could be turned and detached, allowing the microphotograph to be removed and changed for a different image.

Meanwhile, on 18th July 1861 Louis-Marie Berthier made a patent application for a new type of double-image microviewer. Berthier was an optician employed by René Dagron, and his design involved a simpler and more effective method than that originally conceived by his employer. Within three weeks Berthier had ceded the rights of Patent No. 50469 to Dagron, who then applied for additional changes to the patent in his own name. Whether this was part of an agreed employer/employee relationship, or whether Berthier had originally intended to market his design independently is a matter of conjecture, but from August 1861 Berthier's process was put into production at *Dagron & Cie*.

By September 1861 Dagron had experimented with a total of four different methods of producing microphotographic viewers. Finally, he retained one process for viewing a single microphotograph, and Berthier's design for a double image viewer. A report for *Le Comité de la Société de Photographie* was produced by M. Girard on 18th October 1861, after he had paid a visit to Dagron's workshops. He provided an explanation of Dagron's manufacturing process for a single image microviewer.

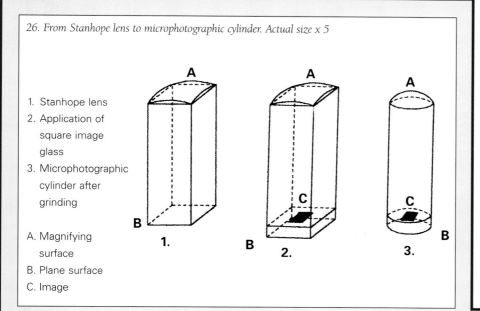

26. From Stanhope lens to microphotographic cylinder. Actual size x 5

1. Stanhope lens
2. Application of square image glass
3. Microphotographic cylinder after grinding

A. Magnifying surface
B. Plane surface
C. Image

1.   2.   3.

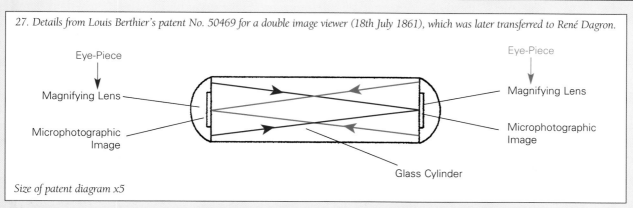

27. Details from Louis Berthier's patent No. 50469 for a double image viewer (18th July 1861), which was later transferred to René Dagron.

Eye-Piece

Magnifying Lens

Microphotographic Image

Eye-Piece

Magnifying Lens

Microphotographic Image

Glass Cylinder

Size of patent diagram x5

Expanding the Market

28. Image from a shell pinholder of the "Famille Impériale" of France: Napoléon III, the Empress Eugénie and Prince Eugène Louis, c.1860. (Private Collection.)

29. Image from a bone monocular: "Souverains Européens", c. 1861. (Terence Taylor

Girard wrote: "For a single image, a tiny rectangular prism with square ends is cut from optical glass, and one end is given the required curve on an optician's grinding machine. A small square of glass holding the microphotographic image is glued to the opposite end. Finally, the lateral edges of the prism and the image glass are ground to produce a smooth cylinder." (See Diagram 26).

Apart from the "small square of glass holding the microphotographic image", this description discloses the familiar form of the Stanhope lens, invented half a century before by the 3rd Earl Stanhope. In fact, Dagron always referred to the lenses awaiting the addition of the image squares as "Stanhopes". This method of producing a "microphotographic cylinder" remained unchanged until the final demise of the Stanhope industry.

Berthier's process for a double-image magnifying viewer also began with a rectangular prism of optical glass, but two thicker squares of glass holding the images were glued at either end. The whole unit was placed in a grinding machine, which rounded the outside plane surface of each image glass into a convex lens. Each lens focused on the image at the opposite end, so that when either end of the viewer was held to the eye, the opposite image was seen. Meanwhile, the nearest image was too tiny and so far out of focus that it became invisible to the eye. (See Diagram 27). Girard admired this "extremely ingenious process, of which M. Dagron is the owner, but which was invented by M. Barquillé, one of his workers". "Barquillé" is a very rare name in France, and is not recorded elsewhere in primary sources about microphotography. Also, the name on this patent is definitely that of Berthier. It is most likely that Girard recorded the name incorrectly in his article, thereby denying Berthier the recognition he deserved.

During the summer of 1861, Dagron decided to exhibit at the prestigious *Salon de Photographie* held in the *Palais d'Industrie* on the Champs Elysées. This huge building had been designed for the 1855 Paris Exposition, and was known as the "Cathedral of Commerce". The Empress Eugénie and the five-year-old Prince Imperial visited the event, where they enjoyed the contrast between the larger exhibits of well-known French photographers, and Dagron's display of miniature images in a variety of novelties.

This time, the *bijoux microphotographiques de M. Dagron* were the *tour de force* of the occasion, as visitors crowded around and exclaimed at the tiny miracles. Even several small thefts could not detract from Dagron's enjoyment of this triumph. A variety of images were on display: an attractive portrait of the French Imperial Family, famous works of art and treasures from museums, monuments, churches and palaces, views around France, and family groups. A calendar for 1861 was a popular purchase, and also a bank note. The most impressive were the composite groups of important personalities of the era: the image of twenty-three "Souverains Européens" was particularly admired.

Many microphotographs were mounted in rings, brooches, pins and pendants, and the popularity of topographical views prompted one journalist to remark that in future all the holiday souvenirs could be carried home in the jewellery box. As well as the inevitable monoculars and binoculars, there was an amazing selection of cheap bone items: crucifixes and rosaries, pen and pencil-holders, manicure sets, needle cases and many other items in daily use by members of both sexes.

It seems amazing that within two years of applying for his first patent, Dagron was supplying novelties to the other side of the world. One newspaper report from August 1861 told how a gentleman in Adelaide, Australia, had received an interesting packet in the mail. The contents were "three gentlemen's breastpins, of simple and well-known pattern, namely two entwined hoops having a gold bar running through them. In these pins, however, the bar represents a telescope, in one end of which is fixed a small piece of glass, and in the other a lens. The diameter of the tube does not exceed the sixteenth of an inch, yet when the eye is brought to bear upon it, a most magnificent portrait of Richard Cobden (half-length) is reflected. Underneath the portrait is his name, in full, and the address of the photographers, *Messrs René Dagron & Cie, Paris*. The portrait is of course obtained by the use of the microscopic camera, an instrument which has now been brought to such a high degree of perfection at home as even to exceed the expectations of the most sanguine professors of the art". Two of the pins contained portraits, and the third showed "a perfect representation of a Bank of England five pound note".

30. A religious image produced by Dagron & Cie, c. 1861. (Dagron Family Archives)

The 1861 Salon brought so much new business to René Dagron that by the end of the year his small workshops in *rue des Bons Enfants* had expanded to give employment to one hundred and fifty workers. The majority of the workforce was female, being able to handle the tiny lenses with great dexterity. Dagron's novelties found a ready market at home and abroad. In the same year French newspapers reported that in Italy fashionable young gentlemen in Rome wore novelty microphotographic charms on their watch chains. The charms were in the shape of gold boots, representing the shape of the map of Italy, and the images revealed eighteen portraits of the *"Défenseurs de l'Italie"*: Napoléon lll, Prince Napoléon, Victor Emmanuel, King of Piedmont; and various French field-marshals and Italian generals, including Garibaldi. These charms were possibly the first examples of political microphotography.

At a very early stage in the business René Dagron accepted postal commissions. In the *Courrier de St. Etienne* (November, 1861), it was reported that one could send him any portrait, even a simple *carte de visite*, and he would reduce the photograph to microscopic size. He began to build up a reputation abroad, receiving orders from England, Germany, Italy, America and even Australia. He was able to offer a vast choice of subject matter, and one reporter was amused to discover the varied preferences of different nationalities. It was said that the English liked miniature calendars and reproductions of banknotes, while the Italians only wanted pictures of religious subjects and angels. However, as for the *"vertueux Allemands, ils n'achètent rien de vertueux"*. ("The moral Germans buy nothing that is moral"!) This comment is the first indication that René Dagron included risqué or erotic images in his selection of microphotographs.

Le développement du marché

Le succès de René Dagron faisait l'envie de beaucoup de concurrents qui commencèrent à déposer des brevets pour leurs propres créations. Dagron acheta alors certains de ces droits afin de maintenir son monopole. En 1861 il exposa certains de ses bijoux photomicroscopiques au Salon de la Photographie au Palais de l'Industrie, où ils furent remarqués par l'Impératrice Eugénie et le jeune Prince Impérial. Les affaires prospérèrent au point que son atelier de la rue des Bons Enfants faisait travailler plus de 100 ouvriers. Dagron recevait également des commandes par la poste, et commença à exporter ses articles vers la Grande-Bretagne, l'Allemagne, l'Italie, les Etats-Unis et même l'Australie en utilisant des images pour répondre aux goûts différents de chaque pays.

En 1862 les concurrents de Dagron devinrent si nombreux que Dagron fut forcé de défendre ses brevets devant la justice. Il publia une collection d'articles intitulée "Cylindres Photomicroscopiques Montés et Non-montés sur Bijoux, brevetés en France et à l'étranger" dans l'espoir d'appuyer sa réclamation. Malheureusement, ses plaintes furent rejetées par la Cour.

La même année également, il exposa à l'Exposition Universelle de Londres. Sur le plan familial, son beau-frère s'était marié à une anglaise et habitait à Sunbury-on-Thames, où il avait fondé une importante académie militaire.

Expanding the Market

Richard Cobden (1804-1865) was known in mid-Victorian Britain as "the Apostle of Free Trade". In 1860 he negotiated a Commercial Treaty between France and Britain, whereby British duties on silk and wine from France were reduced, in return for limited French import duties on British goods. Cobden was a well-known and popular figure on both sides of the Channel when the microphotographic image described in this newspaper report was produced by Dagron in 1861.

Henri de Parville, writing in *Le Constitutionnel* (4th February 1862), noted that twelve thousand microviewers per day were being produced in Dagron's workshops at this time. The speed of his business expansion was noted by other Parisian photographers, who were keen to capture a share of the souvenir market. Anyone with experience of microphotography had the ability to make a reasonable copy of his souvenirs, and soon there were many such items on sale all over the city. René Dagron was determined to uphold his patents, and took legal action against a group of fifteen Parisian photographers who had been selling similar novelties to his own. At the hearing Dagron stated that he did not consider himself the inventor of microphotography, nor of the microviewer with which to magnify them. However, he did insist that he was the first to achieve viewers of such minute proportions, and that it had been his idea to incorporate them in novelties and trinkets. He claimed exclusive rights to manufacture and sell all such viewers, but was shocked to lose his case. He was no longer able to include the word *"breveté"* (patented) in the captions on his microphotographic images.

It is interesting to note that the judgement quoted Sir David Brewster's article on microphotography from the 1857 version of "The Encyclopaedia Britannica", where he described its use in jewellery: this was used to nullify Dagron's patents. He was forced to pay the legal costs but was charged no fee for damages, the Court recognising that he had acted in good faith, and had after all succeeded in making magnifying viewers smaller than ever before achieved.

This unfortunate lawsuit was the likely reason for Dagron's first sortie into print. In the summer of 1862 he published a small booklet of thirty-six pages, with a title almost longer than the book itself: *"Cylindres photomicroscopiques montés et non-montés sur bijoux, breveté en France et à l'étranger"*. ("Microphotographic viewers mounted and unmounted in trinkets, patented in France and abroad.") Although one might assume it describes the variety and method of production of such items, the reader is presented with a collection of newspaper and magazine articles in praise of Dagron and his novelties. They date from 25th November 1860 to 2nd March 1862.

In his foreword, Dagron wrote that although his novelties had met with immediate success, the general public did not know enough about them, and needed to be warned against unscrupulous competitors who produced inferior copies. To safeguard his reputation, he reproduced a number of articles published in the French Press by eminent journalists, scientists and men of the Church. They had all been to visit his establishment to view the method of manufacture of microphotographic souvenirs and he had been very touched by their letters of support. Dagron added nothing more, certain that the articles were a defence in themselves. They make interesting reading, for they record the progress and increasing popularity of microphotographic novelties in France and elsewhere during this short period of a mere sixteen months.

Shortly before his death in 1861, Prince Albert attempted to revive the spirit of the 1851 "Great Exhibition" by arranging another international event in London: "The International Exhibition of Art and Industry". Unfortunately, the breath-taking "Crystal Palace" had been dismantled and moved to a new site in Sydenham after the 1851 exhibition. A decade later the organisers chose a less decorative design for the main building erected in Cromwell Road.

31. *Image from a bone whistle, with a view of the Crystal Palace at its later site in Sydenham, c. 1865. (Note the incorrect spelling of the caption.)*

32. *Image from a bone monocular of the London International Exhibition, 1862. (Terence Taylor)*

33. A significant image from a bone monocular: "A Nation Mourns the Loss", probably dating from early 1862. (Jull Collection.)

Dagron applied to exhibit at the event which, due to the royal funeral arrangements, did not take place until the summer of 1862. He received the backing of M. Girard, who was a member of the *jury d'admission*, and had written encouraging articles in France about his microphotographic novelties. These were also mentioned in the official programme of the exhibition, together with a repeat of the story describing the theft of the ring specially made for Queen Victoria. His readiness to publicise this in London itself lends credence to an actual event, rather than a far-fetched publicity arrangement. The Royal Archives at Windsor have no trace of surviving Stanhope jewellery. However, it is known that Queen Victoria made many gifts of sentimental photographic items to her family and friends.

It was noted that English and French visitors bought vast numbers of Dagron's *"fantaisies charmantes"*, and one of these must have been the bone monocular containing the earliest dated Stanhope image so far discovered. It was produced by *Dagron & Cie* of Paris, but the image is captioned in English. The view shows the main exhibition building: "INTERNATIONAL EXHIBITION 1862 FROM THE EXHIBITION ROAD".

It is probable that Dagron visited or even stayed with his brother-in-law and young family in Sunbury-on-Thames during his attendance at this exhibition. With the advantage of her English mother tongue, Mme. Sophia Lendy may even have checked the caption translations for him. Dagron produced several commemorative microphotographs for sale to the predominantly English-speaking crowd. The population shared Queen Victoria's grief at the unexpected death of Prince Albert in November 1861, and

pitied her fatherless children. Patriotic mourning souvenirs found a ready market, and as usual René Dagron was well prepared. Although undated, a monocular showing the royal widow seated beneath a portrait of her late husband, and surrounded by cameos of her nine children, may have predated the exhibition souvenirs.

René Dagron was awarded a Certificate of Honourable Mention at the 1862 International Exhibition, but Sir David Brewster, ever supportive of microphotography, expressed regret that the Jury for Awards had neglected to present him with a medal. He paid tribute to the ingenuity with which the Frenchman had offered an entirely new article for manufacture, and wrote about "one of Dagron's photomicroscopes containing a photograph of Sir Walter Scott, and sold at Messrs. Knox, Samuel and Johnson's for one shilling. The cylinder lens is only one-third of an inch long, and its diameter one-tenth of an inch. It is placed within the eye-end of an ivory tube, which screws onto a larger piece, so as to resemble a minute opera glass through which we see the portrait as large and distinct as if it were an oil portrait on the wall."

Unfortunately René Louis Dagron did not live to enjoy the mounting success of his son, having died in 1852 at the age of eighty years. Dagron's own family now numbered six children: four daughters and two sons. (Pauline, the eldest daughter, was aged thirteen when Georges René entered the world on 17th April 1861, to become the final addition to the Dagron household.) Their father's success enabled the family to live in some affluence for the next few years, while their mother was much involved in running the financial side of the business.

5 "Mail Order" Microphotography

Although René Dagron had lost patent protection for his microphotographic novelties, he was determined not to lose a near monopoly of the market. His unique flair for publicity ensured that *Dagron & Cie* remained in the public eye and retained a major share of the industry. Trade fairs and exhibitions were used to display his miniature products in ever-changing variety, so that the general public and retailers in France and abroad were keen to place substantial orders. His visit to the "International Exhibition of Art and Industry" in London had certainly proved to be a profitable venture. The overall attendance at the 1862 event was more than six million, to view a total of twenty-eight thousand exhibits. Sales of souvenirs during the exhibition and orders from retailers and distributors ensured that business was thriving for *Dagron & Cie*. A continual supply of prepared Stanhope lenses was crucial to the success of the current operation and future expansion, but opticians in Paris and elsewhere struggled to meet the demand. René Dagron decided that the best solution was to set up his own factory solely for the production of Stanhope lenses, and the chosen site was at a considerable distance from Paris.

At first Dagron had considered a location in *le pays des lapidaires*, or gem-cutting region. This was the area around Mijoux and St. Claude in the heart of the Jura Mountains, which had been renowned for the quality of its work since the end of the seventeenth century. The population was sparse and the small number of skilled lapidaries could command high wages. The gem-cutters were mainly outworkers, for winter conditions in the mountains isolated them in their homes for several months each year. Dagron preferred to establish a large workshop, where production could be checked and controlled, as it was in Paris. His chosen site was Gex, then a small village, at the foot of the Jura and close to the Swiss border near Geneva. His investigations had revealed that the area had a plentiful supply of cheap labour but no established industries. The local lawyer, from whom Dagron had decided to rent a building, assured him that by setting up a factory at Gex he would "do the area a great service, as a large number of young people were unemployed".

The Dagron family archives have preserved a series of enthusiastic letters from Dagron to his contacts in Gex, which chart the progress of the new enterprise between October and November 1862. Caroline Dagron was also involved, and was so keen for work to start that she despatched their foreman, M. Frontant, from Paris before her husband had returned from Geneva to deliver his final instructions. Several exasperated letters from Dagron deal with missed meetings and retrieving tools and equipment sent to the wrong railway station!

M. Frontant was kept busy ordering, collecting and installing thirty-seven optician's grinding wheels, tools, emeries and plates of "crown" or best quality optical glass.

All this equipment was sent down by rail from Paris to Geneva by *Dagron & Cie's* normal suppliers, and resulting delays caused much annoyance to the busy foreman. It was planned to start production in February 1863 in the ground floor of the workshop, which was to be occupied by the women workers. Frontant was so well organised that despite all the difficulties the installation was almost ready by the end of October 1862. Dagron was able to write to his lawyer in Gex: "We will need the upper storey sooner than I had thought, so please do whatever is necessary. My intention being to employ at least sixty people, please notify the local authorities, as you yourself wanted to undertake the arrangements for this factory, which will produce a specific type of optical equipment."

By the end of November Frontant had already marshalled his local labour force and begun production. Apparently some of the techniques were proving difficult to master, and Frontant sent some of the early examples to be finished at the Paris workshops. Dagron counselled patience, for it was a type of work unknown in the area, but assured Frontant he was pleased with the results so far and was certain that before long all processes involved in the manufacture of Stanhope lenses could be completed in the Gex workshop. Dagron had confidence in his foreman, writing: "I am counting on you and your energy and intelligence to manage our workshop." Soon the factory was in full production, and the completed lenses were despatched to the Paris workshops, in preparation for the remaining processes involved in the manufacture of *cylindres photomicroscopiques*.

The price of Stanhope novelties seems to have been very cheap during this period, and having considered Frontant's cost prices, Dagron decided against paying his labour force by piecework. The workers were paid 10-12 francs per day, which was an acceptable wage in that area. Many years later, René Dagron's daughter-in-law Lucile noted that the factory in Gex continued for as long as Dagron himself ran the company. It gave work to the population of the entire village, and Lucile's husband told her that the villagers hoped Dagron would be made *député* for the region (their local political representative in the French Government).

Dagron's designs were being duplicated in increasing numbers by competitors in Paris and possibly elsewhere. Although his exhibition success and subsequent orders ensured that his name was probably the best known for these souvenirs at home and abroad, Dagron realised it was time to diversify and seek new markets. It was particularly important to maintain the volume of orders to support the production of Stanhope lenses at the Gex factory. Photography had become an internationally popular hobby for amateurs, and Dagron knew his expertise was a valuable commodity. As he regarded himself as the foremost authority on microphotographic viewers and the techniques needed to produce them, his next project was to write a textbook on the subject. Although in theory this would enable many others to reproduce the process themselves, Dagron was counting on the fact that some parts of the process needed specific equipment and materials. By offering to supply these needs at reasonable prices, Dagron would gain far more than the sales price of his little textbook. It would promote his new venture and help to build up a larger customer base. He also aimed to provide an alternative and most useful option: if his customers wished, most of the difficult work could be undertaken in his own workshops, enabling them to obtain individually designed souvenirs with minimum effort, and at very low cost.

Microphotographie en vente par correspondance

En 1862 Dagron ouvrit à Gex dans l'Ain une usine consacrée à la production des lentilles Stanhope. Il y envoya son con-tremaître, les outils et tout le matériel nécessaire de Paris. Il y avait peu d'industries dans la région gessienne et les gens du pays furent heureux d'accueillir cette nouvelle possibilité de travail .

En 1864 Dagron écrivit un 'Traité de Photographie Microscopique' où il expli-quait sa méthode de production des microphotographies. Le livre était une excel-lente publicité pour Dagron et Cie. Ainsi des photographies ordinaires envoyées à la société Dagron pouvaient être réduites et reproduites sur des lentilles Stanhope et Dagron proposait des prix avantageux pour des commandes importantes. D'autre part, Dagron pouvait également fournir tout l' équipement nécessaire pour monter un ate-lier de microphotographie.

En 1864 Dagron fut autorisé à utiliser le titre de ' Photographe de Sa Majesté l'Em-pereur'. Il reçut beaucoup de commandes officielles et privées pour des portraits pho-tographiques, dont le plus célèbre est son portrait de l'ambassadeur du Siam. En 1867 il exposa ses nouveautés micropho-tographiques à l'Exposition Universelle de Paris, et produisit quelques compositions étonnantes des chefs d'Etat du monde entier.

His *Traité de Photographie Microscopique* (1864) con-tains thirty-six pages of diagrams and information, and sold for only 50 centimes when it was first published. It was the world's first book on microfilm techniques, and was most valuable to the early photographic enthusiasts. He described his process as quick and easy to learn, and he was certain that many people would benefit by learning the

processes used in his workshops, "as nobody else practises this industry on such a scale as we do."

Dagron described his methods in detail, but also included a price list of all the necessary accessories and materials to carry them out. Every item could be purchased from *Dagron et Cie*, and "nothing was despatched without rigorous testing in the laboratory". Stock included the reducing camera he had designed for the production of multiple images. This camera had already been described in Dagron's first book by *Dalloz*, correspondent of *Le Moniteur* in an article printed in February 1862. It was made of brass, and was screwed into place at one end of a large box-shaped tube strongly constructed of wood. At the far end was a rectangular opening over which the glass negative plate was clamped. This held the image that was to be microphotographed and multiplied many times. The tube was placed against the window, with the glass plate in full daylight.

On the front of the camera was the microscope viewing lens and control that enabled the photographer to focus on the image plate. Behind this was a chamber enclosing a sensitised glass plate held in a movable copper frame. Dagron disclosed that he did not use the "wet plate collodion" method, but preferred the "Taupenot method" to prepare a glass plate. After it had been sensitised with collodion, it was covered with a film of albumin or eggwhite. This prevented the plate from losing its sensitivity to light as it dried out. The Taupenot "dry collodion" process enabled the photographer to store prepared glass plates for some time.

Light was reflected onto the plate through groups of small lenses behind the camera, and after each exposure the frame could be moved horizontally according to a sliding scale, to allow another portion of the plate to face the bank of lenses. Another adjustment allowed a vertical movement of the plate, providing another series of images. Dagron suggested that the time of exposure would vary between one and three seconds, "depending on the weather"! If a photographer only wished to produce a few copies of a microphotograph, a camera with only one lens was sufficient, as this would reproduce eight identical images on the plate. In 1864 *Dagron & Cie* also sold cameras with three, six, nine or even fifteen lenses, at a cost of 10 francs extra per lens. The largest surviving Dagron cameras have twenty-five lenses. The frames can be moved into six positions horizontally and three vertically, and are therefore capable of producing 450 images on a single glass plate (25x6x3). These would only have been used by professional microphotographers such as Dagron himself, when the volume of work justified the expense.

In 1864 the price of a microphotography "starter kit" was 110 francs, and included the camera and all its spe-cialised attachments, plus the wooden casing and some optical glass for cutting into plates. However, this could be augmented with several other items of equipment. Dagron's technical instructions were quite precise and everything he mentioned could be purchased from his company.

A diamond cutter ("price: 12 francs") was used to cut the glass plate to the required size, which in Dagron's original instructions had to measure 2cm x 7.5cm in order to fit the frame in the camera. Later, larger glass plates were available to hold groups of 450 images.

"Mail Order" Microphotography

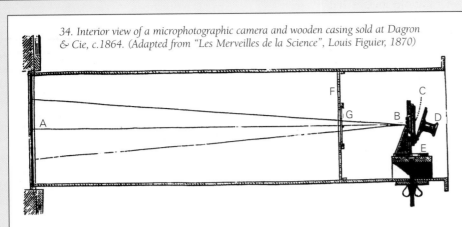

34. *Interior view of a microphotographic camera and wooden casing sold at Dagron & Cie, c.1864. (Adapted from "Les Merveilles de la Science", Louis Figuier, 1870)*

A. Image on glass plate to be microphotographed

B. 20 microphotographic camera lenses

C. Collodionised glass plate on which the microphotographic images will be reproduced

D. Microscope and camera viewfinder

E. Clamp and support holding camera in place

F. Diaphragm (wooden screen)

G. Sliding shutter

35. *A complete Dagron camera. (Preserved at the Musée Nicéphore Niépce, Chalon-sur-Saône, France)*

36. *A Dagron camera, showing the multiple lenses. (Preserved at the Musée Nicéphore Niépce, Chalon-sur-Saône, France).*

Once the glass plate covered in multiple images had been processed, a suitable hand magnifier ("price: 30 francs") was needed to ascertain if all the images had developed properly. Any images not meeting the quality requirements were scratched from the plate at this point. Dagron's own double convex hand magnifier is preserved by his descendants.

A diamond was also used to mark and cut the lines of images on the plate into strips, and then into 3mm x 3mm squares, each holding one microphotograph.

The next stage described the miniature magnifier, which Dagron himself termed a "Stanhope". He admitted that few people would be skilled enough to make these themselves, but he was able to provide Stanhopes ready prepared with a curved magnifying lens at one end and a flat surface at the other. These were very cheap in price, being supplied from the Dagron factory at Gex. To attach the tiny 3mm squares each holding a microphotograph to the rectangular Stanhope rods, Dagron's optical adhesive was *"baume de Canada"* or "Canada balsam". This is the yellow resin from a Canadian fir (Abies balsamea), which becomes transparent when dry. Its refractive index is almost the same as glass, which made it an ideal adhesive for Dagron's process. It was supplied at a cost of 5 francs per pot. Dagron suggested that if little bubbles of air appeared under the image, the Stanhope should be warmed slightly to make the adhesive more fluid, after which the square of glass could then be pressed firmly onto the square end of the rod.

A little grinding was necessary to smooth the lateral edges of the rod, so producing a neat curved cylinder to insert in a round hole in the required mount. *Dagron et Cie* could supply an inexpensive optician's grinding wheel for this purpose for a mere 15 francs, but a more elaborate model costing 105 francs was recommended for those who wished to develop business on a larger scale. Dagron was also aware that not everyone would be able to undertake all the work involved in his process, so he offered to simplify the task. *Dagron et Cie* would reproduce any photographs sent to them, either in positive or negative form, and mount them on Stanhopes. A single proof would cost 5 francs but discounts were offered for larger orders: a dozen proofs would cost only 12 francs. Dagron claimed: "At very reasonable prices, we offer everyone the means of producing easily and economically the little cylinders known as 'Stanhopes', those mysterious objects within which anyone can enclose that which he holds most dear in the world".

Dagron and his contemporaries sometimes referred to Stanhope novelties as *"bijoux photomicroscopiques"*, which can be translated as "microphotographic jewellery or trinkets". However, he also invented "microphotographic jewels", in which the image itself is embedded in facetted coloured glass or a cut semi-precious stone. He advertised these "jewels" in his book, pricing them at 10 francs each or 50 francs per dozen. Several examples of these attractive objects are preserved in the Dagron family archives. The square of clear glass holding the image was glued onto a larger block of coloured glass. This was cut into facets to imitate a jewel, and the end opposite the image glass was ground into a convex magnifying lens. Once these operations were completed, it became extremely difficult to distinguish the small area of clear glass, as it was camouflaged by reflection and refraction from the expanse of coloured glass. The stones were cut from bright green, blue, red and pink glass, and others were cut in clear glass to resemble "diamonds".

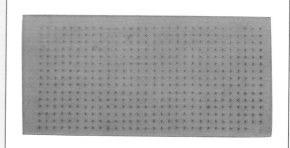

37. A glass plate holding 450 microphotographs. Dimensions: 8.2cm x 4cm. (Preserved at the Musée Nicéphore Niépce, Chalon-sur-Saône, France.)

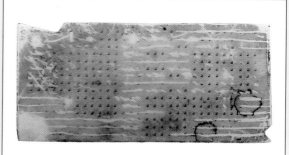

38. A glass plate with multiple images, showing the photographer's scratches to obliterate those of inferior quality. Actual size: 8.2cm x 4cm.

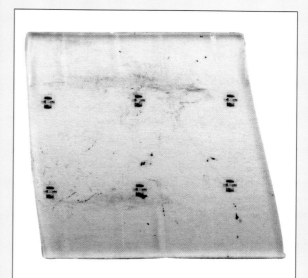

39. A plate showing measurement marks before being cut into strips and then squares, each containing one microphotograph. (Dagron Family Archives.)

"Mail Order" Microphotography

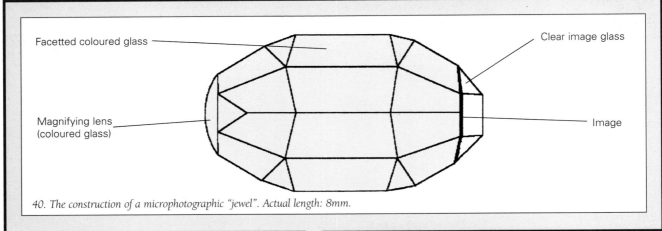

Facetted coloured glass

Clear image glass

Magnifying lens
(coloured glass)

Image

40. *The construction of a microphotographic "jewel". Actual length: 8mm.*

41. *Greatly enlarged glass "jewels", revealing the microphotographic images. (Dagron Family Archives)*

When the images were mounted in rings or other items of jewellery, they were glimpsed against a background of reflected colour. Although many of the microphotographs were of religious subjects, a larger proportion of images in coloured glass reveal more exotic views. Loosely draped models were posed in positions imitating classical paintings and sculptures, each image being given a title to reassure the viewer that it was tasteful art. The captions show that they were made by *"Reproductions Dagron & Cie, Brevetés Paris"*, which indicates that Dagron was selling novelties of this type before he lost his patents in 1862.

Dagron wrote that his workshops could provide mounts "of infinite variety" for microphotographs: gold, gold-plated and silver jewellery, and novelties in mother-of-pearl, ivory, etc. His craftsmen aimed to create elegant and innovative trinkets, and were particularly noted for the variety of their watch-keys. The latter could be separated into several pieces, so that photographs of members of the family, friends and "everyone you hold dear" could be united in the one mount, without increasing its size in any way.

It is clear from his *"Traité de Photographie Microscopique"* that René Dagron intended to cover every aspect of the "do-it-yourself" microphotography market. He provided expertise, equipment and materials to those who wanted to make money from a business, or enabled the amateur to produce a single unusual item or souvenir. His business would no longer be threatened by competitors, although their trade would be adversely affected once the processes of microphotography were freely available. In fact, he hoped they themselves would decide to purchase photographic supplies from *Dagron & Cie*, once they realised his prices were so reasonable. Yet again, René Dagron was one step ahead of the market.

Dagron & Cie continued to thrive, and in January 1864, René Dagron was authorised by the Emperor Napoléon lll to use the title *"Photographe de Sa Majesté l'Empereur"* (Court Photographer) and this was proudly included on the *cartes de visite*. Unfortunately, the course of history only allowed him to use the title for the next six years.

Dagron's success in microphotography began to influence his career as a photographer and he was inundated with orders for portraits and official commemorative photographs of important visitors to France. His portrait of the Siamese ambassador robed in lustrous silks received particular praise. The ambassador and his entourage were the centre of attention during their visit to France. When they attended the French court, the exotic visitors progressed across the chamber to the feet of Napoléon lll on hands and knees.

42. *A carte-de-visite produced by Dagron & Cie, 1864-1870.*

43. Visit of the Siamese Ambassador to the French Court, 1865. From "Le Second Empire 1851-1870", Armand Dayot. (Ashley Lawrence Collection)

Apart from family portraits, that of the Siamese Ambassador is the only image on a glass plate retained by Dagron for posterity, indicating his pride in this important commission. The Dagron family archives also preserve a Siamese award of merit and an elaborate letter of thanks. Other wealthy and influential visitors from abroad flocked to his elegant premises, and he became the *"véritable photographe à la mode"*! He advertised: "this establishment is remarkable for the unusual location of its immense studios and its magnificent salons, occupying the second floor of the imposing building at *66, rue Neuve des Petits-Champs"*.

Microphotographic novelties were exhibited at all the important international fairs in Europe. In 1865 at the *Exposition de Porto* Dagron was awarded a medal, Second Class, followed by another Honourable Mention at the 1867 *Exposition Universelle* in Paris. The latter was a most prestigious event, which occupied forty-one acres in central Paris on the *Champs de Mars*, scene of French national celebrations since the Revolution. Alexandre Gustave Eiffel was just starting his architectural career, and his impressive design was chosen for the main building. It was an enormous ellipse, with seven concentric galleries around a central garden. The *Galerie des Machines* on the outer ring was the largest, and the whole showground housed more than 43,000 exhibits.

44. Image from a bone monocular, produced by Dagron & Cie: the 1867 Exposition Universelle in Paris, viewed from the Palais de Trocadéro, on the opposite bank of the River Seine. (Terence Taylor)

Impressive composite microphotographic images were produced for this event, although the captions do not include the name of *Dagron & Cie*. Views of the exhibition site were given added impact by a frame of individual portraits of monarchs and Heads of State from around the world. All the major world leaders of the time were represented: Napoléon lll of France, Queen Victoria of England, Tsar Nicholas ll of Russia, Emperor Franz Josef of Austria, Pope Pius IX and Andrew Johnson, President of the United States. Portraits were also included of the Kings of Bavaria, Belgium, Sweden, Prussia and Portugal, and the rulers of Brazil, Turkey and Malta. It is unlikely that all these illustrious leaders were able to visit the exhibition in person, but their arts and industries were certainly on display in the vast halls. Different versions of this picture have been discovered: one displays fifteen such portraits and another shows seventeen. The latter shows the same fourteen foreign leaders, but the three members of the

French Imperial Family are added to make up the larger total.

The 1867 *Paris Exposition Universelle* attracted more than six million visitors: an extraordinary number, given the difficulties and expense of travelling at the time. Amongst the many newspaper articles describing the event, one referred to "those astounding 'microscopic photographs' invented by M. Dagron, whereby he places a monument in a ring and a portrait on a pinhead". Persistent souvenir-sellers passed among the crowds, pestering visitors to buy their microphotographic novelties for just 50 centimes. The journalist commented: "How strange when one must consider banal and pass by without stopping before marvels, just because they have been in existence for perhaps a dozen years!" Although the length of time since Dagron's first patent was only eight years, the newspaper report illustrates that by 1867 Stanhope novelties were being produced so cheaply and in such numbers that they were considered commonplace by most of the population.

45. Two versions of composite microphotographic images from bone needle cases, with portraits of Heads of State surrounding a view of the site of the Exposition Universelle, 1867. (Right: Terence Taylor).

Once René Dagron's *"Traité de Photographie Micro-scopique"* had been published (and translated into English), the export trade became a most important aspect of his business. His foresight opened the route to a very lucrative overseas market, and he began to export all necessary items to keen photographers abroad. He could also set up agencies in other countries to facilitate international trade. In 1866, Edward Wilson in "The Philadelphia Photographer" wrote about the three main centres producing microscopic novelties at that time: "At Manchester, England, there is a very large establishment engaged in producing not only portraits, but all sorts of copies, views, etc., on slides for the microscope. In Paris there is a similar establishment, under the care of M. Dagron". The third business mentioned by Wilson was that of John H. Morrow of New York City, who "obtained his instructions from head-quarters, that is, from Dancer, Manchester, and Dagron, Paris."

From the following description of Morrow's workshop, it is evident that novelties containing microphotographs were being assembled in the U.S.A. at this time. "We were shown opera-glasses, watch-charms, finger-rings, breast pins, eye-glasses, knives, canes, penholders, pencils, pipes, porte-monnaies, etc. in great variety. The most beautiful application of this elegant process is to finger-rings. No matter what color the stone may be, it may be so ground as to be used for a microscope for viewing the picture of the one you love best or the least. The process is very simple and easy, and the instruments used low in price and not complicated. Fifty-six pictures have been made in one minute by a girl working six instruments at once." Again, it seems that female workers were better suited to the manipulation and insertion of the Stanhope lenses. Morrow also offered training courses for those who wished to learn the techniques and then set up their own business.

From available evidence it appears that, having corresponded with both Dancer and Dagron, John H. Morrow obtained enough expertise to set up his own business. However, it is debatable whether this was entirely independent of the two European experts. Nevertheless, photographic materials and equipment were easily available in the U.S.A., and several American photographers had already experimented with preparing glass plates of multiple images. Morrow himself had a microphotographic camera and could produce images. He was also aware of what type of novelties would appeal to the specific American market. Indeed, Edward Wilson informed his readers that "Mr. Morrow is now manufacturing largely for Messrs. Gurney and Son, and others, in New York." However, it is probable that he still imported some of the components from France, such as ready-ground Stanhope lenses and specially designed mounts and novelties. Certainly many American microphotoscopic images, particularly those of Niagara Falls, exist with the caption "MADE IN FRANCE", and this would only be added to items made for export. Despite much research, I have yet to find an example of an American manufacturer's name written on the image itself in any microphotographic novelty from the nineteenth century. I shall be delighted to learn of evidence to the contrary.

It is known that Dagron's novelties had been exported to Australia within a couple of years of his patent application, but they were not sent as separate components for a considerable time. In September 1869, Customs officials seized a case of jewellery and watchmaker's tools, which had been imported by an Adelaide jeweller. Inside was a packet of watch keys, "each containing a diminutive photograph with magnifying power which, upon being held close to the eye, represented the most obscene and disgusting pictures"! The watch keys were confiscated, and in addition to "these exceedingly filthy articles", the jeweller was deprived of a large quantity of watches, brooches, earrings and other jewellery. The images were punched from the watch keys, which were later sold at auction with the other goods seized by the Customs officers. Dagron had found a ready market for erotic microphotographs on the other side of the globe, but collectors have found few examples there. Perhaps the vigilant Customs officers ensured that the line of supply was discontinued!

6 Tributary Crafts of the Stanhope Industry

In *"Traité de Photographie Microscopique"* René Dagron wrote: "In five years (i.e. from the application for his patents in 1859 to the date of publication in 1864) microscopic photography has become a real industry, drawing in about thirty tributary crafts, especially in the trinket trade." His own workforce numbered one hundred and fifty employees. These included skilled glasscutters, lens grinders and a large proportion of female workers, whose nimble fingers glued the tiny squares of glass to the ends of the Stanhope lenses, assembled the small components of various novelties and inserted the completed Stanhopes. In addition *Dagron & Cie* provided work for a variety of small businesses and individual artisans.

Dagron's workshops were still situated in the *rue des Bon Enfants*, where he had produced the prototypes of his *"cylindres photomicroscopiques"*. The area was within walking distance of his professional salon at *66, rue Neuve des Petits-Champs*. The narrow crowded street was adjacent to the *Jardin du Palais Royal*, an area of fascinating small shops and galleries, which attracted the fashionable citizens of Paris and wealthy foreign visitors alike. Besides superb jewellery, enamels and ivory work, the small boutiques offered all manner of less expensive trinkets in brass, gilt and non-precious metals, bone, mother-of-pearl, wood and corozo nut, or "vegetable ivory". All these delightful pieces were termed *"articles de Paris"*, and certainly some of them were produced by skilled artisans in cramped workshops at the same premises. However, many items were transported to the Palais Royal area from other parts of France specialising in particular types of craftwork. Exquisite ivory carving from Dieppe was sold in Paris, but its place of origin was its guarantee of skilled workmanship. Other items, such as turned bone and cut shell novelties, were sent to Paris for the final stages of manufacture. For items to qualify as *"articles de Paris"*, any details of painting or gilding, the addition of clasps and other small metal accessories and the final packaging were all added in the numerous busy workshops of central Paris.

When extending the range of his microphotographic novelties, René Dagron turned to the artisans of the Palais Royal for inspiration and help. He would have been able to choose from an enviable selection of items suitable for both sexes, and made from an assortment of materials. Jewellers supplied mounts for rings, brooches and cravat pins, and the ever-popular watch charms, in gold, gilt and silver.

Métiers associés à l'industrie Stanhope

La plupart des souvenirs en os de Dagron étaient fabriqués à Méru dans l'Oise. Pendant de nombreuses années les artisans locaux produisirent un grand nombre d'objets à partir d'os importés des Amériques. Les objets étaient envoyés à Paris pour la finition ce qui leur valait l'appellation 'Articles de Paris'. Ces bibelots comprenaient des brosses à cheveux, des éventails, des articles de couture et beaucoup d'autres petits objets en os. Des trous étaient percés dans des objets pour insérer des lentilles Stanhope. Des jumelles miniatures furent produites spécialement pour l'industrie microphotographique et demeurèrent populaires pendant près d'un siècle. Les artisans travaillaient aussi des noix de corozo importées d'Amérique du Sud qui devenaient essentiellement des articles de couture.

Le Musée de la Nacre et de la Tabletterie à Méru est une source extraordinaire d'informations au sujet de cette industrie.

46. Location of Dagron's workshops, salons and homes in central Paris, 1859-1897. (Extract from Baedeker's *"Paris and Its Environs"*, 1891.)

(1) 22, rue Poissonière (c.1849)

(2) Workshops in rue des Bons Enfants (1858›)

(3) 66, rue Neuve des Petits Champs, corner of rue d'Antin (1859-c.1873)

(4) 34, boulevard Bonne Nouvelle, corner of rue d'Hauteville (1873›)

These were provided for his wealthy customers, but Dagron also catered for the extensive demand for cheap souvenir items. At this time these were not necessarily tawdry, and many were delicate and attractive,

During the fifteenth and sixteenth centuries the adventurous sailors of Dieppe had supplied Paris with gems, precious metals and luxurious fabrics from the New World and the East Indies. They also returned with elephant tusks from Africa, but kept this scarce commodity for local artisans. Seafarers from Dieppe and nearby Fécamp had developed considerable hand-carving skills, and specialised in intricate floral designs and religious motifs. However, it is rare to find a Stanhope lens inserted in an ivory item of genuine Dieppe origin, for these works of art did not need to be enhanced by the addition of a souvenir microphotograph. Neither the cost nor the slow production time was viable for the type of cheap souvenirs Dagron intended to mass manufacture.

Fortunately, an inexpensive and easily available substitute for ivory existed in bone. This material did not merit painstaking hand carving, but small turning machines could speedily produce a variety of items with a limited range of decoration. The use of bone devalued the skill of

the Dieppe ivory carvers and was largely ignored by the artisans from this area, but several communities further inland had been using bone for almost two centuries. Indeed, at the beginning of the nineteenth century, many French prisoners-of-war, held in gaols around the English coast, had been able to augment their meagre diet by making and selling large numbers of bone items.

One region noted for its specific skills in turned bone ware was centred on the town of Méru, about thirty miles north of Paris in the Oise region. In fact, the proximity of the French capital was a major influence on the development of industry in the area. Large numbers of useful, decorative or religious articles were despatched regularly from Méru and the surrounding small towns and villages to receive the final touches in city workshops, after which they could be classified as *articles de Paris*.

From the early eighteenth century the area had been involved in the manufacture of *"tabletterie"*, *"brosserie"* and buttons. *"Tabletterie"* originally referred to the thin sheets of bone covered in a fine layer of wax, on which notes and messages could be written. Later the name embraced all types of writing equipment, boxes and games. Méru itself

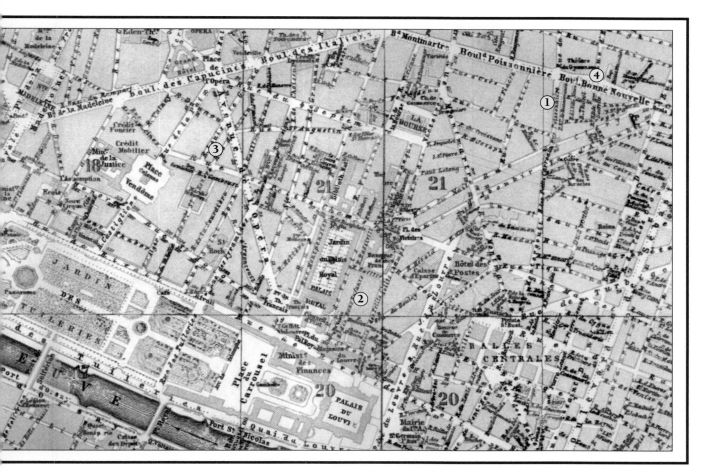

Tributary Crafts

was known for its skilled *"dominotiers"*, or domino-makers. *"Brosserie"* included hairbrushes, toothbrushes and all types of grooming accessories. The large-scale button industry mainly used varieties of mother-of-pearl shell. Other villages were involved in small enterprises specialising in boxes, wafer-thin pierced fan leaves, combs, manicure tools, penholders and a range of needlework tools. Individual items were also made by home-workers and itinerant artisans, who made use of the bone and mother-of-pearl off-cuts discarded by the bigger workshops. In the nineteenth century Méru and the surrounding region provided employment for thousands of workers, and was a hive of industry in the heart of the French countryside.

Bone was the cheap material that René Dagron chose for the majority of his souvenir novelties. The bone workers were willing to supply whatever he ordered or designed, and the introduction of Stanhopes was a major cause of increased activity in the French bone industry during the latter half of the nineteenth century. French sources could not supply enough beef leg bones for the industry, and once the rail industry began to spread throughout France, the bone workers began to seek supplies abroad. Vast numbers of bones were shipped across the Atlantic from the great cattle centres of Chicago and Argentina, eventually arriving in Méru for distribution to the centres of production. Thorough boiling to remove any remaining tissue was a pungent but necessary prelude to any handling of the bones, and the smell of cut bone impregnated the homes and surroundings of the workers. It was an industry that linked both the Old and the New Worlds, and Dagron's invention enabled it to survive into the twentieth century, Bone articles made in rural France found their way into homes around the world.

Miniature bone monoculars and binoculars to be suspended from watch chains were among the first and cheapest of Dagron's Stanhope souvenirs. The turning was so precise that more than one hundred years later each component is easily unscrewed to reveal the Stanhope hidden inside. Most of them still have the fragile metal frames and pendant loops. They were produced in such vast quantities that collectors can find examples relatively easily and they are not always appreciated because of their similar designs and availability. A substantial number has even been purchased by doll makers and collectors, who use them as accessories for antique dolls and dolls' houses.

Bone has a structure formed of microscopic tubes. Cutting and turning unavoidably exposes the ends of the tubes, eventually allowing dirt to become ingrained and other surface discoloration to take place. Some examples of old bone can appear singularly unattractive and unworthy of a place in a Stanhope collection. However, as monoculars and binoculars were produced from 1859 onwards, the images sometimes reveal some of the gems of early microphotography. Pictures of all the early international exhibitions were commemorated in these tiny souvenirs, and also some of the most attractive royal portraits. Collectors should study the subject of the image within; despite the unprepossessing holder, the microphotograph may provide you with a lot of pleasure in researching its history.

Sometimes very attractive mother-of-pearl binoculars can be found, like miniature opera glasses. Méru imported

47. A mother-of-pearl and brass filigree pin-holder, with Stanhope. The image is of St. Geneviève, patron saint of Paris. Actual size: 4cm x 3.5cm x 1cm.

49. A selection of monocular and binocular watch charms, 1860-1950. Actual size.

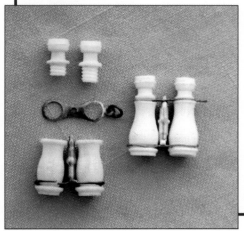

48. Components of miniature bone binoculars containing Stanhopes. Actual size.

vast quantities of mother-of-pearl shell, or *"nacre"*, from the islands of the Pacific, to support the area's pearl button industry. It is likely that the mother-of-pearl Stanhope binoculars originated from home workers using shell off-cuts. There were also examples made in gold, rolled gold, cheaper metals and bog oak, while plastic binoculars appeared in the twentieth century.

Religious articles made of bone had been made long before the introduction of microphotographic viewers. Crucifixes and rosaries echoed the strong faith of the artisans themselves, and were distributed throughout France, Spain, Italy and other Catholic countries. The small round beads were skilfully turned, and decorated with a repetitive dot and circle design. They were interspersed with flat heart-shaped beads cut from smooth plates of bone, and the surfaces scored with lines and concentric circles. All components and the crucifix were linked together by a thin brass chain.

The crucifixes were cut from flat bone plates, with notches around the edges. Although the general designs appear similar, it is evident that these were made by hand and bear the imprint of the individual bone worker. Later examples were often stained a vivid red colour. One of René Dagron's first ideas had been to pierce the crucifixes in the centre, and insert a Stanhope with a religious image. Such rosaries and pendant crosses became popular and revered souvenir items, often sold at religious shrines in France and elsewhere. In the majority of crucifixes the Stanhope lens is found set in a metal mount, as described by Dagron in his early patent applications. The microphotographic images included views of churches and shrines, religious paintings, statues of saints and battlefield memorials. Images in crucifixes without apparent religious connections should be carefully checked for signs of a replacement Stanhope.

Apart from rings and other jewellery, cylindrical needle cases were among the earliest trinkets specifically produced for women. For many years the bone turners had produced useful tubes with well-fitting screw-threaded tops, and many examples can be found in this original form. They were decorated with simple but attractive dot and circle designs or symmetrical scored lines. Dagron used the same needle tubes, but with a hole pierced near one end to allow a metal-mounted Stanhope to be inserted across the diameter of the cylinder. A more ingenious and attractive version included the addition of a circular turned bone bead. A small sphere, drilled through the centre to hold the Stanhope, would be screwed into the end of the needle tube. Occasionally, collectors may be puzzled by a cylindrical bone needle case with a screw-threaded hole at one end. These indicate the loss of the terminal bead and the cases are invariably empty, for needles would soon be lost from such a container. Collectors should not be tempted to buy such an item despite a cheap price, for it is almost impossible to find a replacement for the bone ball holding the Stanhope.

Another adaptation of the basic cylindrical needle case incorporated a "closed fist" design. Sculptures of a hand with slim, bejewelled fingers, and an elegant wrist encircled by a bracelet, were popular parlour ornaments of the time, and the motif was also used in jewellery and other objects. The width of the folded fingers in a closed fist easily permitted the insertion of a Stanhope.

A French bone needle case design, which does not appear to exist previously without a hole specifically drilled to hold a Stanhope, is the miniature parasol. By the 1860s, full-size parasols had become an important feminine fashion accessory. The fabric canopies were neatly pleated, the ferrules slim and pointed and the handles were long and decorative. The bone workers imitated this fashion in small parasol-shaped needle cases, which became popular gifts for women. The handles were turned in a variety of designs but always incorporated a wider section to hold the Stanhope.

50. A selection of bone crucifixes with Stanhopes, 1860-1930. Actual size.

51. A larger bone crucifix mounted on a pedestal, similar to roadside shrines in rural France, c. 1880. Actual height: 9 cm.

Tributary Crafts

The latest fashion in full-size parasol handles was repeated in the miniature versions, such as the vogue for bone rings through the stem. Although the ring appears unbroken and even has some movement in the handle, the glass cylinder passes from one side to the other, a little optical illusion which would have been much appreciated in Victorian England. The "closed fist" motif was also used. Later versions were stained in shades of red, purple or yellow, and others hand-painted with garlands of flowers.

Certainly the large number of needle cases with Stanhopes available to collectors today is evidence of their mass production and popularity in the latter half of the nineteenth century. There are enough clues in dates and style of the photographic image to indicate that they were among the first Stanhope souvenirs produced in the early

1860s. It is also interesting to note that often the microphotographs inserted in them commemorate many of the most important historic events and occasions of this period, at a time when women were beginning to concern themselves with political issues.

A sharp pointed stiletto was a tool used in several forms of craftwork from earliest times, even before needles were invented. Its function was to pierce a series of holes through fabric or leather so that a cord or leather thong could be threaded through. By the late nineteenth century a stiletto was used by needlewomen to pierce holes in finer fabrics and was combined with the sewing needle to produce certain forms of embroidery. Stitching was worked around the edges of the holes for strengthening and decoration, making them a specific feature of the design.

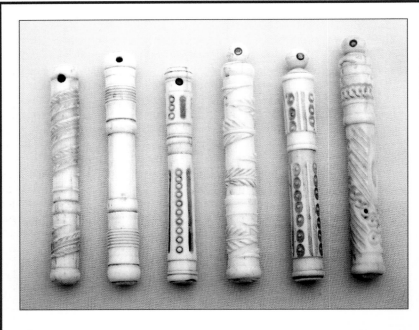

52. Cylindrical bone needle cases with Stanhopes, 1860-1890. Actual length, including ball: 10 cm.

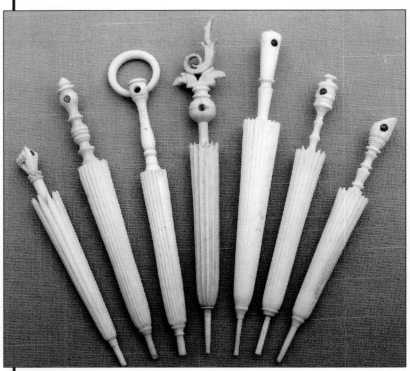

53. Bone needle cases with "closed fist" decoration, 860-1880. Actual length: 10 cm. (Jull Collection).

54. Parasol needle cases of bone, 1860-1910. Actual length: 9.5-14 cm.

Stilettos were generally made of steel, brass or bone and are still included in the contents of most workboxes. Stanhopes can sometimes be found in bone stilettos, although they then tend to make these sewing accessories most impractical. As the tool needs to be gripped quite firmly to produce the required hole, the lens is likely to be damaged or dislodged.

"*Articles de bureau*", or desk accessories, were still being produced by the bone workers long after the end of the nineteenth century. They included pen and pencil holders, and paper knives. It is difficult to date them precisely, apart from those containing dated Stanhopes, but some idea of age can be gained by studying the style of decoration. Although the general shapes remained the same over the years, later examples do not display the same degree of complicated drilling and turning found on the early items. Intricate patterns of interlocking holes were cut right through the bone to the opposite side, often producing a hollow core. This motif was used to good effect on combination paperknives and penholders, where the nibbed end was reversed and screwed into the hollow handle when not in use, and could be glimpsed through the lattice of drilled bone. The Stanhope is usually found in a ball or seal-shaped knob at the end of the item.

Surprisingly, bone whistles containing Stanhopes were very popular in the latter half of the nineteenth century, and many reveal microphotographic images of relatively early date. There are considerable variations in design, and they can be combined with other accessories, such as mechanical pencils. Smaller examples have small metal

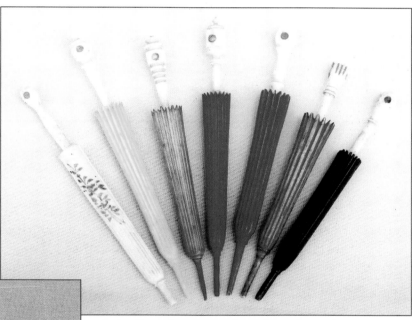

55. Stained and decorated bone parasol needle cases, 1870-1910. Actual length: 10.5-12.5cm.

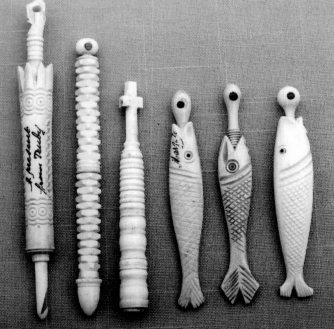

56. Decorative bone needle cases. The example on the left has a crochet hook "ferrule", 1860-1920. Actual length: 8.5–13.5 cm.

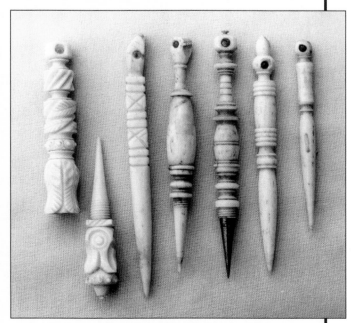

57. Bone stilettos, 1860-1890. Actual length: 7.5–9 cm.

Tributary Crafts

loops for attachment to a watch chain. Bone whistles are frequently discoloured and display the dirt-speckled surface of aged bone.

Although the majority of bone items were mass-produced in tens of thousands, workers in bone occasionally found the time and inspiration to express their individuality and skill in unusual "one-off" pieces. A large accessory for the needlewoman was a turret-shaped combination of tape measure and plump silk pincushion. Such pieces are rare, and may seem less attractive when one remembers they are made from hollow sections of beef thighbone! The knobs to wind the silk measure exist both with and without Stanhope lenses. These items can be found in different sizes, but the method of decoration is similar, pointing to one or just a few craftsmen producing such pieces.

Possibly only a single worker in bone was responsible for the extremely rare drum-shaped gaming containers, which have been discovered with sets of dominoes or dice. Like the pincushion/measure combination piece, the body of the "drum" is cylindrical and formed from a section of beef thighbone. The pierced sides point to a craftsman familiar with the techniques used in cutting the teeth of bone combs or producing delicate lattice-work on fan blades, both of which were made in great numbers in the Méru region of France. The top and base are formed of circular bone plates that screw easily onto the central cylinder, and the miniature dominoes or dice were probably cut from chips of bone left over from mass-produced bone items. The dominoes and dice are another link with the master *dominotiers* of Méru. The style of the string threaded herring-bone fashion around the "drum" is yet another clue to an individual craftsman. To find such an item with a Stanhope is a particular prize, treasured by fortunate collectors around the world wherever these pieces have surfaced.

Many articles containing Stanhopes were made from a different ivory substitute, derived from the vegetable rather than the animal kingdom. "Vegetable ivory" is a term applied to items made of corozo or tagua nut, the fruit of two species of tropical palm. One variety (Phytelephas Macrocarpa) grows in central and South America, and the other is found in parts of central Africa (Hyphaene Palm). Corozo nuts have a very white but extremely hard kernel when ripe, but are inedible, lacking in useful oils and fairly heavy. They only began to appear in Europe when used as ballast on early sailing ships.

Sometimes they were referred to as "iron nuts", and in the mid-nineteenth century it was discovered that their

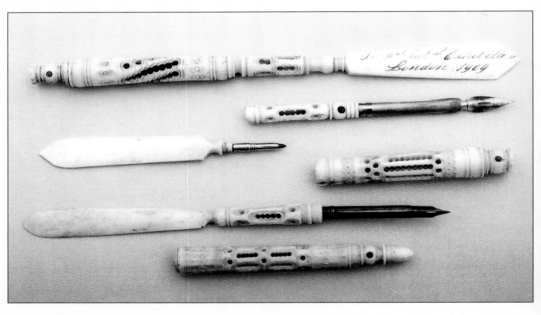

58. Combination pen and pencil holders with letter openers, 1860-1920. Longest item: 22.5cm.

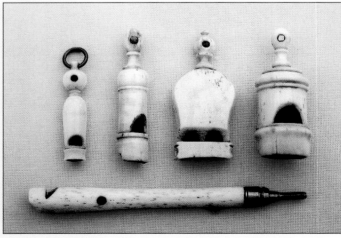

59. Bone whistles, 1860-1890. The longest item is a combined whistle and mechanical pencil. Actual lengths: 4-10 cm.

kernels were hard enough to be cut and drilled by machine. Corozo nuts began to be imported in large amounts for the button industry in Britain. Some of the Méru bone turners decided to use their skills on this new material, and sacks of corozo nuts began to arrive from faraway South America. Yet again, workers who may never have visited Paris or even travelled beyond the confines of their villages, were using their skills on a material originating from thousands of miles away.

The main disadvantage of corozo nuts is their relatively small size, with a diameter averaging less than two inches. This limits both the size and the shape of items made from them, but the craftsmen found they were ideal for making chunkier novelties. In fact, they were better than bone for making tape measure containers and thimble holders, and these were produced in large numbers in the shape of barrels, acorns and pears. The clever use of two or more

sections linked by screw threads but made from different nuts even allowed the craftsmen to make the longer shapes required for needle cases.

Surprisingly, the spindles onto which the measuring tapes were wound, and the tiny rings retaining the tape ends, were rarely turned from corozo, and small pieces of bone were substituted for these components. At the time of manufacture, the three components of the tape measure (i.e. container, spindle and ring) would all have been the same ivory-white colour, although made from the two different substances. However, corozo nut mellows with age, darkening to shades of honey, amber and light brown, while bone remains the same creamy colour. Over the years the difference in colour between the holder made of corozo and the small bone attachments becomes quite marked. In early items the bone spindles are very slim and with narrow handles, but to incorporate Stanhopes more substantial

60. A bone combination pincushion and measure, c.1870. Actual height: 5.5 cm.

61. A gaming container with miniature dominoes. Actual height: 2.5cm. (Kessler Collection).

62. "Vegetable ivory": from corozo nut to finished article. Actual size.

Tributary Crafts

bone knobs were needed. In thimble cases oval bone knobs were screwed directly into the lid of the corozo container. It is unfortunate that to use either the tape measure or a thimble case, the knob holding the glass Stanhope must be grasped firmly, often resulting in a lost image or the entire lens.

French bone manufacturers' catalogues displayed illustrations of articles also made of corozo, either with or without holes for Stanhope lenses. In the late nineteenth century several French souvenir shops advertising microphotographic novelties included items made of the same material. Some corozo articles have also been discovered in other countries with "France" stamped on the base of the container, indicating that the complete novelty was exported from a French source. Even so, France did not have a monopoly on corozo articles, for some British manufacturers also produced vegetable ivory souvenirs, inserting Stanhopes they had obtained from France by mail order. It is not always possible to be certain about the country of origin of many corozo souvenirs with Stanhopes.

Workers in bone and vegetable ivory formed the main tributary crafts of the Stanhope industry, which provided the livelihood of the populations of entire rural communities. In addition, several other small enterprises in and around the Paris area had reason to be thankful for the market generated by the international popularity of microphotographic souvenirs.

63. Bone and corozo measures. Actual size: 4-6 cm.

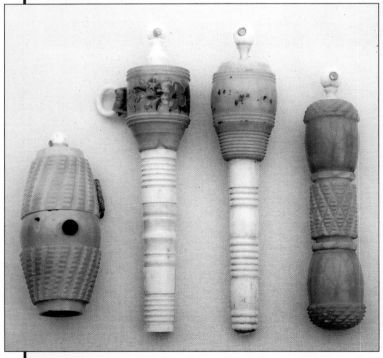

65. Corozo thimble cases, the smaller version with a matching thimble. Unusually, the knob holding the Stanhope is an integral part of the container lid, rather than a bone addition. Actual size: 5.0-5.8cm.

64. Bone and corozo combination sewing accessories: a measure with thread container (private collection) and three measures with needle cases. Actual size: 6.5-11 cm.

7 Dagron and the Franco-Prussian War

During the summer of 1870, René Dagron was forced to suspend most of his business activities, due to the outbreak of war. Napoleon lll was angered by the expansion of the Prussian Empire, and was determined that France should not lose her leading position in Europe. With little cause for aggression, and even less preparation, the Emperor declared war on Prussia on 19th July, but only six weeks later he and much of the French army were forced to surrender at Sédan. Many citizens fled the country, including Dagron's wife Caroline and their children. Earlier that year their daughter Renée had been sent to England to learn the language, possibly with the intention of helping the export business of *Dagron & Cie*. Now she was joined by the rest of the family, who found refuge with Caroline's brother, Captain Auguste Lendy at Sunbury-on-Thames in Middlesex. Pauline, the eldest daughter, had married Jean-Baptiste Poisot, a painter, and he remained in Paris with his father-in-law.

French families, including the Comte de Paris and the Duc de Chartres. In the 1871 census, Captain Lendy was listed as the Principal, living there with his wife and five children. The household also comprised eleven military students and thirteen assorted servants. Madame Dagron and her six children joined the household and anxiously awaited news from Paris.

By 19th September Paris was surrounded, and for the next four months and ten days the city was cut off from the rest of the world. No tourists came to Paris and the souvenir trade came to a halt. *Dagron & Cie* ceased production of Stanhope novelties, for the majority of the workforce had either left Paris or been conscripted. Dagron and Poisot prepared to help defend the city, unaware that they would soon be required to fulfil their most important microphotographic commission to date. Dagron's expertise would enable him to play an unexpected but most significant role in the Franco-Prussian War, and would cause his name to

66. *Sunbury House, 1859 (By courtesy of the Sunbury and Shepperton Local History Society.)*

Auguste and Sophia Lendy occupied a position of some consequence in the area, for Sunbury House was one of the most important and grand houses in the parish. Previously it had provided sanctuary for the exiled Orléans family, who had often been visited by Queen Victoria. Now the Military Academy founded there by Captain Lendy was flourishing, and several students came from aristocratic

be remembered more for this than any of his other achievements.

As the Prussian army advanced on Paris, normal lines of communication were severed. A number of ministers, including M. Steenackers, Director of the Telegraph Service, hurriedly left Paris for Tours, to set up a provisional Government in unoccupied France. Baskets of carrier pigeons

PARIS ASSIÉGÉ

REVOLVER
GALAND
3, rue Richer

OSSEÏNE

Au Bureau de L'ÉCLIPSE,16,Rue du Croissant,PARIS   Imp.Coulbœuf, Paris.

LES EFFETS DU BOMBARDEMENT.
_ Ni hommes, ni femmes, tous Ambassadeurs Siamois !

*67. The Parisians avoid the
Prussian missiles, Siamese
fashion! From"Souvenirs du
Siège de Paris", Draner.
(Ashley Lawrence Collection)*

had been taken by train to Tours, with the aim of transporting official despatches from the provinces to the capital. This communication system was set up almost immediately. At first the messages were written by hand, in very small script on the thinnest of paper. Even so, each pigeon was able to carry very few messages at a time, on account of the weight. This laborious method was used until mid-October, when it was suggested that many more despatches could be sent if they were first reduced by photography. This task was begun by a local photographer at Tours. The reduced proofs were printed on both sides of a small sheet of fine-textured paper, which was then transported to Paris by the feathered couriers, to be read under a microscope.

In Paris the situation worsened, and in some areas the population came under fire. Jules Renard, under the pen name "Draner", began publishing a series of cartoons illustrating how the Parisians had their own ways of coping with various difficulties and deprivations. One of these was a reminder of the visit of the Siamese ambassador several years before.

Before the outbreak of war, the French photographer Félix Tournachon, known as "Nadar", had been experimenting with aerial photography from gas-filled balloons. Now he used his contacts and expertise to organise escapes from the city, and new balloons were being made at the rate of almost one per day. A number of them were able to ascend out of the capital carrying passengers and post, and fly over the blockade to unoccupied France or even further afield. Return trips into Paris were impossible, for even favourable winds could not be relied upon to carry balloons to a specific site. As soon as the balloons landed, passengers and post continued the journey, using the quickest route by rail and boat.

René Dagron used the *"ballons montés"* (manned balloons) to send letters to his wife in England, and one of these remarkable documents is now preserved in the Dagron family archives. It is a thin sheet of folded notepaper only 10cm by 13cm, covered on both sides with minute handwriting, and was posted on 19th October. It left Paris at 11.30 a.m. on 22nd October 1870,

68. Dagron's letter sent by "balloon post" to his wife in England. Actual size and folded. (Dagron Family Archives)

carried by Balloon No.17, "The Garibaldi", together with the pilot and one passenger. The journey was surprisingly uneventful, for the wind was blowing in a favourable direction and the balloon drifted over the Prussian lines without mishap. It travelled for about forty kilometres before descending at Quincy-Voisins, near Meaux at 1.30 p.m. The bags of letters were delivered to the local post office, and Mme. Dagron's letter continued its journey to England by the normal route, arriving at Sunbury House on 2nd November.

Dagron wrote that it was the seventh letter he had sent by this route, and he had been discouraged to learn from the newspaper that at least one balloon had come down in Prussian-held territory, together with all the mail. He described the current situation in the besieged city; morale and patriotism were high, but although many wanted to enlist in the National Guard, there were no more rifles. The main food source in the city was horsemeat, and there was talk of rationing. He and Poisot were happy enough, but news from the family would make the situation more bearable. He hoped that the children were using the time to learn English, and reminded Caroline that she herself knew "how useful it is to know this language". He spoke of courage and hope, and his love for all his "little family", and signed the letter from *"Ton mari dévoué, Dagron"* ("Your devoted husband Dagron"). Another letter to Mme. Dagron *"chez le Capitaine Lendy"* was posted on 25th October, and also reached its destination safely.

Some official despatches sent by carrier pigeon from Tours had arrived in Paris by mid-November, but the isolated population was desperate to receive news of family and friends from beyond the Prussian lines. The Government in Paris realised the importance of maintaining morale by keeping lines of communication open, and decided to augment the Tours despatches with a more extensive service based at Clermont-Ferrand. René Dagron was asked by M. Rampont, Director of the Post Office, to establish and operate this additional system of microphotographed messages carried by carrier pigeon. He made plans to leave Paris at the earliest opportunity, although the first part of the journey would involve a perilous balloon flight over the Prussian lines.

Dagron et la guerre Franco-Prussienne

Juste avant le siège de Paris, René Dagron envoya en Angleterre son épouse et ses enfants, qui trouvèrent refuge chez son beau-frère à Sunbury-on-Thames. Il leur envoya, par ballon monté, des lettres qui décrivaient la situation à Paris. L'histoire du ballon postal et des pigeons voyageurs est bien documentée, et dans cette affaire Dagron fit preuve d'un courage et d'une abnégation exemplaires. À l'âge de cinquante et un ans il accepta la mission qui consistait à s'échapper de Paris pour aller à Tours et améliorer le système de transmission de messages élaboré par le service postal français. Avec quatre autres personnes et un important matériel photographique, il réussit à parcourir une certaine distance en ballon. Malheureusement le ballon atterrit en territoire occupé par les Prussiens mais Dagron put terminer son périlleux voyage jusqu'à Tours à travers les lignes ennemies sans être capturé.

En microphotographiant des messages sur des films très légers, Dagron permit aux pigeons de transporter deux millions de messages officiels et personnels vers la ville de Paris assiégée. Il rendait ainsi un très grand service à son pays et relevait le moral des Parisiens pendant cette période difficile pour la France.

Malheureusement après le siège, il ne reçut aucune reconnaissance officielle pour cette mission réussie. En 1871 il écrivit son troisième livre 'La Poste par Pigeons Voyageurs: Souvenir du Siège de Paris'.

Dagron and the Franco-Prussian War

SOUVENIRS DU SIÉGE DE PARIS.

Au Bureau de L'ECLIPSE 16 Rue du Croissant.PARIS   *imp.Coulboeuf.Paris*

AÉROSTIER — Mon Laisser-passer? Tiens, le v'la!

DEPOSE — Tous droits réservés.

69. The perils of balloon travel in 1870! From "Souvenirs du Siège de Paris", Draner. (Ashley Lawrence Collection)

The balloons were inflated with highly inflammable coal gas, an additional hazard for the passengers. Dagron was fifty-one years of age at this time, but his sense of duty seemed to overcome any fear of danger. However, he had been offered a generous financial contract for all despatched messages, and he was certainly aware that the resulting publicity would prove invaluable for his business once hostilities ceased.

On 12th November 1870 two balloons were prepared, appropriately named *"le Niépce"* and *"le Daguerre"*. The former carried Dagron, Poisot and three other passengers: M. Gnocchi, his photographic assistant, M. Pagano, a young sailor who was the *"aéronaute"* or balloon pilot and M. Albert Fernique, who was Dagron's official partner in the operation. The balloon was also loaded with six hundred kilograms of photographic equipment. *Le Daguerre* contained another three passengers, several baskets of pigeons, a consignment of post and the remainder of Dagron's pho-

tographic supplies. The balloons drifted eastwards with the prevailing wind, but as they passed over Prussian-held territory not far from Paris, heavy gunfire forced *Le Daguerre* to descend. All the passengers and contents fell into the hands of the Prussians.

Le Niépce managed to continue for almost one hundred miles east of Paris, but was still within Prussian-held territory when it came down near Vitry-le-Francois. First to arrive was a group of sympathetic peasants, who provided the Parisian passengers with more suitable clothes and helped to load the equipment onto two farm-carts. Although Prussian soldiers soon arrived on the scene and captured one of the carts, they overlooked Dagron and the other aeronauts in rural peasant garb, thinking the balloon's passengers had already fled. The group split up to lessen the chances of capture, and Dagron managed to leave with the other cart containing most of his precious photographic supplies.

For the next week the five Frenchmen managed to evade the Prussian troops as they endeavoured to continue their route southwards. The weather was atrocious, making the arduous journey even more hazardous. They had several narrow escapes, and more of Dagron's photographic equipment was lost, but eventually the little group managed to cross into unoccupied France at Mont-Saint-Sulpice. From there they received orders to proceed to Tours, which they reached on 21st November.

Dagron's welcome was less than rapturous, for M. Steenackers and other officials of the Telegraph Service were unwilling to change current arrangements for the new orders he brought from the Director of the Postal Service. The impossibility of speedy two-way communication between Paris and Tours resulted in a conflict of priorities. Only those trapped in Paris really understood the devastating effect of total isolation. M. Rampont knew that the besieged population could only withstand the physical hardships if their anxiety about loved ones was eased by a better mail service, yet officials in Tours considered their present efforts to be more than adequate.

Dagron was asked to provide a specimen microphotographed message to compare with those being produced on paper in Tours. Despite the loss of equipment and materials, Dagron was able to produce good results with collodion film, using a thicker coating that could be peeled intact from the glass plate. His method needed a very short exposure time, permitted a greater rate of reduction and produced a message that was lighter in weight and more legible when enlarged. The reluctant officials had to accept that the Dagron process was superior, and his team set to work to clear the backlog of messages that had collected in Tours from all parts of free France. However, enemy forces were nearing the area and the Government Delegation was compelled to flee. On 11th December a special train carried them to Bordeaux, accompanied by Dagron with his personnel and equipment.

At Bordeaux the system was rapidly reorganised by officials of the Post and Telegraph Services to include three centres for collecting and preparing printed sheets of messages, but René Dagron undertook all the microphotography himself. Within a few days the backlog of despatches had been cleared, and the "pigeon post" system became well established. Dagron produced microfilm of both official and private despatches. Local amateur photographers provided him with further supplies to enable him to continue the operation. Each piece of microfilm measured 3.6 cm x 6 cm and contained an average of three thousand miniature messages. Each pigeon could carry between fifteen and eighteen such pieces of film, for they weighed less than a gram in total. The films were rolled up tightly and pushed into a piece of goose quill 5cm in length. A waxed silk thread attached the quill tube to the fifth large tail feather of the pigeon, so that its centre of gravity was not affected in flight. Provided no disasters befell the bird, a carrier pigeon could take about twelve hours to cover the distance to Paris.

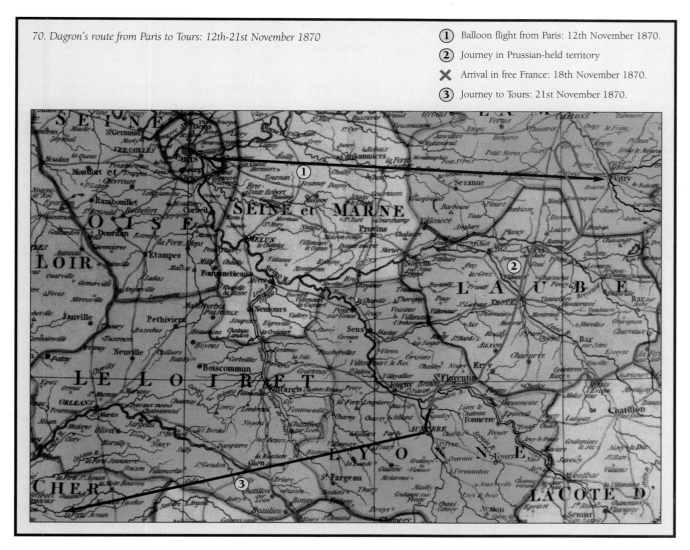

70. Dagron's route from Paris to Tours: 12th-21st November 1870

① Balloon flight from Paris: 12th November 1870.

② Journey in Prussian-held territory

✖ Arrival in free France: 18th November 1870.

③ Journey to Tours: 21st November 1870.

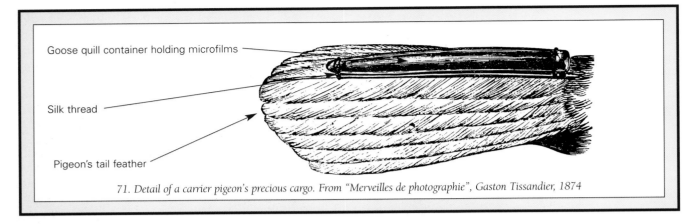

Goose quill container holding microfilms

Silk thread

Pigeon's tail feather

71. Detail of a carrier pigeon's precious cargo. From "Merveilles de photographie", Gaston Tissandier, 1874

When a carrier pigeon arrived at its pigeon loft in Paris, the message tube was taken to the main Telegraph Office. The microfilms were removed and placed in a basin of water, together with a little ammonia. This caused the films to unroll, and they were then dried and placed between two plates of glass. M. Jules Duboscq's *"Megascope"*, a powerful "magic lantern", was used to project the films onto a screen, from where the messages were read and transcribed by a group of copiers. The complete operation for each batch of microfilms took about nine hours.

A stamp on the pigeon's wing, giving dates of departure and receipts of completed messages, completed this service. Further balloons continued to be sent out of Paris carrying post and more baskets of pigeons.

Dagron recounted the rapid progress of one microfilmed order for photographic chemicals sent to a firm in Paris. The carrier pigeon left on 18th January 1871, and once the message was received, the supplies were despatched by the next balloon out of the city. They were delivered to his workshop in Bordeaux on 24th January, and Dagron was proud to note that the ordinary telegraph and railway route of peacetime could not have fulfilled his order more quickly. Unfortunately this swift delivery was a rare exception, for usually the entire despatch and receipt process took several weeks. Meanwhile, Mme. Dagron was able to receive letters from her husband by normal postal routes from Bordeaux, and presumably to reassure him in turn that the rest of the family were living peacefully in England.

Sadly, the loss of pigeons was very high. Members of *"L'Espérance"*, a group of Paris pigeon fanciers, offered their birds to supplement the service. Officers of the society accompanied their pigeons aboard the balloons, in order to look after the birds in Tours. Once the pigeons had flown back to Paris, they rested only a short time before being sent out of the city again by balloon. Then they were fitted with another message container and required to repeat the hazardous flight. Of the 360 or so pigeons sent from Paris, only fifty-seven were still alive by the end of the siege, the majority of them having perished during the winter weather or from artillery fire. Nevertheless, several heroic birds survived more than one flight, and each arrival was greeted with joy in the city.

To ensure successful delivery, most messages were sent several times before their receipt in Paris was acknowledged. Some were even sent more than thirty times. Dagron later calculated that, before the siege came to an end in late

72. Transcribing despatches carried by pigeon to Paris. From "Merveilles de photographie", Gaston Tissandier, 1874.

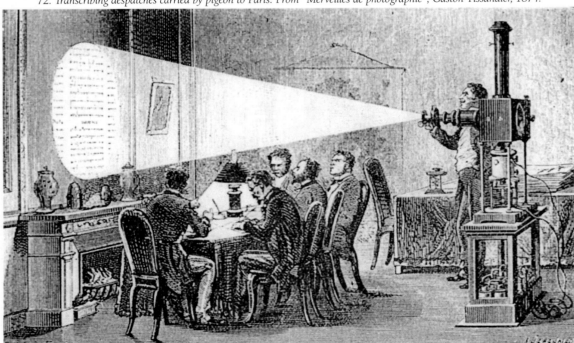

74. Balloons leaving Paris, with passengers, post and baskets of pigeons, 1870-1871. A contemporary engraving. (Ashley Lawrence Collection)

January, more than two and a half million despatches had been sent by this route. The stressful events of the previous months took their toll and severe illness forced him to remain in Bordeaux until mid-April. His family then rejoined him from England, but found Paris much changed. The Imperial Family was in exile and the political situation had become very unstable. The citizens had become embittered and scarred by their experiences, and amid general unrest, declared a Commune. After a period of street riots, burning buildings and virtual civil war, the insurrection was strongly suppressed by the French government. The Dagron family could no longer feel safe in the capital and decided to leave Paris again, so that their father could recover his health in a more peaceful environment.

The period of rest proved useful: to enable the public to appreciate the incredible achievements of the "pigeon post", René Dagron started writing a booklet about his wartime escape from Paris and subsequent adventures. In *"La Poste par Pigeons Voyageurs: Souvenir du Siège de Paris"*, the author described himself as the "official Government photographer of all microfilmed despatches". In the account one detects a slight whiff of revenge. While he was pleased to mention those patriotic Frenchmen who came to his aid during his escape to Tours, René Dagron had no scruples about naming and shaming those who were more helpful to the enemy, or who endeavoured to hinder the completion of his assignment.

Dagron was unaware that several other participants involved in the "pigeon post" operation had hastened to

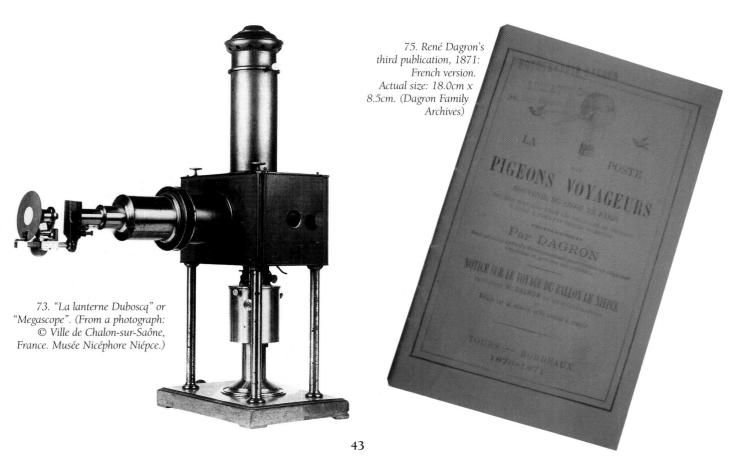

73. "La lanterne Duboscq" or "Megascope". (From a photograph: © Ville de Chalon-sur-Saône, France. Musée Nicéphore Niépce.)

75. René Dagron's third publication, 1871: French version. Actual size: 18.0cm x 8.5cm. (Dagron Family Archives)

Dagron and the Franco-Prussian War

76. René Dagron, c. 1872 (Dagron Family archives)

publish their own versions of events in Tours and Bordeaux. M. De Lafollye, Chief Inspector of the Telegraph Service, was one of the first, producing a comprehensive memoir full of detailed facts and figures while still in Bordeaux in February. On his return to Paris, René Dagron was angered to discover that others were claiming credit for the success of the "pigeon post". His manuscript had already been delivered to the printers, but he added a postscript in which he stressed that his was the true version of events and the terms of his contract could be verified officially. Dagron's book underlined the importance of both the quality and the quantity of his microfilmed despatches in maintaining communications between besieged Paris and free France. Ever mindful of catching the public interest, into the centre of each book was attached a small card frame holding a piece of microfilm identical to the microfilms carried by pigeons during the siege of Paris and signed by Dagron. It bore an official Government stamp and was authorised for reproduction by M. De Lafollye.

In August 1871 René Dagron submitted his report and claim for payment to M. Rampont. Unfortunately, the generous financial terms promised in the initial contract with M. Rampont did not materialise. The agreed rate of 15 francs per negative for a minimum number of two hundred negatives per day had caused consternation among the provincial officials when they became aware of his phenomenal output. In December 1870 Dagron had been obliged to sign a renegotiated contract, based on a fee per block of messages, and even this was decreased towards the end of the siege when demand for messages carried by pigeon diminished. Unlike Fernique who had insisted on payment in advance, Dagron did not even receive the initial payment until he had survived the risks of the journey to Tours. In addition to the loss of equipment worth almost 10,000 francs, he had incurred considerable expense when setting up the operation, paying his assistants and accommodation.

When he presented his final bill, critics accused him of profiteering from the war, but his family and friends were adamant that he had barely received enough payment to cover his losses and costs. Certainly, documents preserved by the Dagron family show his meticulous account of expenses and microphotographic work carried out.

By the time the family returned to Paris, Dagron's fortunes had suffered a serious setback. He was unable to meet the high payments for the studio where he had carried out *"photographie de luxe"* and petitioned for a reduction in the rent. His lack of portrait customers was matched by the decline in the microphotography business. It would take time before tourists returned to Paris and the souvenir trade recovered. Influential friends endeavoured to advance his cause with the French Government, and finally his two sons were awarded scholarships to pay for their higher education. It seems poor recompense for Dagron's magnificent achievement in restoring peace of mind and hope to the people of Paris while they were enduring the terrible conditions of life under siege. A further insult occurred when Fernique was awarded the *"Légion d'honneur"* for services to his country, while Dagron himself received no decoration or official recognition for his bravery and tireless efforts during the war.

As a postscript to the Franco-Prussian War, it should be noted that the balloon pilots and even the carrier pigeons themselves received more substantial recognition than René Dagron. Frédéric-Auguste Bartholdi, designer of the Statue of Liberty, produced an impressive monument in bronze to commemorate their historic flights. It consisted of a hot air balloon, supported by four pedestals holding pairs of carrier pigeons. It was placed at the Porte des Ternes, not far from the Arc de Triomphe, and was unveiled in January 1906. In 1944, during the German Occupation of Paris, the bronze monument was melted down and nothing more remains.

77. "Monument des Aéronautes du Siège de Paris": Porte des Ternes, 1906-1944. (Ashley Lawrence Collection)

253. PARIS-NEUILLY — Monument des Aéronautes du Siège de Paris   C. M.

8 Back to Business

In the early 1870s fun and frivolity were scarce in Paris, and tourists were reluctant to revisit the city. The Dagron family finances were helped by the commercial success of his book: *"La Poste par Pigeons Voyageurs"*. Dagron also decided to publish an English translation, and this soon appeared in identical format to the French version. Unfortunately his translator lacked experience, for there are a number of mistakes in the text, including the title itself: "The Post by Travelling Pigeons" uses a direct translation instead of the correct term "carrier" or "homing" pigeons. Nevertheless, both versions attracted considerable interest, and continued to be sold at the Dagron business premises for almost thirty years.

Another popular souvenir was a specially designed card frame holding a reproduced sheet of microfilmed messages like those inserted in the books. From the 1870s onwards, Dagron used the motif of a gas-filled balloon labelled *"Le Niépce"* on his *cartes de visites*, together with the words: "Sole Government photographer for microfilmed despatches by carrier pigeon post during the siege of Paris".

During this decade the Dagron family moved from their previous premises on the corner of *rue Neuve des Petits Champs* and *rue d'Antin* to another corner site: *34 boulevard*

Bonne Nouvelle and *1, rue d'Hauteville*. This was a most prestigious address, classified as one of the "Great Boulevards" of Paris. It was one of the Inner Boulevards, constructed on the site of ancient fortifications which formerly surrounded the city. In 1891 Baedeker's Guide to Paris and Its Environs noted: "These imposing streets are nowhere surpassed in the handsomeness of their architecture, the briskness of their traffic and the attractiveness of their shops". The tree-lined boulevards were at least thirty metres wide, and as their paving stones had been removed to build barricades during the French Revolution, they benefited from "macadamised roadways and asphalt sidewalks for foot-passengers".

Dagron & Cie had been out of contact with their overseas customers for several months during the period of the siege of Paris, and it took time to re-establish the export network. However, gradually the work force returned, the tributary industries started sending components to Paris again and new equipment and supplies were obtained for the microphotography department. Mail orders for Stanhope images and mounts were completed and despatched to established and new distributors and soon *Dagron & Cie* was busier than ever. Dagron's daughter Renée had

78. The English translation of "La Poste par Pigeons Voyageurs", René Dagron, 1871. Actual size: 18.0cm x 8.5cm. (Ashley Lawrence Collection).

79. Souvenir card frame for reproduction microfilms from the "Pigeon Post" during the siege of Paris. (Dagron Family Archives)

Back to Business

completed her education in England, and in 1872 returned to the family in Paris. Many years later, she wrote to her sister-in-law Lucile: "When I returned the microscopy was doing very well. There were many book keepers...and I was busy helping Mama in the business."

René Dagron had always preferred microphotography to studio photography, although his wife did not share this enthusiasm. After the siege he began to investigate the commercial use of microphotography for more serious purposes. He wrote several articles for French and British photographic journals, describing his particular method of preparing microphotographic despatches on "dry" collodion film. His process attracted much interest, not only among other photographers, but also among those who were concerned with safeguarding or transporting valuable documents in time of war. Unfortunately he did not take out a patent on what later proved to be a major advance in microphotography: his process for the microfilm itself. It is possible that Dagron's financial difficulties following the siege of Paris prevented expenditure on patent costs, or he may have overlooked the importance of the film in promoting the microphotographic process itself. During the following century, shortly before World War ll, experiments to produce quality microfilm were taking place both in Britain and the U.S.A. Dagron's descendants noted these developments and in 1937 Renée wrote from America to her sister-in-law: "I know he did not take out a patent, as it was necessary to pay a large sum of money because the name of microfilm had already appeared."

This may have been a major opportunity lost, but Dagron was more concerned with the subject matter of microphotography. His wartime experiences in microfilming documentation had convinced him that whatever scale of reduction could be achieved for written or printed records, unless clarity of text was maintained, the exercise would be worthless. Like Sir David Brewster some years before, the vast amounts of printed matter accumulating and stored around the world in business records, libraries and government departments excited his inventive mind. He had influential friends and government contacts, and hoped to gain lucrative contracts for projects that had nothing in common with cheap souvenirs. In 1872 he was paid to microfilm all the records and policies of an insurance company, and later he was commissioned by Baron Rothschild to microfilm all the Bank's accounts. Dagron also entered into negotiations with the French Government to copy all official documents onto microfilm, but this project does not seem to have succeeded. Another use of microfilmed documents was in teaching, and he was able to produce for students of religion a microphotographed version of the Koran on small glass plates. An example is retained in the family archives.

Retour aux commerces

Après la guerre, des émeutes se produisirent sous la Commune, et peu de touristes vinrent à Paris. Dagron développa plusieurs projets pour gagner sa vie; son dernier livre fut traduit en anglais, il reproduisit les microfilms portés par les pigeons et les vendit dans des cadres souvenir. Il étudia aussi d'autres utilisations pour la microphotographie, et fabriqua le 'télémètre - microphotographique'. C'était une visionneuse portable pour des cartes de France sur microfilms, qu'il espérait vendre à l'armée française. Malheureusement, les autorités militaires ne retinrent pas ce procédé. Le gouvernement fut davantage impressionné par son invention d'une encre indélébile pour marquer les uniformes des militaires. Il inventa également une sorte de pâte permettant de tirer plusieurs copies d'un même document. Ces inventions étaient généralement couronnées de succès, mais Dagron dut vendre les droits de production pour résoudre ses problèmes financiers immédiats. D'autres en profitèrent et firent fortune à partir de ses inventions.

Dagron exposa à l'Exposition Universelle de Paris en 1878, et reçut une médaille d'argent pour la microphotographie. Il inscrivit cette récompense sur ses cartes de visite. Quelques années plus tard l'entreprise Dagron sépara ses activités. René Dagron maintint son intérêt pour la microphotographie, et son épouse devint responsable de la 'Photographie Dagron'.

80. Ink bottle from
"Dagron & Cie", c. 1880.

In 1873 Dagron and two colleagues, Dallemagne and Triboulet, were granted the patent for a microfilm viewer for use by the French Army (No. 100735). This was a small hand-held instrument holding an entire set of microfilmed maps of France. They could be projected onto the wall of a tent during military operations, and Dagron hoped they would be made available to every French officer. (The lack of maps had been a major grievance during the Franco-Prussian War, and some sources blamed the French defeat on this omission.) The instrument was known as a *"télémètre-micrographique"*, but its approval for military use was refused.

Government ministers were more impressed by another of Dagron's inventions which owed less to his knowledge of photography than his scientific background. The army had been losing money because of the widespread theft of uniforms, and one of the reasons for this was the easy removal of identification markings. Dagron invented a type of indelible ink that marked the fabric permanently, and this went into widespread production later. Another idea on which he worked for some time was a type of paste that enabled many copies of a document to be printed. He referred to this as a "facsimile" process, and hoped to encourage interest and financial backing to start up production. It is not clear why he decided to sell the patent rights, or grant the manufacturers use of the name *"Dagron & Cie"*. It is possible that in view of his financial difficulties after the "Pigeon Post" mission, he preferred to accept an immediate lump

sum instead of long-term recompense. The manufacturers did indeed enjoy great commercial success in France, and in future years this type of ink became a household name. Dagron's own business became *"Photographie Dagron"* from this time.

Renée Dagron described her father as "a man of genius who succeeded in all his inventions", and even today, members of the Dagron family refer to their ancestor as *"l'Inventeur"*. René Dagron continued to experiment with new microphotographic novelties, and despite his many

81. *Image from a bone parasol needle case: single view of the popular Palais du Trocadéro with its gardens and fountains. (1878 Exposition Universelle in Paris.)*

inventions, none was as popular or financially successful as the Stanhope souvenirs. This process was always associated with the Dagron name, and it never failed to retain his initial enthusiasm. Whatever else Dagron became involved with, he rarely lost an opportunity to promote his latest novelty.

It was planned to hold another *Exposition Universelle* in Paris in 1878. However, France had suffered a humiliating loss of important territory after the Franco-Prussian War, and had been forced to pay an enormous indemnity to Germany. The government could ill afford the cost of such an event, yet national pride dictated that France should still be regarded as a major power in Europe. Nevertheless, the authorities were aware that the economy would benefit from the expected large numbers of tourists, who still remained absent from the city following the political unrest after the siege. The event was held in the same area as before, but it was extended to cover about 66 acres, and divided into two sections. A huge rectangular structure was built on the original *Champs de Mars* site, so that most exhibits were housed under one roof. The rest of the exhibition could be visited on the opposite side of the River Seine, in the *Palais du Trocadéro*. Many souvenirs show twin views of the double site. Another interesting image was the *"Vue Générale"*, showing the complete exhibition site on both sides of the river. It pictures a busy scene with much water traffic on the River Seine and a gas-filled balloon tethered above the showground. This was M. Girard's captive balloon, used for aerial photographs.

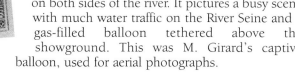

Back to Business

82. *Cartes de visite produced by "Photographie Dagron" after 1878. Note Caroline Dagron's initials below the portrait.*

The 1878 *Exposition Universelle* was devoted to "World Peace", the first time an official theme had been announced. It became the world's largest international fair to date, with more than sixteen million visitors touring more than fifty thousand exhibits during the six-month period of its opening. The French Government was delighted with the financial success of the event, and once more Paris was the centre of fashion, art and pleasure. René Dagron was an exhibitor, and this time was awarded a Silver Medal. His cartes de visite were proudly inscribed *"Medaille d'Argent, Paris Exposition 1878"*.

One incident at this event was to infuriate René Dagron, however, recalling the bitter memories of his treatment after the Franco-Prussian War. To his disgust he discovered that in the *Palais du Champs-de-Mars*, among the exhibition of photography, was a display by Albert Fernique that included a microfilmed sheet of messages for the "Pigeon Post". He concluded that Fernique's intention was to infer that he alone had been responsible for the operation. This time Dagron felt that letters of rebuttal to the Press and to Fernique himself were insufficient to right the wrong. Unless he took a more positive action, the volume of visitors viewing the offending display would remain ignorant that Dagron was the actual microphotographer who produced every microfilmed message. He produced his 1870 contract and solicited letters of support from those who had been involved in the operation eight years before. Then he published his *"Dépêches du Siège: Revindication"*, a pamphlet of documentary evidence to reclaim his reputation. His indignant words informed the public that for several years M. Fernique had attempted to claim credit as the inventor and the producer of the microfilmed messages. In the interests of truth and historical accuracy, and for the sake of his children, the author had found it necessary to publish the facts and events as they really happened. Dagron's parting shot alluded to Fernique's medal, commenting that as he had received the honour, he could at least allow Dagron the credit for completing the mission for which it was awarded. The pamphlet seems to have succeeded in its objective, for it is now universally accepted that René Dagron was the sole producer of the microfilmed messages carried by pigeons into Paris during the Franco-Prussian War.

Towards the end of the 1870s changes occurred in the Dagron family situation. Caroline Dagron had always been involved in the business affairs of *la maison Dagron*, and may have become unsettled by her husband's numerous inventive projects. She had always preferred the *photographie de luxe*, but Dagron relished the challenges of new enterprises and resisted his wife's attempts to curtail his overwhelming interest in microphotography. There are also hints in family correspondence that Mme. Dagron did not approve of the nude microphotographic images. Novelties containing "exotic" views had always been part of the stock in trade at *Dagron & Cie*, and had probably made a considerable contribution to the firm's profits. However, the family had become well known in Paris, and had many influential friends, so she may have wished her husband to put an end to the less respectable aspects of the business. Sadly the differences caused a rift between them and they began to live apart, although they always appeared together at important family or formal occasions. Mme. Dagron took over *"Photographie Dagron"*, which she continued to manage until shortly before her death.

Stanhope novelties and unmounted lenses with microphotographic images produced for mail order still formed the major part of business, but the elegant portrait studio was still in operation. In the 1880s photographic portraits taken for *cartes de visite* included a small motif of Caroline Dagron's entwined initials, and she began to undertake commissions and exhibit her work under the name "Mme. Dagron".

It is not known who retained control of the Stanhope factory at Gex, but it is most likely to have been René Dagron himself, given his interest in optical and other experimental work. However, within a few years the factory passed out of the ownership of the Dagron family. Certainly the factory continued in production, for microphotography was still a thriving concern, both for the Dagron business and for its several competitors, and Stanhope lenses were needed in large quantities. Perhaps the most important competitor was the firm of *E. Lizé et Costil*, whose shop was nearby at *48 rue de Turbigo*, with workshops at *347 rue St. Martin*. The business was described as *"Microscopie et Tabletterie"*, with a similar background to *Photographie Dagron*. Advertisements promised that "Stanhopes" could be ordered from this shop on a variety of subjects, including "views of Paris, the surroundings of Paris, cities of France and abroad, ports, seaside resorts and spas, places of pilgrimage at home and abroad, religious subjects, famous personalities, actresses and events in the news". The wording is an indication that René Dagron was no longer the sole supplier of Stanhopes with applied images by mail order.

Lizé et Costil also provided a huge choice of items in which microphotographic lenses were already mounted: "pen-holders, étuis, parasols, crosses, measures, knives, binoculars, lorgnettes, bracelets, whistles, etc.", which were made from silver, bone, ivory, corozo nut, coconut, wood and mother-of-pearl shell. Examples of all these items can now be found in collections of Stanhope novelties around the world, together with many more unlisted objects and other types of material. Plastic is not mentioned, although more than one variety had already been invented in the latter part of the nineteenth century. They were produced when manufacturers sought substitutes for natural materials, which had become scarce and therefore more expensive. By the beginning of the 1880s imitation ivory and tortoiseshell were widely used, and once the versatility and low cost of plastic were recognised, this substance would supersede most of the other natural and more beautiful materials.

Advertisements for *"Photographie Dagron"* also mentioned "portraits (life size) on cloth, hand-coloured in oils or in black and white." Many of these were painted by Jean-Baptiste Poisot, who had married Pauline Dagron. He was an artist who was employed in the family business until the rift between Caroline and René Dagron inevitably forced their children and other relations to take sides. The situation worsened when some customers cancelled their orders or refused to accept the paintings because of the poor quality. René Dagron had always been close to his

83. Formidable ladies! Front, from left to right: Mme. Lendy, mother-in-law of René Dagron; Mme. Caroline Dagron, his wife. Back, from left to right: Mme. Pauline Poisot, eldest daughter of René and Caroline Dagron; Mlle. Poisot, sister-in-law of Pauline. c. 1885

eldest daughter, and Poisot decided to discontinue working for his mother-in-law. Lucile Dagron, writing in 1937, described further efforts by Dagron to provide work for his son-in-law. He experimented to achieve photographic images on enamel articles, which were then hand-coloured by Poisot, in an attempt to reproduce the effect of Limoges enamels. The results were not particularly attractive and Dagron abandoned the process. He was more successful with another artistic experiment, whereby canvas was treated with sensitising chemicals and the photograph of an old painting was developed on it. The prepared canvas was sent to a workshop in Holland where the exact colours of the old painting were reproduced.

In the late nineteenth century the company founded by René Dagron no longer monopolised the souvenir trade in microphotographic novelties, but the factory established by him at Gex still provided the tens of thousands of Stanhope lenses needed to maintain the businesses of many entrepreneurs in France and abroad. An increasing number of Stanhope souvenirs were being made elsewhere and had no connection with France, apart from the microphotographic lenses produced there.

9 Stanhopes in Souvenir Ware

Although Dagron and his competitors were able to supply a vast selection of microphotographic jewellery and trinkets from their Paris workshops, not all Stanhope souvenirs originated from this source. Many were too specialised for reproduction in Paris, using particular materials or artisans skilled in a craft practised in just one region. Stanhopes ordered by mail order widened the market to include such souvenirs from other regions of France or even abroad. Distributors were able to send regional photographs to their Parisian contact, and a supply of completed Stanhopes with local views would be returned to them as soon as possible. Having decided on a suitable position to drill the hole, a Stanhope could then be inserted in the local product.

Local craft products had been sold at markets throughout Europe for several centuries, and once people began to travel long distances for pleasure, they purchased regional souvenirs to remind them of their experiences. Railway transport accelerated the spread of tourism, and all manner of articles were offered at the popular resorts and watering-places, shrines and historic sites. Most regional souvenirs were being made several decades before microviewers had been invented, but the addition of a miniature photograph of the local scenery or architecture updated the existing souvenir. Dagron and his fellow photographers usually ensured that credit for the image remained with them by including the caption "MADE IN FRANCE". Today's collector sometimes finds it a little disconcerting to see these words when the microphotograph portrays views of some location in a completely different country.

The majority of regional souvenir ware is made from natural materials available locally, and provides an opportunity for the visitor to take away a memory of the area in tangible form. Examples of carved wooden ware, objects made of nuts, fruit stones or animal horn and samples of attractive rocks or minerals were very popular in the nineteenth century. When such a souvenir reveals a hidden Stanhope, we can trace the footsteps of the intrepid Victorian traveller.

Wooden "Tyrolean" Ware is unmistakable, and items of the same design exist both with and without Stanhopes. They were produced in the alpine areas of Switzerland, Austria and Northern Italy, and examples can be found in all the main collectors' categories of sewing accessories, writing equipment and smokers' requisites, as well as jewellery and ornaments. A "chalet industry" of woodcarving grew up in the mountains, when deep winter snow isolated villagers in their homes and local valleys. Brienz, a small town in the Bernese Oberland, has been a centre of the Swiss woodcarving industry for more than two centuries, and is still famed for its woodcarving school today. Many attractive items also originate from the nearby Grindelwald area.

In the late 19th century attractive items carved by individual craftsmen were collected and sold through retailers in the lakeside town of Interlaken, where wealthy visitors came to enjoy the beautiful scenery and clear mountain air. Alpine souvenirs were also distributed further afield to the cities of Lucerne, Bern, Montreux and Geneva. It is most likely that the distributors rather than the individual artisans were responsible for sending photographs of local views to Paris, for application on to Stanhope lenses. They would then arrange for them to be inserted into the finished articles.

When the supply of hand carved items could not cope with demand, small turning machines helped to increase production, and most late nineteenth century Tyrolean

84. Twin images from a souvenir cigarette holder in horn, c. 1890. Mountain climbing and exploring glaciers was becoming a popular sport, especially with British visitors to Switzerland in the late nineteenth century.

ware includes a combination of both skills. Often two colours of wood were used together, with darker sections cut away to reveal a lighter background. Alpine areas produced designs inspired by delicate edelweiss flowers, whilst bunches of grapes and vine leaves were favourite motifs of craftsmen in the warmer lower valleys. It needs a practised eye to find Stanhopes in Tyrolean ware, for the tiny glass lenses are more difficult to spot against a dark wood background, than against cream-coloured bone.

In Ireland many souvenirs were carved from an unusual material known as bog oak, or "Irish ebony". Fallen logs from primeval forests became submerged in peat bogs, and over the millennia the wood was preserved and darkened by minerals in the peat. The resulting dried black wood became very attractive when hand carved with traditional Irish emblems of harps and shamrocks. In the mid-nineteenth century there were eight "bog oak ornament manufacturers" in Dublin, and others near the popular Lakes of Killarney. These small factories were equipped with turning lathes and good woodworking tools, and the products included large items such as jewel caskets, writing "suites" and candelabra. There was also a range of smaller bog oak items: needle cases, penholders, thimble containers, whistles and crosses. These were ideal for the

Les Stanhopes en articles de souvenir

Bien que la majeure partie des ventes de Dagron et Cie. fussent des pièces complètes, la société exportait également des Stanhopes non montés à des commerces de souvenirs à l'étranger.

Des objets de bois sculptés provenant des montagnes suisses et des pièces faites à partir du chêne noir des marais d'Irlande furent également percés pour être équipés de lentilles françaises.

Quelques souvenirs britanniques furent aussi fabriqués à partir de pierres, tels que le jais, l'agate et le granit. Dans la région des chutes du Niagara aux Etats-Unis des objets souvenir furent réalisés dans du feldspath. Des noyaux de fruits et d'olives et des noix de coquilla furent également taillés comme souvenirs pour touristes.

Image from a carved wooden bookmark: Geneva, Switzerland. c. 1890 (Jull Collection)

86. A selection of "Tyrolean" bookmarks carved with Swiss flowers. Average length: 5cm. 1880-1920. (Jull Collection)

"Tyrolean" carved wooden needle cases. Switzerland, 1880-1910. Lengths: 9.5cm-14.0 cm.

88. The carved wooden thimble holder combined with a needle case holds a Stanhope. Other versions were made without lenses. Switzerland, c.1890. Length: 4cm.

Stanhopes in Souvenir Ware

insertion of Stanhopes containing a limited variety of views of the most picturesque Irish locations, such as the Giant's Causeway, Killarney and Glendalough.

It is relatively easy to find a variety of extremely small bog oak charms containing Stanhopes. They were produced in great numbers from tiny off-cuts of bog oak, and many are of fairly crude appearance. Most of them were chip carved at home by individual workers using basic implements. Their makers were paid a pittance for their efforts, but even this was a welcome supplement to the meagre income of many poverty-stricken families at that time. The motifs were often those associated with good fortune: pigs, black cats, four-leafed clovers, and owls. The Stanhopes in bog oak miniatures do not always contain Irish views, for most of them were exported across the Irish Sea to Britain as "lucky charms". They were sold at most British resorts, and show pictures of the locations popular in late Victorian and Edwardian times.

Turned olive wood articles originate from several areas around the Mediterranean Sea, especially from the Holy Land. Victorian travellers visited Jerusalem and other sites associated with the Bible, and returned home with olive wood souvenirs. These frequently contained Stanhopes, but the lenses are often difficult to distinguish against the dark wood. The most popular were combination pen holders and letter openers, similar in style but larger in size than those carved in bone from France. Baedeker's "Palestine and Syria" (1898) notes that " a staple product of Jerusalem is carved work in olive wood and oak, usually with the name 'Jerusalem' in Hebrew letters, of which the best specimens may be purchased at Vester's". It is significant that the same merchant could provide photographs "at 8-10 francs per dozen".

The Garden of Gethsemane on the Mount of Olives was a popular view in Stanhope souvenirs from the Holy Land. Some images depict an enormous olive tree with a broad, gnarled trunk. Baedeker notes: "The Garden contains eight venerable olive trees, which are said to date from the time of Christ; their trunks have split with age and are shored up with stones. The olive oil yielded by the trees is sold at a huge price, and rosaries are made from the olive stones". Rosaries do exist with larger dark-brown beads than the bone versions from France. The carving is more intricate and the pendant crucifixes are made of olive wood. These are more than likely to be the olive stone rosaries described by Baedeker, and would have been popular and revered souvenirs for Catholic pilgrims to the Holy Land.

The vogue for inserting Stanhopes does not appear to

89. A parasol needle case, penholder and a whistle made from bog oak. Ireland, 1880-1900. Length of penholder: 18.5cm

90. Image from a bog oak penholder: Killarney, Ireland.

91. A selection of "good luck" charms made of bog oak, c. 1890. Actual size.

92. Penholders and letter openers made from olive wood, 1880-1900. Longest item: 23.5cm.

have influenced the Scottish souvenir trade in wooden "transfer ware", for as yet no examples with microviewers have been found. A range of novelties had been made in and around the town of Mauchline, Scotland, since the beginning of the nineteenth century. These articles were made of pale-coloured sycamore wood and decorated with black transfer prints, before receiving several coats of protective varnish. By the time Dagron had invented his microphotographic viewers, Mauchline ware was well known, and most British resorts and a number of overseas venues were pictured on wooden souvenirs from this source. Yet although many transfer ware items had suitable places where a hole could be drilled to insert a Stanhope, this did not happen. Apart from the possibility of damaging the varnished finish of the article, it was unnecessary to add a Stanhope: the same scene would be clearly visible in transfer form on the article itself. Repetition of the image was surplus to requirements, and would needlessly add to the cost of the article.

Stanhopes were inserted in some German transfer-printed souvenirs, where a plain wood handle made a suitable location for the microphotographic lens. Most of these were large wooden parasol-shaped needlecases, with "canopies" in light-coloured wood and handles in a darker

variety. Black transfer prints of different resorts, or advertising some business, were used to decorate the main body of the parasol. These souvenirs exist in versions with and without microphotographic lenses.

Mauchline products included other different finishes on the wood, and the most popular of these was "tartan ware". Thin tartan paper was glued to the surface of a range of articles, and the name of the appropriate clan applied in gold. A few tartan ware items have been discovered with inserted Stanhopes, but these are extremely rare finds. It is possible that the Stanhopes were not inserted as part of the original manufacturing process, but it would be possible for some retailer to add local interest to a tartan ware souvenir if he had obtained a supply of lenses. Two of the known tartan ware novelties containing Stanhopes are covered in paper reproducing the Buchanan tartan. The knobs where the lenses were inserted are painted black, and unlike other Mauchline items do not have a smooth varnished finish.

In addition to olive stones, another source of souvenirs usually associated with the Holy Land and other Middle Eastern countries is provided by the coquilla nut. Like the corozo nut (vegetable ivory), it is the fruit of a type of palm tree (attalea funifera), but the hard outer shell instead of

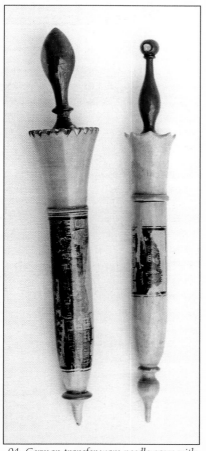

93. Rosaries made from (left to right): bog oak, bone and olive wood, 1880-1900. Half actual size.

95. A barrel-shaped measure, needle case and "rolling pin" novelty in tartan ware. British, 1890-1910. Actual size. (Jull Collection.)

94. German transfer ware needle cases with and without a Stanhope lens, 1890-1910. Length: 14.0cm. (Version with Stanhope from Jull Collection.)

Stanhopes in Souvenir Ware

the inner kernel is used for turned items. The coquilla nut is reddish-brown in colour with few varieties in shade, and it takes a high polish. It is larger than the corozo nut, and because of its size and shape, one of the earlier uses of turned coquilla was for making containers for rosaries. These were egg or pear-shaped, and unscrew in the middle; occasionally matching rosaries can still be found inside. The specific decoration on coquilla ware takes the form of concentric circles, interlocking crescents and dots. Stanhopes are found in several types of coquilla articles, and the subjects are usually religious shrines or sites in the Holy Land. Coquilla sewing accessories are the most attractive and include needle cases, pincushion baskets and thimble holders. Coquilla pincushion baskets often have handles of matching carved beads threaded onto firm wire. The central bead at the top of the handle is usually larger than the others, and often contains a Stanhope. A familiar style of needle case in this material is shaped like a fish, possibly indicating its Christian associations. Unusually, the lens is not placed in the eye of the fish, but near the tail, disguised among the circles and crescents imitating scales.

The largest coquilla items are "sand shakers", measuring up to 12 cm in height. They were made from three components screwed together, each turned from a different nut. The base was made from an upturned half nut and the central section is the oval shape of a complete nut. The top is made from part of a small nut, capped with a plate of olive wood. This is pierced with several small holes, from which the sand can be shaken out. The Stanhope is held in a round knob, also carved from olive wood. In the past, fine sand was shaken onto documents to dry the ink, but even in late Victorian times this would have been considered somewhat old-fashioned. Local craftsmen probably kept reproducing designs they were accustomed to make, and tourists would purchase them for their unusual appearance rather than usefulness.

Articles incorporating fruit stones were popular in Victorian times. The majority consisted of dried and polished peach stones, but nutmegs and cob nuts were also used. Most contained Stanhopes, and many originated from the Irish distributor, McKee of Dublin. The Stanhopes are held in identical metal components screwed into the apex of the fruit stones, transforming them into pendant watch fobs or miniature mechanical pencils. Rare examples are found with the Stanhope inserted into a hole drilled into the nut itself.

The use of carved or turned bone as a natural material was not confined to France; it was used to a smaller extent

96. Two needle cases made of coquilla nut, c. 1880. (Actual size.)

98. Watch fobs and mechanical pencils made from fruit stones, 1890-1910. British. Actual size.

97. Coquilla nut sand shakers with Stanhopes, 1880-1900. Actual height: 10-11.5cm.

99. Miniature alpine chalets made of bone, 1880-1910. Actual size.

100. Knitting needle guards made from chamois horn. Switzerland, 1880-1910. Actual size. (Jull Collection)

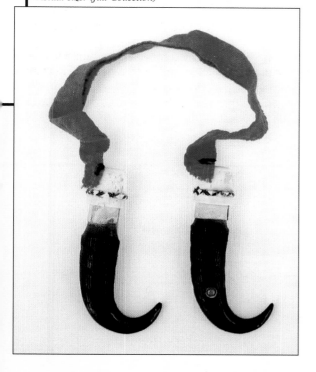

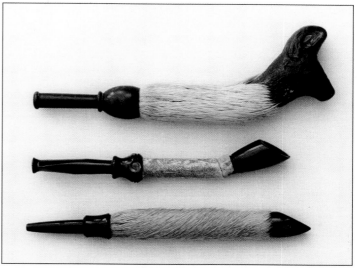

101. Cigarette holders and a mechanical pencil made of plastic and goatskin, to imitate chamois hooves, 1910-1930. Actual size.

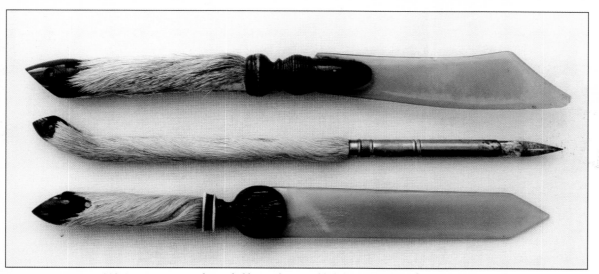

102. Letter openers and a penholder in plastic and bakelite imitation hoof. Length: 19 cm.

Stanhopes in Souvenir Ware

in other parts of Europe. Craftsmen from the Brienz and Grindelwald region of Switzerland produced cylindrical bone needle cases and automatic pencils, which were stained and decorated with alpine motifs of edelweiss flowers and chamois. More unusual novelties made of bone are thimble holders in the form of miniature alpine chalets. Many of these can be found with Stanhopes, usually situated in the miniature chimney. They were constructed from thin plates of bone glued together to resemble the familiar mountain architecture. The images in these charming bone chalets are views of alpine scenery from Switzerland, Austria or the Mont Blanc region of France, although as yet it has proved impossible to establish if any of these areas was the place of manufacture. In view of the design I think it is unlikely that they were made in the bone-turning region of Méru, France.

Another type of souvenir ware produced in mountainous regions was made from horn, often using tiny chamois hooves, or the tips of their curved antlers.

These were adapted for a number of ingenious uses, from knitting needle guards, whistles and cigarette holders, to the larger spoons and salad servers. As real horn became scarcer, this material was simulated in turned wood or types of plastic, such as bakelite, with goatskin strips glued to the surface. Some versions were made in Britain, and sold as souvenirs in highland areas, particularly Scotland.

Collecting geological and mineral specimens was a popular Victorian pastime, and tourists enjoyed visiting areas where the local rocks were attractively coloured. Items of stone ware began to be produced for the souvenir trade in several parts of the British Isles, and the smaller novelties were often drilled with holes for Stanhopes. Jet has been mined at Whitby, on the north-east coast of England, since Roman times. This shiny black stone was considered suitable for mourning jewellery, and when Prince Albert died, demand for jet increased, until there were nearly two hundred small workshops where it was cut and polished. It was suitable for turning and hand carving, and a range of souvenirs in varying sizes was produced. Stanhopes have been found in jet penholders and pendant charms, often book-shaped. Occasionally the name of an individual jet manufacturer may be found in the caption of the microphotograph. One of these was Thomas Bryan, who also produced jet novelties for "McKee of Dublin".

Large urns and tables of dark green Connemara marble were displayed at the 1851 Great Exhibition in the Crystal Palace, but later only smaller items were made, such as brooches and small ornaments. They were cut and polished by hand, often using the motifs of harps and shamrocks. Marbles of different colours were found elsewhere in the British Isles, and smaller items were more popular because of the weight. Charms and pendants in the form of miniature books made attractive gifts, especially those holding Stanhopes, and they were often sold far from where the rock was obtained. Agate, with its bands of

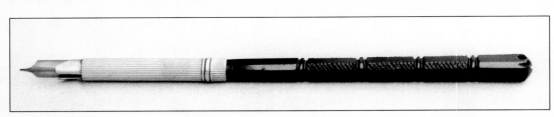

103. A souvenir penholder made of jet from Whitby, Yorkshire, c. 1880. The im... shows six views of the res... of Whitby. Actual size: 16.5cm. (Jull Collection)

104. Attractive agate pendants, 1870-1910. British. Diameter of heart: 3.4cm. (Kessler Collection)

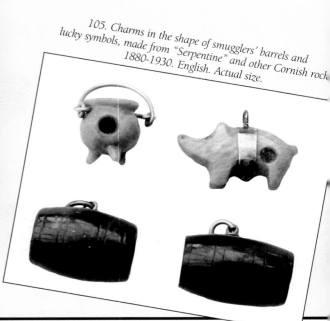

105. Charms in the shape of smugglers' barrels and lucky symbols, made from "Serpentine" and other Cornish rock... 1880-1930. English. Actual size.

56

different colours, produces a particularly attractive appearance when polished, and miniature books made of this type of mineral were so popular that they too were often sold far from where the rock originated. They were some of the earliest Stanhope souvenirs not made from bone, for book charms of carved agate have been found commemorating "A Memory of Dublin 1875" and "A Memory of Windermere 1876".

"Serpentine rock" is a type of Cornish granite, in dark grey with attractive red patches or the rarer dark olive green, speckled with light green, grey and white. The latter is found almost exclusively in wild and beautiful Kynance Cove, where hand-crafted rock souvenirs have been produced since the mid-nineteenth century. There were also cutting and polishing workshops at Penzance. The granite was mostly used for small ornaments shaped like lighthouses, and items of jewellery. Stanhopes are often found in barrel-shaped charms, which may be a reminder of Cornwall's smuggling past, when barrels of French brandy were landed at secret haunts along its rocky coastline. The images are mainly views of famous Cornish tourist attractions, such as Land's End, the Lizard Lighthouse and Kynance Cove itself.

Similar mineral charms were produced on the opposite side of the Atlantic, near Niagara Falls, but carved from a particular variety of gypsum found in that area. When cut and polished it displays a fibrous quality with a satin sheen. It is known as "satin spar" and is particularly attractive when set in jewellery. Souvenirs of this type were very popular with tourists to Niagara Falls at the end of the nineteenth century. Examples include necklaces, watch chains and fobs, brooches, bracelets, hatpins and cravat pins. The majority of such items are linked to a small barrel-shaped charm containing a Stanhope. This time the barrel commemorates the many attempts to survive a plunge over the mighty waterfall in a barrel. It is not surprising that most Stanhopes in this type of souvenir display images of Niagara Falls and the surrounding scenic area.

Semi-precious stones are found as pebbles around the British coast, and Victorian enthusiasts consulted their guidebooks to visit the best beaches to find colourful examples. Amethyst and citrine could be found on the "crystal beach" at Marazion, Cornwall, and they searched for jasper, agate, amber, chalcedony and cornelian at Sidmouth and Budleigh Salterton, Devon. The seaside pebbles could be taken to workshops in these towns to be cut and mounted as required. Many attractive examples were drilled to hold a Stanhope, and either left as mineral oddities or mounted as a pendant for a necklace.

106. Cornish views from a Stanhope in a barrel charm.

108. Images of Niagara Falls from "satin spar" barrel jewellery.

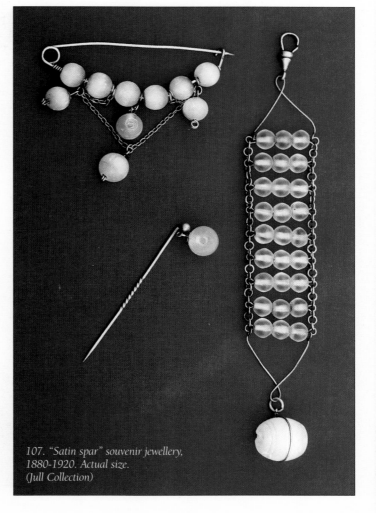

107. "Satin spar" souvenir jewellery, 1880-1920. Actual size. (Jull Collection)

10 The Mystery of the "Pursall" Thimble

The popularity of items incorporating miniature viewers was evident to manufacturers of everyday objects, as well as novelty souvenirs. Thimbles were not included in the range of Stanhope articles produced in France, but the idea eventually occurred to one or more thimble manufacturers in Britain. There were certain limitations to the design of a thimble fitted with a Stanhope. The main purpose of a thimble is to protect the fingertip inside it, which would leave very little space in the apex to incorporate a magnifying lens. Nevertheless, "Stanhope thimbles" do exist, dating from the latter part of the nineteenth century. They are difficult to find, and can command high prices among specialist collectors of both thimbles and Stanhopes. In fact, there are probably less than forty examples worldwide in private collections.

Until recently it was assumed that all "Stanhope thimbles" were the work of William Pursall, an English thimble maker from Birmingham. He was the owner of the "Electrum Works", which had been established in 1830 by Benjamin Terry. This factory produced plain serviceable brass thimbles at inexpensive prices, but it seems that Pursall had plans to increase demand by introducing novelty thimbles. On 10th January 1880 William Pursall applied for a patent to manufacture brass thimbles with his own design for a magnifying viewer in the apex. His specification described an invention relating "to a novel application of the hereinafter described parts to the tapered end of sewing thimbles for magnifying, microscopic and advertising purposes". He described how he would pierce a small hole in the end of a thimble, below which would be

110. Side view of two versions of antique brass thimbles with Stanhope holes. The example on the right is the rare design. Actual heights: left, 2.6cm; right, 2.4cm.

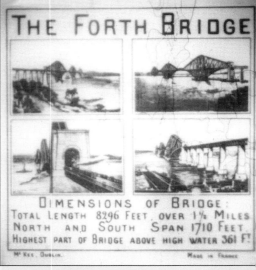

109. The most common image found in an antique brass Stanhope thimble: the Forth Bridge, completed in 1889.

111. Apex view of the same two thimbles. The example on the right is the rare design. Actual diameters at apex: left, 1.2cm; right, 1.4cm.

inserted a metal washer, with a disc of paper, silk, metal, glass or enamel, which could be decorated by printing or microphotography. "A microscopical or magnifying glass" would be placed over the disc and secured by a metal lining. Pursall's expertise as a thimble manufacturer is evident from his intention to make the entire thimble himself, as well as the viewer: "I raise or form the body by means of dies and tools as hitherto."

William Pursall had taken the precaution of adding "I do not limit myself to the precise details herein given" and that "various modifications may be made". As a thimble with a magnifying viewer corresponding exactly to his specification had yet to be discovered, popular opinion assumed he had decided that it was less complicated and cheaper to obtain prepared Stanhope lenses from France. The antique "Pursall" thimbles all seemed to share the same characteristics. They are all made of brass, and are slightly taller than similar designs of the same period. They share the same unadorned, serviceable design, with a rolled rim, plain band and rounded indentations. The finger size is also indicated on the band, and collectors have discovered that these numbers vary. For this reason, Stanhope thimbles have been recorded with slightly different heights and different diameter measurements at the base. On all of them, however, the inside depth measures about 5mm shorter than the outside height, and the interior apex is curved to fit the fingertip. At the exterior apex, the diameter of the hole incorporating the Stanhope lens is 3mm and the edges are flat and smooth.

Most of the microphotographic images in these thimbles include the captions "MADE IN FRANCE" and "McKee Dublin". A large proportion of these also display the same series of four views of the Forth Bridge in Scotland, together with precise details of its dimensions.

The Forth Bridge is a railway bridge across the Firth of Forth in Scotland, designed and constructed in late Victorian times and still in regular use today. It was the world's first major bridge made of steel, and Sir John Fowler and Benjamin Baler's plans used the balanced cantilever principle. It is 1.5 miles in length, and is composed of three double-cantilevers supported on granite piers and connected by "suspended" girder spans. Construction began in 1883 and was completed in 1889, although not formally opened until 4th March 1890. On that occasion, HRH Edward Albert, Prince of Wales, tapped into place a "golden" rivet. The Stanhope image enables the bridge to be viewed from all angles, and the most attractive photograph shows a steam train about to cross the bridge, trailing a plume of smoke.

Other Stanhope images in antique thimbles include several Scottish sites, with captions such as "A Memory of Aberdeen" and "Bought at the Wallace Monument, Stirling". There are also a few with English locations, usually with the favoured "McKee" of "Dublin" arrangement of six views around a title beginning "A Memory of…" In view of the high prices of Stanhope thimbles, prospective purchasers should pay particular attention to the image, both its subject and its fit. It is always possible that a Stanhope lens from a cheaper or damaged item might have been inserted into the empty hole of a missing lens in a brass thimble.

Recently a different type of brass thimble has come to light, which had previously been thought to contain a Stanhope cylindrical glass lens with a missing image. Close examination revealed certain details that were not apparent in other Stanhope "Pursall" thimbles. Slight differences in the overall measurements and design of this thimble were discovered, which are nevertheless significant. The lower edge is flat instead of rolled, while the band is milled in vertical lines instead of being left plain. There is no indication of finger size, which may indicate that it was made in only one size. The hole pierced in the apex is 4mm in diameter, which is wider than the standard lens used in other Stanhope thimbles, and it has a neat rolled edge that stands slightly proud of the thimble surface. The inside profile is flat, resembling Pursall's "metal washer", and the edge around the interior hole is also rolled.

A study of William Pursall's patent specification and design drawings shows that he described three components: 'C' was a washer with a turned up edge, 'D' was a thin curved lens and 'E' was a washer with a hole and turned up sides. When the three parts were placed above each other, Pursall noted: "the first process known as rolling or closing over is applied to the edge, thus securing the parts together". The complete unit was inserted into the apex of a pierced thimble, with the turned up edge of

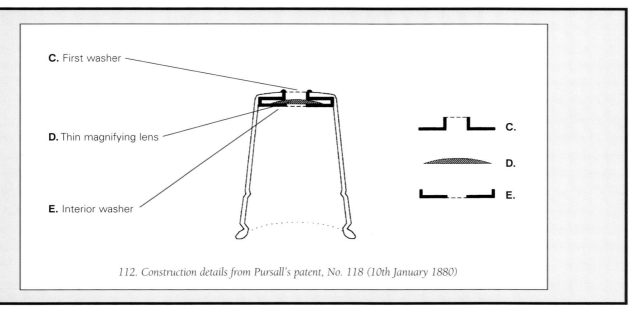

C. First washer
D. Thin magnifying lens
E. Interior washer

C.
D.
E.

112. Construction details from Pursall's patent, No. 118 (10th January 1880)

The Mystery of the "Pursall" Thimble

Le mystère du dé à coudre de Pursall

Les anciens dés à coudre en laiton sont très répandus mais il est rare d'en trouver avec une lentille Stanhope insérée dans l'extrémité. On a cru que ces dés avec Stanhope avaient été fabriqués par un fabricant britannique du nom de William Pursall. En 1880 Pursall avait déposé un brevet pour un dé incorporant deux éléments - une lentille grossissante et une image miniature. La méthode qu'il décrivait n'employait pas la lentille Stanhope, mais on pensait que finalement il trouva plus facile et meilleur marché d'importer de France les cylindres photomicroscopiques Stanhope à la place de sa propre solution brevetée.

Cependant un dé en laiton, récemment découvert, correspond beaucoup plus aux caractéristiques techniques du brevet de Pursall que les prétendus 'dés de Pursall avec Stanhope'. Malheureusement l'image manque et il n'est pas possible d'affirmer que Pursall a réellement réalisé le dé qu'il avait breveté ; d'autres recherches et comparaisons effectuées par des collectionneurs pourraient à l'avenir éclaircir ce mystère!

the top washer protruding through the hole: "this is also secured by closing over". This description can be applied exactly to the mystery brass thimble, with its rolled edges both inside and out, and the flat surface at the inside apex like a flat washer. By comparison, standard Stanhope thimbles have no rolled edges around the holes, and inside the profile is rounded to suit the finger shape, rather than flat.

These facts alone do not prove that this unusual thimble was manufactured to the design described in William Pursall's patent. No magnified image had been visible, but the existence of glass in the viewing aperture implied that some type of lens was in place. However, further evidence emerged when the thimble was accidentally damaged: instead of a loosened glass rod, the lens shattered into a great number of tiny glass shards. Some of these fell out of the hole, but enough remained in place to reveal there had been a wide and thin curved lens inside the apex of this unusual thimble. At the moment it is still only supposition that this may have been an example of a true William Pursall thimble; the only way of proving the truth is to discover another example intact with its lens and image. However, as with all collectables, when one "unique" item is recorded, others come to light soon afterwards. I eagerly await the imminent appearance of the next true Pursall thimble for "magnifying, microscopic and advertising purposes"!

Meanwhile, who made the other antique brass thimbles containing the Stanhope lenses? It is evident that the Stanhopes were "Made in France", and that "McKee" of "Dublin" imported them, but there is no positive link between McKee and Pursall. Indeed, it would have been easier and more profitable for Pursall himself to obtain Stanhope lenses directly from France, and he could have used the opportunity to advertise his own name and thimble company. As he would have been in a position to make and sell the novelty thimbles in bulk to his own distributors, the inclusion of a third party in Ireland would have incurred unnecessary costs and time.

A more logical explanation is that another thimble manufacturer apart from William Pursall was involved, who agreed to supply "McKee" of "Dublin" with thimbles already pierced in the apex for the insertion of Stanhopes. As yet, no other registered design or patent for a thimble with an inserted Stanhope has come to light from a different thimble manufacturer, but this is not particularly significant. Such an application would be unnecessary when the manufacturer only needed to pierce a hole in an existing thimble, as this was not a major design change. Other novelties existing in versions both with and without Stanhopes were produced without applying for modifications to the original design. Sooner or later evidence will come to light to provide a confirmed link between McKee, the distributor in Dublin who obtained his completed lenses from *Dagron & Cie*, and a thimble manufacturer who provided the pierced thimbles. That manufacturer may or may not have been William Pursall.

One interesting point about "Stanhope thimbles" concerns the size of the lenses inserted by or for McKee of Dublin. These were only 5mm in length, to conform to the 5mm difference between the inner and outer depths of the thimble. From another source I learned that 5mm was the smallest size of lens produced at the Gex factory, and they were ordered rarely and in small numbers. Judging from the few examples of thimbles containing Stanhopes in collections world wide, they were not particularly popular souvenirs. In this case at least, practicality appears to have overcome novelty.

Late twentieth-century Woodsetton versions of brass thimbles with microphotographs are described elsewhere in this book. In these, the images are always viewed from the outside, looking through the apex into the body of the thimble. It was originally thought that all antique Stanhope thimbles should be viewed from the opposite direction, i.e. from inside the body of the thimble, with the apex against the light. This was considered a definitive method of distinguishing between antique and modern examples. However, recent research has revealed some antique thimbles, where the rounded magnifying lens is situated at the outer apex of the thimble, permitting the images to be viewed only from the outside inwards. Although less light reaches the end of the lens, the image is better protected inside the thimble. However, should the thimble be used for its true purpose of sewing, the point of the needle would slide off the curved surface of the lens, which would be more dangerous for the needlewoman.

When the flat surface of the lens lies at the outer apex, it is safer to sew, but the point of the needle can scratch the flat glass, or even dislodge the tiny image plate at the end of the lens. Certainly William Pursall intended his patented design of magnifying thimbles to be viewed from the outside inwards, as the specification clearly shows the curved surface of the lens facing the hole in the outer apex. This may be another clue leading to the discovery of a genuine "Pursall Magnifying Thimble". When this occurs, I predict that the subject of the image will cause the liveliest debate, particularly should the caption bear the words "Made in France" or the name of the omnipresent McKee!

11 Stanhopes and the Victorian Traveller

From the mid-nineteenth century onwards travel by land and sea became a popular and pleasurable activity for those who could afford it. In Britain and throughout Europe, families embarked on rail journeys to coastal resorts for sea bathing and to mountain areas for scenic beauty. Inland spas were visited for the health, and pilgrimages were made to religious shrines. Everywhere people travelled, they were able to purchase a variety of decorative or novel souvenirs to remind them of an enjoyable visit, or to take back as a small gift for those had not been able to experience such a journey themselves. Soon most homes throughout the land displayed some sort of novelty on the mantelpiece that had originated many miles away. Inevitably, a number of these mementoes contained Stanhopes, enabling the owner to display not only the souvenir but also a picture of the place visited.

It had been intended to include a substantial but certainly incomplete list of tourist venues from various countries featured on Stanhopes as an appendix to this book, but recent research at the *Musée Nicéphore Niépce* proved this to be superfluous. The collection of artefacts from the defunct *Lizé* business in Paris includes a large notebook listing alphabetically all the microphotographic images available for their customers. As two of the earliest entries are listed under "Paris" as "*Tour Eiffel*" and "*Exposition*", 1889 is a likely date for the commencement of this valuable inventory. The date 1950 is written beside one entry: "*Pie XII Anno Santo*" (Pius XII Holy Year), so the *Lizé* list would seem to span more than a half century of continuous Stanhope production. The notebook records in elegant copperplate handwriting topographical and other views from France, Britain and other European countries. In addition, cities and resorts from the United States, Canada, South America, Australia, New Zealand, the Eastern Mediterranean and India are represented, many of which have not yet been recorded by collectors of Stanhope novelties. The inventory numbers more than seven thousand entries, and when one considers that an even more comprehensive list would also have been in existence at *Dagron & Cie*, the spread of tourism in the nineteenth century is illustrated very clearly. The inventory is even more amazing as evidence of the global influence of the microphotographic trade.

Despite the length of the list, it is interesting to note that the majority of places are as popular with today's visitors as they were with travellers in Victorian and Edwardian times. Until the late eighteenth century the pleasures of sea bathing were not appreciated, and even then the only fashionable places were those at short distances from the capital cities of London and Paris. Inland "watering places", where visitors came to drink the waters gushing from local mineral springs, achieved status for their health-giving properties and became favoured meeting places for wealthy families. This genteel situation began to change with the introduction of rail travel. The railway network spread rapidly across Britain and Europe throughout the nineteenth century, and the population was on the move.

In 1830 rail travel was expensive and there were only 120 miles of track in Britain. A decade later this had increased to almost 1500 miles and the fashionable world found it easier and quicker to travel by train. Travellers discovered the existence of many picturesque fishing ports or scenic mountain villages and returned home to publicise their attractions. Unexpected but welcome prosperity enabled the inhabitants to flourish, and "tourism" began to affect ways of life that had remained unchanged for centuries. The pace accelerated when the extended railway network became cheap enough for most people to enjoy the pleasures of train travel. Five years after Queen Victoria ascended the throne, the railways were carrying almost sixty million passengers per year, and by 1880 there were over fifteen thousand miles of track linking cities, towns and villages inland and around the coast of Britain. Thomas Cook had started to organise group rail travel on a grand scale, and by 1866 his company had already transported 40,000 tourists to Scotland.

Les Stanhopes et le voyageur du 19ème siècle

La croissance du transport ferroviaire en Europe et aux Etats-Unis a permis le développement de l'industrie de la microphotographie. Les gens commencèrent à prendre des vacances au bord de la mer, dans les stations thermales et dans les villes et les sites historiques. On trouvait des souvenirs Stanhope dans la plupart des endroits touristiques

Thomas Cook organisa des voyages en groupe à l'étranger à partir de 1878 et la France et la Suisse devinrent des destinations populaires pour les touristes britanniques. De plus de longs voyages en train et en bateau amenaient les voyageurs en Terre Sainte, où ils pouvaient acheter des souvenirs Stanhope fabriqués en bois d'olive avec des vues de Jérusalem et d'autres lieux saints mentionnés dans la Bible.

Towns beside the sea enjoyed the greatest rise in prosperity, and thirty years after the 1871 Census the number of seaside resorts listed had grown from 48 to 200. It is interesting to research why certain places became more popular or were considered less fashionable than others. Various Baedeker Guidebooks of the time are most useful

Stanhopes and the Victorian Traveller

in helping to build up a picture of the spread of tourism throughout Britain and Europe, and give some idea of the attractions which made individual resorts popular enough to be recorded on microphotographic images. Baedeker's descriptions can provide fascinating and often humorous quotes. "Fashionable watering-place" was the necessary accolade of the era, but one British resort was described as "cockneyfied"! Brighton had been a popular resort since Regency times, when Brunswick Square was the most fashionable address for a seaside visit, and by Victorian times the town was still "the most frequented seaside resort in the British Isles".

neighbourhood is Portland Island, with its convict prison and quarries"! Great Yarmouth also seemed a little down-market, as "in the height of summer it is flooded almost daily with excursionists". Nevertheless, these would have been the ideal customers for cheap Stanhope novelties, and images portray the resort's main attractions of the harbour and "Pegotty's Hut". This was featured in Charles Dickens' novel "David Copperfield", and Great Yarmouth was keen to promote its literary connections.

113. Brunswick Square, Brighton: view from a bone monocular, c.1870.

*115. Great Yarmouth: image from a letter opener, c.1890.
(Charles Horton, Lishman Collection.)*

Budleigh Salterton was considered "a charming little watering-place". One historical image of this seaside town displays a row of wheeled "bathing machines" along the sands. When a respectable lady wished to swim, she would enter the hut on one side to change her clothes and then be towed into the sea. She would exit on the opposite side, and a formidable female attendant would ensure that she was totally submerged in the water!

All the popular resorts promoted their own special attractions. It was essential to have a pier, and Yarmouth had three! Ryde Pier, on the Isle of Wight, was renowned for its length, being half a mile long "with an electric tramway line along one side".

114. Bathing machines along the bay: image from a bone stiletto, c. 1870.

*116. Ryde Pier before the installation of the "electric tramway":
image from a bone seal, c. 1880.*

Weymouth, which had enjoyed early popularity in Regency times when George III introduced sea bathing there, was considered somewhat passé by a late-Victorian Baedeker Guide: "the chief object of interest in the

Bexhill-on-Sea appealed to the younger generation with its "cycling boulevard", while Eastbourne advertised "a roller-skating rink, croquet lawn, lawn-tennis courts and swimming baths". Folkestone had "hydraulic lifts up the cliffs" and "motor-omnibuses", but even more enticing were the "rowing boats for hire, with or without men, from one shilling and sixpence per hour". Blackpool gained a reputation for fun and entertainment soon after the introduction of the "Bank Holiday" in 1871. For the first time the hard working factory employees in the industrial cities of Northern England were able to take a train journey to visit the seaside. Soon Stanhope souvenirs were on sale with multiple images of Blackpool's fine esplanade, three piers and gigantic wheel, while late nineteenth century versions include the resort's reproduction "Eiffel Tower", five hundred feet high.

118. A port instead of a resort: images from a letter opener, c.1895. (Charles Horton, Lishman Collection)

117. A late nineteenth century Blackpool landmark: a single image from a parasol-shaped needlecase.

Some towns beside the sea were important for other reasons, and being unable to promote a sand and sea-bathing image, sold Stanhope novelties with less frivolous images. Portsmouth, home of the British Royal Navy, provided views of the dockyard crowded with the tall masts of sailing ships, including the historical and venerated "Victory" and "Wellington".

Buxton, Harrogate, Tunbridge Wells, Leamington and Bath featured on many Stanhopes, and were the main inland watering-places or "spas", where visitors came to drink the health-giving mineral waters. Baedeker noted that the Buxton hot-springs were "efficacious in rheumatism and other ailments", but recommended that it should also be visited in winter, when "sleighing, tobogganing and skating are in vogue". Harrogate was designated "the most aristocratic of all the great English spas", whose sulphur springs had been known for over three hundred years. The waters at Tunbridge Wells came

from the chalybeate springs, and were priced at "one penny per glass, two shillings per week". "Tunbridge Ware" wooden novelties were on sale there, but like Mauchline Ware they did not contain Stanhopes. However, Baedeker noted that the "import of cheap foreign goods" (which surely included Stanhopes from France) had instigated the decline of the local souvenir industry. Many tourist areas became popular in Victorian times because of their historical or literary associations, particularly Scotland, which was much admired by Queen Victoria herself. These included Ayr, where "the whole countryside is full of associations with Burns' poems", Dunfermline, where Robert the Bruce is buried, Edinburgh, "one of the most romantically beautiful cities in Europe" and Forfar, with nearby Glamis Castle, reported to be haunted by the ghost of Macbeth

119. Memories of Scotland in a bone parasol-shaped needlecase, c. 1890.

English historical towns featured on Stanhopes include Chichester, "a town of great antiquity, dating from pre-Roman times" and Salisbury, with nearby Stonehenge, "the most imposing megalithic monument in Britain". Baedeker commented caustically that "Stratford-on-Avon owes its prosperity chiefly to the memory of the great dramatist born here in 1564, whose name and form have been

Stanhopes and the Victorian Traveller

120. Stratford-on-Avon: images from a metal mechanical pencil, c.1900.

imported into the trademark of almost every saleable article in the town". These, of course, included Stanhope novelties, some of which been the subject of recent reproduction in the U.S.A.

Coventry, an ancient and historical city, was already home to many industries by the late nineteenth century. However, it was still visited for its romantic connection with an eleventh century legend. Lady Godiva, wife of the Earl of Mercia, took pity on the poor of the city when her husband wished to charge them heavy tolls. In protest, she rode through the streets draped only in her flowing hair, while the population turned their backs on her modesty. (Apart from one, who was forever after known as "Peeping Tom"!) During the Victorian era the poet Tennyson commemorated her gesture, and Lady Godiva's statue in the Guildhall became a popular tourist attraction for those with a literary interest, and others.

121. Lady Godiva's statue, Coventry:
image from a bone parasol-shaped needlecase, c. 1890.

The Lake District was another popular Stanhope subject, where nineteenth century visitors came to admire the scenery that had inspired the "Lakeland Poets". Baedeker felt it was being commercialised as "Wordsworthshire", but advocated walking tours to encompass "the rugged fells" and "charming little falls". The wild scenery of Wales was also "discovered" by Victorian travellers, and the Snowdon region enjoyed great popularity with tourists. In 1894 a rack and pinion railway was constructed to take passengers to the summit of Mount Snowdon, ascending a winding route of four miles in little more than an hour. The "Snowdon Mountain Tramroad Company" also built two small temporary constructions (the "S.M.T. Hotels") to house those enthusiastic tourists who wished to experience the fine panorama of mountains, lakes and the distant sea at sunrise or sunset. However, Baedeker warned: "The summit is often swathed in mist for days at a time"!

122. The attractions of Snowdon featured on a Stanhope image from a fish-shaped needlecase: an unusual mountain souvenir! c. 1900.

Meanwhile, Thomas Cook's thoughts were already occupied with tours beyond the British coast, and he organised the first international excursion from London to Paris in 1878, to enable his clients to visit the *"Exposition Universelle"* that year. More than 75,000 travellers were transported to the continent on hundreds of special trains and ferries on the first of "Cook's Tours" abroad. In addition to the Stanhope souvenirs on sale at the exhibition, tourists could purchase items with images of many famous sites in and around Paris. Many years before postcards appeared, Stanhope souvenirs enabled visitors to take home a photographic memory of their holiday. However, the most well known landmark of Paris in modern times was absent, for the Eiffel Tower was not constructed until 1889. Although many multiple view Stanhopes can be found with up to eleven sites in Paris surrounding a central image of the Eiffel Tower, these can only post-date that era.

123. The Tomb of Napoleon: images from a paperknife, c. 1900.
(Charles Horton: Lishman Collection)

The Tomb of Napoleon, and the chateau of Malmaison, where the Empress Josephine remained after their divorce, received many visitors and a popular microview on sale was the *"Souvenir de la Malmaison"*. Saint Geneviève, the patron saint of Paris, can be found on some Stanhopes. She appears as a shepherdess, surrounded by her flock and guarded by a sheepdog. She is usually shown spinning wool, using a distaff and spindle.

124. St. Geneviève, Patron Saint of Paris: an image from a mother-of-pearl pinholder, c. 1890.

Other important French cities on Stanhope microphotographs include Marseilles, Rouen and Lyon, but the majority of Stanhope views portray the ports and seaside resorts of the Channel coast. Pictures of the ferry ports of Calais, Le Havre, Dieppe, Cherbourg, and St. Malo, where steamers carried travellers between Britain and France, are

frequently found, as are the smaller resorts of Le Tréport, Cabourg and Deauville. These novelties found a ready market with British visitors, and it is not surprising that so many have been found in Britain by collectors.

125. The caption of this microphotograph also includes a rare advertisement for a French retailer: Soullard, 122 Grand Rue. It comes from a bone needlecase, c. 1900.

Lourdes had been an important place of pilgrimage since 1858, when young Bernadette Soubirous experienced visions of the Virgin Mary near a small spring. After reports of its healing powers, thousands visited the grotto to drink the water and hope to be cured. A vast souvenir industry developed at Lourdes, and this included Stanhope novelties. These contain views of the shrine, the grotto and associated churches, together with representations of *"L'Apparition"* (the vision of Mary) and Bernadette herself. The images are usually multiples of five or eleven views. Rosaries, religious jewellery, penholders and paper knives with appropriate transfer prints on the handles were all popular souvenirs.

126. Details from an image of Lourdes in a souvenir penholder, c.1900.

Stanhopes and the Victorian Traveller

After his successful trips to Paris, Thomas Cook began to organise tours to Switzerland, beginning with Geneva and following with Interlaken and Lucerne, all of which became long-term favoured destinations for British travellers. One of the most common Stanhope images found in Tyrolean Ware is the *Rigi Kulm*, at 5905 feet the highest point in a mountain group overlooking Lake Lucerne, Switzerland. During the second half of the nineteenth century, this area was a popular venue for those who enjoyed walking holidays in the mountains. Many tourists arranged to stay in one of "Schreiber's Rigi Kulm Hotels", which were often pictured in Swiss Stanhope souvenirs. The hotels had been erected on a plateau just below the summit, to enable guests to observe the magnificent views at sunrise and sunset. Baedeker Guidebooks of the time assured the traveller that "although the colours of the sky are finest at sunset, dawn gives the clearest sight of the 400-mile panoramic view". An alpenhorn sounded a reveille half an hour before dawn, to awaken the guests early enough for them to be guided to the summit in time to observe the superb mountain range gradually emerging from the night mists

The spectacular scenery at the *Chute du Rhin* (Rhine Falls) attracted many tourists, then as now. Situated on a bend of the River Rhine near Schaffhausen, the most powerful cataract in Europe tumbles over three rocky ledges, and in the summer months the roaring volume of water is swollen with melting snow from the mountains. Baedeker advised Victorian travellers to visit the falls at early morning or late afternoon, when numerous rainbows "are formed by the sun in the clouds of silvery spray".

128. A pair of images from a wooden souvenir bookmark, c. 1890.

127. The Rhine Falls: image from a horn cigarette holder, c. 1890.

Literary connections also contributed to the popularity of Switzerland as a holiday destination for British visitors from the nineteenth century onwards. The Chateau de Chillon, at the opposite end of Lac Léman from Geneva, was the setting for Byron's poem and fable "The Prisoner of Chillon" (1817).

It is not surprising that a considerable number of Stanhopes with Swiss views have been found by British collectors. Examples from Italy, Germany, Spain and other European countries form a much smaller proportion in collections of Stanhopes, but it does not follow that only a few novelties featuring places in those countries were actually produced. In fact, examination of the *Lizé* inventory lists views from a great number of cities, shrines

and spas from all parts of Europe. The more likely reason for the scarcity is that European collectors have yet to show a positive interest in this sphere of antiques collecting. Once a few are noticed, more will swiftly follow!

The more adventurous travelled even further abroad with Thomas Cook, especially to the Holy Land. Baedeker dispensed advice on every aspect of the journey in the Guidebook to "Palestine and Syria" (1898) The journey entailed either a long steamer voyage from London or an overland train route through Europe. This was followed by a second steamer voyage to Jaffa, from where a train left each day for Jerusalem. Stanhopes from the Holy Land usually contain single view images of just a few places: the River Jordan, the Garden of Gethsemane and general views of Jerusalem and Bethlehem.

129. Panoramic view of Jerusalem: image from an olive wood pen, c. 1900.

The captions are mostly written in French or English, but also feature Hebrew, Greek or Cyrillic inscriptions. A revered site in Jerusalem for Christian visitors was the Church of the Holy Sepulchre. Baedeker described a number of souvenirs that could be purchased in Jerusalem, and noted that "a large choice of these articles is to be found in the space in front of the church of the Holy Sepulchre".

130. Mount Sinai: image from a bone rosary, c. 1900.

The spread of the railroad network in North America had a similar affect upon the population as it had in Europe, enabling travellers to cover the long distances between major cities in comfort and a much shorter time. They were able to admire the contrasts of scenic beauty in their vast homeland, and to enjoy travelling for pleasure instead of a hazardous expedition fraught with danger. Some of the first American photographers took pictures of the great cities of Chicago, St. Louis, New York, San Francisco and Washington and these soon appeared in Stanhope form.

131. Washington: twentieth century image from a camera-shaped charm.
(Milan Zahorcak : London Collection)

However, the greatest volume of nineteenth-century American travel occurred during the well-publicised world fairs, with several million visitors at each event. Great numbers of Stanhope novelties were produced for these occasions, and surviving examples can be found relatively easily in North America.

The most breath-taking tourist attraction for North American and overseas visitors alike is magnificent Niagara Falls, and many Stanhope souvenirs have been found with this image. Most American collectors have several examples, but as one might expect, it is a rarer subject among European collectors. The International Museum of Photography at George Eastman House, Rochester, has three versions of Niagara Falls views on glass plates, each of which has the caption "MADE IN FRANCE" added at the side of the image. The *Lizé* inventory at Chalon-sur-Saône lists twelve versions of images with combinations of six views, three versions with four views and another three single views. Added to variations produced by *Dagron & Cie*, a selection of Niagara Falls microphotographic images could become a specialist collection. In addition, there are two different single versions entitled "Wreckage, Falls View Bridge". Finding an example with this particular view would provide an opportunity for an interesting historical research project for an American or Canadian collector.

Not all travellers were tourists eager to view the world beyond their own shores. Others were in poor health, needing a change of climate and scene for a period of convalescence or hoping to find some new therapy to alleviate their problems. There are many "watering places" or spas around Europe, and during the nineteenth century new railway links brought such health resorts within the reach of a wider public. Occasionally views of some less familiar European location are found on Stanhopes, and a little research will often reveal the existence of a popular spa. A Dutch collector wondered why views of Valkenburg were featured in a Stanhope, when images of the nation's more important cities seemed to be scarce. Research into local history revealed the town's former importance as "Bad (Spa) Valkenburg", which flourished when the main international railway line from Maastricht to Aachen was routed through it in 1853. A similar result was revealed from research by a British collector, who had been puzzled by the name "Essentuki" on a Stanhope charm. The caption refers to a Russian spa town in the Caucasian region, whose local health-giving reputation became more widely known throughout Europe after 1893, when the railway system was extended to reach the town.

Topographical views should not be considered less interesting because of their comparative availability and similar arrangements of multiple views. It is always worthwhile researching the history of the subject of any microphotograph, but geographical details can also prove useful. Guide books of the late nineteenth and early twentieth centuries placed a different emphasis on what would attract tourists to certain areas at that time, and provide clues as to why particular photographic images would have souvenir appeal. Many of the subjects have long since disappeared, and then the Stanhope pictures become a nostalgic link with the past. A little time spent at the library or on the Internet can be very rewarding, and may even help to increase the value of a piece!

12 Distributors and Retailers of Stanhopes

In his book *"Traité de Photographie Microscopique"* (1864), René Dagron offered to reproduce his customers' photographs or negatives in microphotographic form, and then to mount the images onto Stanhope lenses or in semi-precious stones. In fact, newspaper articles of the time indicate that this service had been in operation as early as 1861. Individual customers might require a single item to their own specification, but as Dagron offered substantial discounts on bulk orders, it must be concluded that the majority of prepared Stanhopes were sent to distributors for resale elsewhere. No doubt his competitors would have made similar accommodating pricing arrangements for their mail order customers.

The most prolific distributor of Stanhopes was "McKee" of "Dublin", whose name appears on Stanhope images of places throughout the British Isles. It has been estimated that about 75% of all British named Stanhopes refer to this gentleman. For many years very little was known about McKee, although a few facts emerge from an examination of dated Stanhopes. An agate book-shaped charm, which includes his name on the image, is captioned "A Memory of Windermere 1876". This provides the earliest known date of his business. He was still in business in 1889; this was the completion date of the Forth Bridge, the subject of McKee Stanhopes in several brass thimbles. Another clue reveals that almost every "McKee Dublin" image included the words "MADE IN FRANCE".

Recent research at the National Archives in Dublin has revealed that in Thoms Directory of 1900 he was recorded as William Charles McKee, with a business address at "5 Sackville Street Lower, Dublin City". He was listed as a dealer in "wholesale microscopic photographic views". This description is not a definite indication that he took the photographs himself. However, in the 1901 census return McKee's occupation was given as "wholesale microscopic photographer", and in a footnote on the return he stated: "The only one in Great Britain and Ireland."

Occasionally a Stanhope item is recorded with the inscription "McKee fecit", a Latin version of "Made by McKee". Again, this does not prove that he made both the novelty and the Stanhope image, for these captions still include the words "MADE IN FRANCE". It has been assumed that McKee ordered and inserted the lenses from France, although a link between him and a French manufacturer had not previously been established. In late 2001, among the Dagron Family Archives I discovered a small piece of glass plate on which just a few microphotographs were visible. It had interested me initially because it was marked with fine lines to indicate where the plate should be cut to separate the individual images (See Illustration 39). When the two rows of identical images were viewed through a microscope, all were difficult to decipher, except one. It revealed four views of Cornwall, entitled "A Memory of Penzance", together with the names "McKee" and "Dublin". A fragment of glass less than two centimetres square had provided a vital piece of evidence to establish the link between the French manufacturer and the Irish distributor. The *Lizé* inventory has no mention of McKee's name, although another Dublin customer is listed: "S. W. & Co. Dublin". In the 1901 census return his age was given as sixty, which makes it unlikely that he had entered into a commercial relationship with *Dagron & Cie* before the 1870-1871 Franco-Prussian War. Standard McKee images are easily recognised, consisting of a block of six images which almost always surround a central inscription: "A Memory of ……"

It is not certain whether McKee manufactured the novelties himself or obtained them from elsewhere. The latter is more likely, as the census return does not mention any manufacturing activities but solely his work as a microscopic photographer. Nevertheless, it is amazing that such a large number of retailers throughout Britain obtained their "local" souvenirs from McKee of Dublin. A collector of Stanhopes has discovered proof that McKee definitely supplied retailers with Stanhope novelties, and that he was still in business in May, 1904. It is a fascinating story, and

132. Metal perfume bottles with Stanhopes, 1880-1910.

demonstrates how small details help to build a volume of overwhelming evidence to reveal what happened in the past.

The new owner of a property in Sunningdale, Berkshire, cleared out the front room of a house formerly functioning as a wool shop, and before that as the village Post Office. During the operation a group of six gold-coloured metal perfume bottles was unearthed, together with the business copy of a letter to "Mr. W. C. McKee". The letter dated from May, 1904, when the Post Office had been owned by Mr. F. C. Hodder. The tone of the letter was somewhat irate, complaining about the quality of the Stanhope articles which had been despatched to him the previous month: "I am sorry to say that many of these goods are defective. In a great many cases, especially with the bone goods, the cement used for the views is too intrusive, completely spoiling the appearance of the views, and in some cases

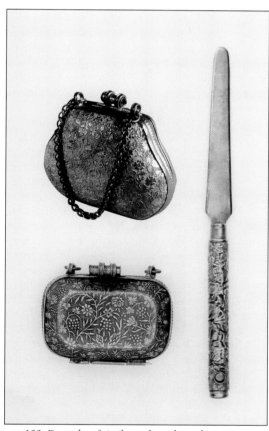

133. Examples of similar embossed metal souvenirs.

rendering them invisible. The enclosed articles have no view at all. Kindly replace them." The retailer then listed seven items that he was returning. Most appeared to be charms: a silver elephant and teapot, a Turkish slipper, a black teapot (probably of bog oak) and a flagon of ink. Two items were larger: a bookmark and combined paperknife, and an "egg-shaped scent bottle" (See Illustration 132). Further research revealed that Mr. Hodder himself was an amateur photographer and took the local photographs to be printed as postcards, and also for McKee to order from France reproduced on Stanhopes.

Judging from the variety of recorded "McKee Dublin" Stanhope items, he supplied an impressive range of souvenirs in many materials. These included bog oak, other wooden ware, bone and vegetable ivory articles, novelties

Distribution et ventes en détail des Stanhopes

Un grand nombre de lentilles Stanhope furent achetées chez les fournisseurs français par des distributeurs et détaillants étrangers, qui saisirent ainsi l'occasion de faire de la réclame pour leurs sociétés. Bon nombre de vues britanniques sont signées 'McKee, Dublin' qui inséra des lentilles dans plusieurs modèles de souvenirs régionaux pour les distribuer ensuite en Grande-Bretagne.

Un détaillant, J.E.Beale, eut ainsi un grand magasin à Bournemouth connu sous le nom 'The Fancy Fair'. Les souvenirs Stanhope de J. E. Beale présentent souvent des vues multiples sur une seule image. Les collectionneurs conservent les noms des distributeurs et des détaillants, car ils permettent souvent d'entreprendre des recherches historiques locales.

made from fruit stones, nuts and geological specimens, and a whole range of items made from silver, brass and plated metal and plastic. Many of these were of British manufacture, but the bone ware was probably imported from France complete with lenses. When the indignant retailer's letter was written in 1904, René Dagron was already dead and the business had been sold out of the family some years before. It is possible that the succeeding French supplier was not as meticulous in quality control as Dagron's workers had been. Also, some of the items listed were definitely of British manufacture, and it is equally possible that McKee's own workers were careless when inserting the Stanhopes. By this time, he himself had been supplying microphotographic souvenirs for about thirty years.

A few Irish images include the rare caption "W. Lawrence Dublin". Thoms Directory for 1900 proves helpful once again, providing interesting details about William Lawrence. An impressive list of his activities is given: "photographic printseller and artists' colourman, toy and fancy merchant, cricketing and tennis outfitters, bog oak carver and jeweller", while another source includes Connemara marble souvenirs – and fireworks. His premises were large, occupying Nos. 5, 6 and 7 Sackville Street Upper, Dublin, and were at the other end of the street from William McKee's business. Their proximity implies that they were either business competitors or trading partners, but no links have been established between the two men to date. As a "toy and fancy merchant, bog oak carver and jeweller" Lawrence could have supplied most types of Stanhope souvenir, yet it is McKee's name that appears on the majority of images. It is unlikely that William Lawrence supplied McKee with novelties that allowed him to claim credit for the photography, for Lawrence himself had become well known as the main supplier of Irish views. His photographic prints were marketed on lantern slides, stereoscopic views and albums of "The ONLY Complete Series of Photographic Views Published in Ireland".

Distributors and Retailers of Stanhopes

Every print bore the initials of William Lawrence, although his numerous commercial commitments left him little time for the photography himself. In fact, it was his chief assistant Robert French who, for three decades, travelled around Ireland taking thousands of photographs on glass plates. It is most likely that French was responsible for the few examples of "W. Lawrence" microphotographs in Stanhopes. The format of the Lawrence image was quite different from the standard McKee rectangular arrangement of six views. It was composed of four separate views in oval frames, with differences in the wording. He used the term "Manufactured in France" and the caption: "Souvenir of ….". Whether it was William Lawrence or Robert French who took the original photographs, they were still despatched to France to be applied to Stanhope lenses.

134. Irish views photographed by William Lawrence: image from an acorn-shaped vegetable ivory tape measure, c. 1890.

Another distributor from Ireland is identified only as "I.B.& M. Co. Dublin", who produced images in the familiar arrangement of six pictures. They included topographical views of a limited number of places in Britain, and occasional commemorative subjects. A dated example commemorates the "Great European War 1914-1918", which helps to establish this distributor in the early twentieth century. Initials also make it difficult to identify an English distributor: "C.R.& Co. London". Many places in Britain were featured on the images, and once again they incorporated six views. The majority of this company's microphotographs were numbered, possibly enabling retailers to specify the required resort from a given list or catalogue. This appears to have been quite extensive, as some examples are numbered higher than one thousand.

The main distributor in North America during the late nineteenth century appears to have been John H. Morrow

of New York. Unfortunately his name has not yet been discovered on any American Stanhopes, and we must rely on contemporary sources to credit him for the manufacture of microphotgraphic novelties. It is known that he had set up a workshop in New York in 1864. Two years later "The Philadelphia Photographer" (September) noted: "His establishment is the only one in this country devoted specially to that kind of work, but he desires that there should be others to make the process popular…..This beautiful application of photography ought to be extended, and we hope it will." In the same year Morrow began to manufacture almost exclusively for Messrs. Gurney and Son, also of New York. Presumably this company then took over the distribution of Stanhopes.

"Made in France" is indicated on a number of images with American views but many others do not specify the country of origin. If items were produced for the home market and not for export, one might not expect to see "Made in the U.S.A." included on the caption. Nevertheless it is unfortunate that the name of an American manufacturer has yet to be revealed to collectors. More research is needed in North America to collate specific American Stanhope subjects, and then to trace their origins.

The names of a number of Victorian and Edwardian retailers have been noted on microphotographs, and a comprehensive list can be found at the end of this book. A considerable number of British souvenirs bear the name of "J.E.BEALE'S FANCY FAIR", the main retailer in Bournemouth during this period. Most British collectors of Stanhopes have found at least one example, but they may not realise that this store still exists on the same site, managed by members of the same local family.

In 1881 John Elmes Beale, an assistant draper from Weymouth, Dorset, paid £400 for a small double-fronted shop in the newly fashionable seaside town of Bournemouth, which at that time was in the county of Hampshire. He called it "The Fancy Fair" and it sold numerous small souvenir items, many of which were imported from abroad. Among them were Stanhope novelties, with topographical views of Bournemouth and the surrounding area. Most were sewing accessories, such as bone needle cases and vegetable ivory measures, but souvenir monoculars and binoculars were also sold at this store. One monocular has been found with a Stanhope of thirteen views of Bournemouth, of which the central image is the shop itself, captioned "The Fancy Fair". This is a rare example of the retailer's business premises being included in the microphotographic views of the resort. The whole microphotograph is entitled "A Souvenir of Bournemouth J. E. Beale's Novelty Stores", and the Stanhope is "MANUFACTURED IN FRANCE". Other souvenir Stanhopes from Bournemouth exist with larger numbers of views, but the name of "J. E. Beale" is not always included.

Business began to flourish in the late nineteenth century, and the size of the shop was increased when Beale purchased adjacent properties. During this period "Bertie", eldest son of Queen Victoria, was infatuated with Lillie

135. "The Fancy Fair", a Bournemouth department store founded in 1881. From a guidebook sold at the same store, c.1888. Inset: John Elmes Beale (By courtesy of Nigel Beale, his great-grandson.)

136. Multiple views of Bournemouth: image from a bone monocular, c. 1890
Inset: detail from another monocular, showing the shopfront of 'The Fancy Fair'.

Langtry, the beautiful "Jersey Lily". The Prince of Wales built a luxurious mansion on the cliffs for his mistress, and visited the area often. It is quite likely that Lillie made purchases at "The Fancy Fair". By the time the heir to the throne had become King Edward Vll, the town was a popular and fashionable resort.

At the start of World War ll, the shop was a five-storey building, with many departments for all types of fancy goods. In May 1943 the original building was completely flattened and burnt during a German bombing raid, but fortunately there was no loss of life as this happened on a Sunday when the store was closed. "Beales" was rebuilt on the same site as soon as possible after the war, and is still a quality department store, although the sale of souvenir items and novelties is not so significant. Beales is now well into the second century of business.

Due to the wartime fire, very few records or items of memorabilia exist from the early years of trading, and Mr. Nigel Beale, great-grandson of the founder, was unable to furnish any invoices or correspondence with manufacturers of Stanhopes in France. However, during a recent study of the *Lizé* inventory preserved at the *Musée Nicéphore Niépce*, I discovered the following early twentieth century entry for numbers 2459 and 2460: *"Bournemouth (13 vues Beale)"*. E. *Lizé* was possibly the largest producer of microphotographic souvenirs in Paris, once the Dagron business had ceased trading. It was personally satisfying to establish this firm link between my hometown and the Paris Stanhope industry, and I hope that future research at the museum will enable me to discover the original photographic plate from the *Lizé* archives.

Distributors and Retailers of Stanhopes

138. "Victoria Falls", the image found in most Stanhope articles sold at Soper's Curios.

137. Carved African animals with Stanhopes from Soper's Curios. Half actual size. (Jull Collection).

Another early twentieth century overseas retailer of Stanhope novelties was J. W. Soper. In 1911 he established "Soper's Curios", a store at Victoria Falls, then in Rhodesia. David Livingstone, the Scottish missionary and explorer, had discovered Victoria Falls in 1855, and they became one of the geographical marvels of the age. With the advent of railway transportation across the African continent, hardy tourists began arriving to view the awe-inspiring waterfalls. Locally made souvenirs were in great demand, and Soper's store supplied the flourishing market. The area was well known for the quality of its teak and ebony, and although the hardwood logs were exported, smaller pieces were used locally for carvings and ornaments. Many of these were inspired by the wildlife of the area, such as antelope, elephants and crocodiles, but small boxes and containers were also popular. Stanhopes have been found inserted in the eyes of carved animals from this area, and invariably display the same fairly crude single microphotograph of a panoramic view of Victoria Falls. It is interesting to note that these images also bear the words "Made at Victoria Falls".

Another regional resource was the African version of vegetable ivory, using the hard nut of the Hyphaene Palm. This was exported to manufacture collar studs and buttons.

J.W. Soper combined the two products of teak and vegetable ivory to produce small trays to hold men's collar studs, etc. and pasted a label underneath to provide all the relevant information.

A surprising addition to these stud trays, a number of which have found their way to Britain, is the insertion of a Stanhope through the vegetable ivory knob in the centre. It is quite unusual to find a Stanhope inserted vertically through a knob, particularly when the opposite end of the lens might be covered by a large circular label. In fact, the label is roughly pierced to enable light to enter the lens from underneath the tray when it is held to the light. Again the Stanhope image is the same single panoramic view of Victoria Falls, together with the words "Made at Victoria Falls". The quality of these identical micro-photographs is very poor, and is likely to be an early twentieth century product of the Stanhope process. Whether J. W. Soper managed to produce the microviews himself on the African continent, or obtained them from elsewhere and just inserted them in his shop near the Victoria Falls, is an unsolved mystery at the moment. "Soper's Curios" still trades in all types of African souvenir near this famous natural feature.

139. Two views of a teak stud holder with a vegetable ivory knob containing a Stanhope. Actual diameter: 8cm.

140. "Soper's Curios" souvenir store in the twenty-first century. (J. Harvey)

An examination of the list of British retailers so far recorded gives some idea of the type of shop where Stanhope novelties could be purchased in the past. Those who were established around the same time as J.E. Beale's "Fancy Fair" were termed "bazaars, "fancy repositories" or "toy and fancy dealers". It is not surprising that several stores were booksellers or stationers, given the number of Stanhopes found in dip pens, paper knives and automatic pencils. Although some retailers advertised only the shop name with the resort, occasionally they also included their exact address. This enables the present owner of such Stanhopes to undertake some interesting research. Although it is very rare to find the shop still managed by descendants of the original owners, or even retailing the same type of goods, the shop itself might still be in existence and a little of its history known. If orders and invoices have survived, information about Stanhope novelties might be unearthed: this was how the letter to McKee of Dublin concerning sub-standard Stanhopes was discovered.

Several Stanhope souvenirs have been discovered with interior and exterior views of "The New Arcade, Birmingham". This covered parade was built in 1875/6, and was the first and most beautiful of several shopping arcades erected in central Birmingham. It occupied a site created by the construction of the Great Western railway tunnel in the city centre, and was more popularly known as the "Great Western Arcade". The original roof and glass dome were destroyed in an air-raid during World War ll, but in modern times it has been refurbished to echo its former glory. "Barnby & Company" was a toyshop in this arcade, and included Stanhopes in the stock of novelties. Another shopping arcade where Stanhopes were sold was in Cardiff, and one image promoted a trade fair and provided publicity for the "toy and fancy dealers" themselves.

French retailers rarely advertised their shops in Stanhopes, but a few examples have been discovered. They include "Soullard" from *122 Grand Rue, Dieppe*, illustrated in the previous chapter, and another showing five views of Cabourg, a small port on the coast of Normandy, near Caen. *"M. Sevestre"* had chosen an appropriate name for the shop: *"Au Gagne Petit"*, or "The Little Bargain"! Perhaps the most apt advertising by a retailer in a Stanhope image is found in a bone parasol-shaped needle case owned by an American collector. It was probably presented as a free gift with the purchase of a full-size umbrella or parasol, and contains a substantial microphotographic caption but no pictorial image. It advertises "William A. Drown & Co.", who were "manufacturers of umbrellas and parasols" in "Philadelphia and New York". It is an interesting detail that the cities of Philadelphia and New York were the first two places where microphotography was established in North America.

The *Lizé* inventory provides more clues about distributors who ordered Stanhopes during the period from 1890 to the late 1930s. "Maccia" from Milan, "Virando" and "Mandelli" ordered large numbers of Stanhopes with Italian views, while "Jantsch" supplied the German market. "Stöger" was a Polish distributor, and "Baline" ordered American views of sites in Ohio, Indiana, California and Washington. "James Potter" specialised in different versions of Niagara Falls images and "Crimminn" placed orders for small numbers of Irish views. The names of "Klein Frères" (Switzerland) and "Aristide Gomès" (Spain) also appeared in the inventory with occasional orders. The names of new distributors and retailers of Stanhopes are continually being recorded, and like all other caption details on Stanhope images, provide much material for future research.

141. Dual images of "The New Arcade", Birmingham, from a carved wooden paperknife, c.1890.

142. Dated advertising image from a vegetable ivory tape measure.

13 Historical Events Commemorated on Stanhopes

During the latter half of the nineteenth and the early twentieth centuries, most events of national importance were commemorated in Stanhope form, particularly in France, Britain and the U.S.A. Images of the most significant historical and political occasions were dated, causing them to be very collectable today. Many of them featured personalities who played leading roles in determining the course of world history during this period.

Images of royalty were very popular, and attractive examples in Stanhopes command high prices. Queen Victoria was an early subject, but microphotographs showing her and Prince Albert together are extremely rare, as Dagron's first patent was granted in 1859 and the Prince Consort died in late 1861. An imposing photograph of Queen Victoria in an elegant lace shawl was taken by the famous London photographer, J.E.Mayall. The picture is inscribed "Mayall fecit" (Made by Mayall), and dated "March 1st 1861". This image was reproduced by Dagron on a Stanhope, with the English caption: "Her Majesty The Queen". This indicates an item made specifically for the British market and it may have been on sale at the 1862 International Exhibition in London. The wording "Dagron & Cie Brev" also dates the item no later than 1862, as Dagron lost his patent rights that year and was no longer entitled to use the word "Breveté" on his images.

Multiple views of royalty on Stanhopes are much prized. One untitled version on a monocular is composed of nine separate royal portraits, with Queen Victoria occupying the central position, flanked by her children in stiffly arranged poses. Although two of the images are impossible to distinguish, the extreme rarity of this Stanhope merits its inclusion. The microphotograph lacks a title, but "Dagron & Cie Paris" is handwritten at one side, together with the word "Breveté" in full, which is itself an unusual feature. This composite microphotograph also dates c. 1862.

One portrait of Queen Victoria was discovered in the Dagron family archives in an unusual and perhaps inappropriate mount: a miniature bone radish-shaped charm, stained red and green! The significance of this choice of novelty article has yet to be established. The image was produced by *Dagron & Cie*, and as the word *"Breveté"* is missing from the caption, it probably has a later date than 1862, and may have been produced for British visitors to the 1867 Paris *Exposition Universelle*.

143. Queen Victoria, 1861: an important Dagron image from a bone monocular. (Terence Taylor)

144. Detail from a nine-image microphotograph of Queen Victoria and her children, from a gold monocular. Those shown here are: Princess Beatrice (middle left), Princes Arthur and Leopold (middle right), and the Princesses Victoria, Alice and Helena (Bottom left, centre and right) c. 1862. (Terence Taylor)

145. Bone "radish" watch charms. Actual height: 1.7cm. (Dagron Family Archives)

In 1863 the Prince of Wales married Princess Alexandra of Denmark, and photographs of the beautiful bride were widely circulated. The new Princess of Wales wore her hair in a distinctive style, and although uncaptioned, her unmistakable likeness in Stanhope form can be found in a gold monocular watch charm.

Photographic portraits of Queen Victoria and her family were taken at regular intervals for the rest of her life, but few of them are found on Stanhopes until the year of her Golden Jubilee. In 1887 she had been the reigning monarch for fifty years, and a large number of souvenirs were produced to commemorate the occasion. Several Stanhopes have been found with double cameo portraits of Queen Victoria: one shows the young girl when she became queen in 1837, and the other portrays a plumper version in sombre garb, as she appeared in 1887. An arrangement by McKee of Dublin is particularly attractive, with the portraits framed in flowers: roses for England and thistles and shamrocks representing Scotland and Ireland.

Twinned with an image commemorating the Royal Jubilee is a more unusual set of four views of the principal residences of the Royal Family at that time. In addition to Windsor Castle and Kensington Palace, home of the young Princess Victoria before her accession to the throne, are pictures of the two places where Queen Victoria spent her happiest times with her family. Osborne House was designed by Prince Albert and was their holiday home on the Isle of Wight. Balmoral, a Scottish castle, was another favourite holiday home of the Royal family, but after Prince Albert's death it became Victoria's refuge from London and the reality of coping with the duties of Queen without the support of her beloved husband.

146. Queen Victoria, c. 1867: a Dagron image from a bone radish-shaped charm.

147. Princess Alexandra, c. 1863: a delicate image from a gold monocular watch charm.

148. A "McKee, Dublin" image from a bone needlecase, commemorating the Golden Jubilee of Queen Victoria in 1887. (Private Collection)

149. More formal portraits of Queen Victoria, produced for the same occasion. One image from a pair of miniature bone binoculars (Lishman Collection)

Les événements historiques exposés sur Stanhope

Beaucoup d'événements historiques furent commémorés sur des microphotographies. Les portraits de la Reine Victoria et d'autres membres de sa famille étaient par exemple très populaires. La famille impériale française fut aussi microphotographiée avant 1870, et aux Etats-Unis les souvenirs Stanhope furent employés dans la campagne des élections présidentielles. Des naufrages, les premiers vols d'avion et les héros nationaux de la Grande-Bretagne et de la France sont aussi présents sur des microphotographies. Des vues impressionnantes des destructions pendant la première guerre mondiale furent également prises. Il est probable que les dernières images royales commémoratives sur Stanhope furent produites pour le couronnement d'Elizabeth II d'Angleterre en 1953.

Historical Events Commemorated on Stanhopes

Dual portraits of the Duke of York and Princess Mary (May) of Teck were issued in 1893 to commemorate their engagement in May and wedding in July of that year. Princess May was to have married Prince Albert, eldest son of "Bertie", Prince of Wales, and Princess Alexandra. Sadly, he died shortly before the wedding that had been planned for February 1892. His brother George, Duke of York, consoled the bereft princess and she accepted his offer of marriage the following year. On the death of his father in 1910, the Duke of York became King George V and his wife became Queen Mary.

In 1897 Queen Victoria celebrated her Diamond Jubilee, having then ruled Britain for sixty years. Special events were arranged throughout the country, and a variety of souvenirs were produced for her loyal subjects. Collectors have found Stanhope images highlighting the length of her reign and her status as a great-grandmother, such as "Souvenir of the Longest Reign" and "The Four Generations".

Queen Victoria died at the start of the twentieth century. There were few mourning souvenirs and a Stanhope has yet to be found commemorating her death. The nation looked toward the future with a new century and a new reign. "Bertie" was due to be crowned on 26th June 1902, and manufacturers began to produce a selection of souvenirs marked with this date and the name he preferred as king: Edward VII. Unfortunately, the king who had waited so long for his crown faced a further delay. He suffered an attack of appendicitis and was so ill after the operation that the nation feared he would not live to be crowned. The Coronation of King Edward VII finally took place on August 9th, 1902.

Apart from the British Royal Family, there are few other regal images on Stanhopes. Most royal sovereigns are shown in composite images, to celebrate large gatherings, such as international exhibitions, or to indicate unity as allies. The French Imperial Family was featured for some years, but after the Franco-Prussian War in 1871 Napoléon III and the Empress Eugénie were deposed, and went to live in exile in England with their young son.

An interesting microphotograph exists with a portrait of Tsar Alexander II, who was crowned Emperor of Russia in 1855. Although a fairly liberal monarch, his government savagely repressed any revolutionary activities, and on 13th March 1881 he was assassinated by a bomb which exploded beneath his carriage. This Stanhope may have been produced to commemorate his death.

In Britain signs of political unrest were reflected in a Stanhope featuring the "London Riots of 1886", which took place on 8th February of that year. A monocular was produced with a single image of rioters marching along the streets of London and waving banners and sticks. According to "The Times" of 9th February, "the most alarming and destructive riot that has taken place in London for many years" had occurred the previous day. The "Illustrated London News" reported that *a rabble of men and youths, bearing little resemblance to any of the London working classes, suddenly poured from Trafalgar Square through Pall Mall, up St. James's Street and along Piccadilly to Hyde Park Corner, turned east of Park Lane, and got into the Grosvenor Square neighbourhood, visiting South and North Audley Street, and everywhere doing all the damage they could to shops and houses."* Prior to this event a meeting of the unemployed took place in Trafalgar

150. An image from bone binoculars. (Lishman Collection)

151. Image from a bone fish-shaped needlecase. Although undated, this commemorative image refers to royal events during the summer of 1893. (Private Collection.)

152. Image from a metal crown-shaped charm. (Townsend Collection)

153. This Stanhope image from a bone cylindrical needlecase is probably one of the last photographs of the Imperial Family taken in France, c. 1870. The Prince Imperial wears a miniature military uniform, and is probably about thirteen years of age.

154. Image from a bone monocular, Tsar Alexander II c. 1881. (Terence Taylor)

155. Political unrest in 1886: an unusually violent image from a bone monocular. (Townsend Collection)

Square, and "The Times" correspondent laid the blame for the disorder on Messrs. Hyndman, Burns and Champion, the "Revolutionary Social Democrats", who had headed the mob in the march to Hyde Park. These and other rioters were later tried for "uttering seditious words" but were acquitted.

An important landmark in French history occurred during the closing decade of the nineteenth century, when France and Russia signed the *"Alliance Franco-Russe"*. The political situation of France within Europe was unstable at this time, with the country seeming to lack strong allies in the event of war. In view of German might, Italian threats and British hostility, the French Government made overtures to Russia. Tsar Alexander lll of Russia was not keen to support the Republic, but military chiefs on both sides recognised the advantages of mutual co-operation. The Tsar expressed a wish to see the French flag flying in Russian waters, so in August 1891 the French Fleet anchored in the Bay of Finland near Kronstadt (Cronstadt), home of the Russian Fleet. French flags flew, and the music of the Marseillaise floated across the waters of the Baltic. After this event the relationship between the two countries became warmer, culminating in a formal pact in October 1893: the *"Alliance Franco-Russe"*. This was signed at Toulon, home of the French Fleet.

156. An attractively designed image from a bone monocular to commemorate a significant historical event in France during the late nineteenth century. (Charles Horton: Lishman Collection)

Historical Events Commemorated on Stanhopes

Several Stanhopes commemorating this treaty have been found, with the same elaborate image of three cameos linked with loops and bows of ribbon. The pictures include French and Russian sailors, with portraits of Tsar Alexander III and President Carnot of France. The captions are in the French and Russian languages. The Franco-Russian Alliance became known elsewhere as the "Dual Alliance", in contrast to the "Triple Alliance" of Germany, Austria and Italy. The friendship between the two nations was further strengthened in October 1896, when the Tsar arrived in Paris, becoming the first Sovereign to visit the new French Republic. Unfortunately, by this time the two Heads of State who had inaugurated the Franco-Russian Alliance were both dead. Alexander III died in 1894, and was succeeded by his ill-fated son, Tsar Nicholas II. In the same year, while visiting the Lyon Exposition, President Carnot was assassinated by an Italian anarchist.

Stanhopes were used to advertise political affiliations very soon after their invention, when Italian students wore watch charms with images of *Les Défenseurs d'Italie* in 1861. Americans also embraced the idea enthusiastically, and cheap watch charms containing Stanhopes were produced for presidential campaigns. The first dated examples so far discovered advertise the 1884 presidential campaign, but it is possible that they were in existence from an earlier date. Giveaway "lucky pigs" made of base metal were widely circulated. These incorporated portraits of both contenders for the post of President of the United States: James G. Blaine was the Republican Nominee, running against Grover Cleveland, the Democratic Nominee. The fact that the image had to be viewed from the opposite end to the pig's snout may have had some political significance!

Grover Cleveland was duly elected and led the country for two terms. Souvenirs of better quality, such as carved bone pens and paperknives, were produced with Stanhope portraits of President Cleveland and his wife and were popular expressions of support during his time in office.

The next President of the United States (1889-1893) was Benjamin Harrison. His Vice-President during the same period was Levi P. Morton, who had previously been the American ambassador to France and given the honour of driving the first rivet into the frame of Bartholdi's Statue of Liberty.

157. An American political image from a metal pig charm, c.1884. (Milan Zahorcak: Kessler Collection)

158. An American commemorative image from a pen with paperknife, 1885-1889. (Milan Zahorcak: London Collection)

159. An American political image from a paperknife, 1889-1893. (Milan Zahorcak: London Collection)

At the end of Queen Victoria's reign Britain was at war in South Africa. The second Boer War (1899-1902) produced two national heroes, whose images were reproduced on many souvenirs. Lord Roberts (1832-1914) had already completed over forty years' distinguished service in India and Afghanistan, and was given the title of "Lord Roberts of Kandahar". He was then made Commander-in-Chief in South Africa. He ended a succession of British defeats and captured the main cities before passing command to Lord Kitchener in 1900. Colonel (later Lord) R.S.S. Baden Powell was also a hero of the Boer War, having successfully defended Mafeking during the siege. He continued a brilliant military career and also founded the worldwide Boy Scout movement.

In Victorian Britain eminent theologians were much respected and important personalities of the day, and it is not unusual to find them commemorated in Stanhopes of the period. The Reverend John Keble was a renowned Victorian cleric and author of many important religious books. In 1865 his wife's ill health prompted a move to Bournemouth, but unfortunately the town's reputation as a restorative resort had little effect; the couple both died there the following year. His colleagues founded Keble College, Oxford, in his memory, and his admirers visited the "House where Keble died" in Bournemouth. It was included as one of six views of the resort's main tourist attractions, revealed in a silver heart-shaped Stanhope charm. Another religious personality was Charles Haddon Spurgeon" (1834-1892). His portrait in a bone monocular is a memorial to a revered British Baptist preacher, whose writings were widely studied in the Victorian era. This Stanhope was probably produced shortly after his death.

There were several enthusiastic and charismatic preachers in Britain and the U.S.A. during the late Victorian era, and none more so than the fiery Dwight L. Moody of Massachusetts. In 1871 he was joined by Ira D. Sankey, whose superb singing voice attracted the crowds to Moody's revival meetings. Two years later they travelled to Britain, and everywhere thousands flocked to hear them. On their return to America. Revivalist fervour gripped the nation, and even President Grant attended their meetings.

160. *British national heroes during late Victorian times: (above) an image from a granite barrel-shaped charm, (Jull Collection); (below) an image from bone binoculars.*

161. *A memorial image from a bone monocular, c.1892.*

162. *Images from a pair of bog oak miniature binoculars: (left) Dwight L. Moody, (right) Ira D. Sankey. c. 1875.*

Historical Events Commemorated on Stanhopes

163. Wooden charms produced to commemora[te] the shipwreck of H.M.S. Montague, c.1906. (Pig charm from the Jull Collection)

164. Commemorative image from a wooden pig charm, c.1906. (Jull Collection)

Commemorative Stanhopes continued to be produced for all occasions, but not all were cause for celebration. In 1906 the battleship H.M.S. Montague ran aground on Lundy Island in the Bristol Channel. Despite great efforts to refloat her, heavy seas finally broke her back and soon very little was left above water. Twiss Brothers, retailers in the seaside resort of Ilfracombe at the beginning of the twentieth century, produced small souvenirs of this naval disaster, usually containing six microphotographic views of the shipwreck before it broke up on the rocks. The images were all the same, and were entitled "In Memory of HMS Montague". The novelties were made of dark wood and roughly carved as charms, such as owls and pigs. It is doubtful whether the timber originally came from the ship, as she was metal-built.

Two images in a pair of bone binoculars commemorate an event of considerable significance in the history of aviation. In one eyepiece is a picture of an early monoplane flying above the "White Cliffs of Dover", with a French inscription commemorating the first aeroplane flight across the English Channel. Louis Blériot (1872-1936) was born in Cambrai, France, and was one of the pioneers of aviation. He designed and built the monoplane for his famous flight. He had made a bet with Hubert Latham that he would be the first to cross the English Channel, and the date was set for Sunday, 25th July 1909. The weather was perfect for the flight, and Blériot decided to make an early start: he left at 4.55 a.m., while Latham was still asleep! By 6.50 a.m. Blériot had landed in England.

165. Blériot's record-breaking flight on 25th July, 1909: image from bone binoculars.

167. The ruins of war: image from a bone crucifix, 1916.

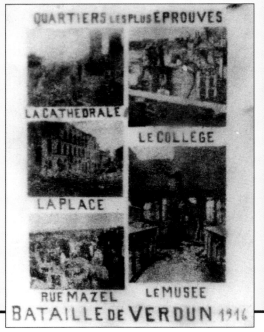

166. Blériot with his family: enlarged detail from an image in the same pair of bone binoculars.

168. "Our allies": composite image from the same pair of bone binoculars. (Townsend Collection)

169: "Our generals": composite image from bone binoculars, c. 1918 (Townsend Collection.)

The other lens in the binoculars shows another view of the monoplane, and a separate group photograph of the famous aviator, his wife and four children, all elegantly dressed in the height of Edwardian fashion. These images may be the examples listed in the *Lizé* inventory as Nos. 2247 and 2247bis: "*Aéroplane: Blériot*".

Five years after Blériot's flight, World War I began, and there were no further opportunities for commemorating joyous occasions or holiday memories in Stanhopes. Photographers on both sides of the Channel were using their skills to record the atrocities of war, and Stanhopes of city landmarks destroyed in the bombardment made macabre souvenirs. The Battle of Verdun (1916) was featured in several different images, showing shattered villages and views of the trenches.

Finally the "Great War" came to an end, but the devastation in France was recorded in Stanhope souvenirs for the visitors to the battlefields. Many were placed in crucifixes, rosaries and pendant crosses, inviting prayers for the millions who had lost their lives in the previous four years. Stanhopes reminiscent of nineteenth century composite views were produced when peace was declared, many of which were inserted in the ever-popular miniature binoculars. "*Nos Généraux*" and "*Les Alliés*" provide interesting research topics for Stanhope collectors.

In 1936 King George V died, and the Prince of Wales succeeded his father as Edward VIII. However, before his coronation took place, he abdicated in order to marry Mrs Wallis Simpson, an American divorcee. His younger brother George became king in his place, and many souvenirs were produced to commemorate the Coronation of George VI and Queen Elizabeth the following year.

Stanhope images do not seem to have commemorated events during World War II and the last royal Stanhope souvenir records the Coronation of Queen Elizabeth II (1953).

170. Commemorative image in a plastic mechanical pencil, 1937.

172. Metal crown-shaped charms produced to commemorate two different coronations: (left) Edward VII, 1902; (right) Elizabeth II (1953). (Townsend and Jull Collections.)

171. Image from a metal crown-shaped charm. (Jull Collection)

14 "World Fair" Stanhopes

Until 1928, when "world fairs" were regulated as to frequency and classification, any country could describe an exhibition in this way, although the events varied greatly in area, size and attendance. Several "international" fairs were simply expanded national trade fairs, rather than universal exhibitions, but many of them were still important enough commercially to be commemorated in Stanhope souvenirs.

In 1876 the United States held its first international exhibition, to celebrate the centenary of the Declaration of Independence. This took place in Fairmount Park, Philadelphia. Unlike the previous British and French international exhibitions, where one or two large halls were constructed to house all the exhibits, the city provided a 236 acre site for numerous separate buildings, all among an attractive garden lay-out. There were more than thirty thousand exhibits from thirty-five countries, which were viewed by eight million visitors. The event

was billed as the "International Exhibition of Arts, Manufactures and Products of the Soil and Mines", and some of the more famous inventions on view were Graham Bell's telephone, Edison's telegraph, the typewriter and the sewing machine. There was also a display of microphotography, and given the fact that John H. Morrow of New York was producing Stanhope novelties by 1866, it is unlikely that he and other photographers ignored such an opportunity to promote their business. Stanhope novelties commemorating this event are probably the earliest dated examples from the New World, and as such should be considered rare collectables.

Two years later the 1878 *Exposition Universelle* took place in Paris, which has been described earlier. This was followed by a series of minor events around the world. In 1883 an exhibition was held in Boston to display "Foreign Products, Arts and Manufactures".

173. Possibly one of the earliest American dated Stanhopes: 1876 Philadelphia Exhibition. Image from a walking stick. (Milan Zahorcak: Kessler Collection)

174. An image from an ivory seal: 1883 Boston Exhibition. (Milan Zahorcak: Kessler Collection)

175. An image from a bone penholder: 1886 Edinburgh International Exhibition.

In 1886 an "International Exhibition of Industry, Science and Art" was held in Edinburgh, the first world fair to take place in Scotland. Given her love of that country, it is not surprising that Queen Victoria was the Patron. The event was opened by her grandson Prince Albert Victor, eldest son of the Prince of Wales. A key feature of the exhibition was the first attempt at large-scale electrical lighting, and the buildings displayed all aspects of Scottish manufacture of the time. The most popular area was "Old Edinburgh", a recreation of historically interesting buildings from the old part of the city. All traders were required to wear appropriate costumes of the period, which suggests that this was a forerunner of the modern theme park!

In 1887 the "Adelaide Jubilee International Exhibition" took place, commemorating Queen Victoria's Golden Jubilee on the opposite side of the world. Bone paperknives were among the souvenirs and these may be the earliest dated Stanhopes from the Australian continent. The following year, Melbourne was the site of the "Centen-nial International Exhibition", and again Stanhopes exist to commemorate this event. The Lizé inventory includes microphotographs ordered for both these occasions.

French international fairs continued to dominate the exhibition scene in Europe. In 1889 another vast *Exposition Universelle* was held in Paris, to celebrate the centenary of the French Revolution. The showground was larger than ever before, attracting more than twenty-eight million visitors to view sixty-one thousand exhibits. The event made more than 8,000,000 francs profit, a source of great satisfaction to the organisers, as the main attraction to the site was the newly constructed but very expensive *Tour Eiffel*. Electricity was the most recent invention exploited at this fair. The gardens, bridges and pavilions were illuminated at night, so that posters advertised the exhibition as *"Le Pays des Fées"*, or "Fairyland". This enabled the exhibition to remain open until midnight and the extension of visiting hours greatly contributed to the financial success of the event.

176. A general view of the 1889 Paris Exposition: image from a bone monocular. (Terence Taylor)

178. The Eiffel Tower and its creator: image from bone binoculars, c.1889.

177. An informative image from a bone monocular: a wordy caption giving details of the Eiffel Tower, c. 1889. (Dagron Family Archives)

"World Fair" Stanhopes

The design of Alexandre-Gustave Eiffel (1832-1923) was chosen from several hundred proposals to build an observation tower for the exhibition. This engineer had achieved world-wide fame in 1886 as the designer of the metal skeleton of Bartholdi's Statue of Liberty. The tower was erected in 794 days on the *Champs de Mars* and faced the *Palais du Trocadéro* across the Seine. It was the wonder of the age, being the tallest construction in the world at that time. National pride required that visitors to the exhibition were made aware of all the relevant facts and figures about *"La Tour Eiffel"*, and several Stanhope souvenirs contain unusually lengthy captions.

René Dagron exhibited at the *1889 Exposition Universelle*, and won yet another Silver Medal for microphotography. He was now seventy years old, and must have reflected with satisfaction upon his part in the spread of commercial microphotography throughout the world. It is interesting that another exhibitor was Mme. Dagron, who was awarded a Bronze Medal in the Photography section.

In 1890 a second Edinburgh International Exhibition took place which had several links with the Paris Exposition Universelle of the previous year. The Guidebook noted that visitors to both events would recognise the "Sliding Railway" and the "Cairo Street Bazaar", both of which had been transported from France to Scotland. The friendly Franco-Scottish relationship was also shown by the display of "Magic Lantern Views of the Paris Exhibition". The

exhibition occupied a fifty-acre site to the west of the city beside the Union Canal. The huge Main Building housed British exhibits, but also included a section for products from France, Austria, Italy, Germany, Russia, Belgium, the Orient and "the Colonies". Electricity was a key feature, from widespread electric lighting to providing the power for various novel methods of transportation. The "Ship Railway" was particularly praised; electric launches on the canal were raised into the air and carried on a monorail overland, to be lowered onto the water elsewhere.

A much greater number of souvenirs was produced for visitors to the 1893 "World's Columbian Exposition" at Chicago, which celebrated the 400th anniversary of the voyage to America by Christopher Columbus. Chicago was chosen because it was an important railway centre, thereby providing easy access for large crowds, and also because this wealthy city could afford to back the event with a substantial sum of money. The fair occupied a seven hundred-acre site fronting Lake Michigan, and canals linked the vast buildings housing the exhibits. These included the Transportation, Mining, Fisheries, Horticultural and Agricultural Buildings and Machinery Hall. Circling the site was an electric railway, and there was also a popular "Movable Sidewalk".

A pair of miniature gilt binoculars has two images referring to this exhibition. One lens has a view of the Transportation Building, but the other reveals a rare and

179. *An image from a wooden parasol-shaped needlecase: 1890 Edinburgh International Exhibition. Note the tethered gas-filled balloon. (Private collection)*

MRS. POTTER PALMER.
President of the Board of Lady Managers

180. *An image from a brass watch fob shaped like an early locomotive: 1893 Chicago Columbian Exposition. (Milan Zahorcak: Kessler Collection)*

attractive picture of a local personality. Research has identified Mrs. Potter Palmer as a leading Chicago socialite of the time, whose husband was a wealthy merchant and real estate promoter. As she was President of the Board of Lady Managers, the "Women's Building", an innovative exhibition of everything to interest women, possibly owed much to her involvement and organisation.

One important exhibitor and provider of liquid sustenance at the 1893 "Columbian Exposition" was the Anheuser-Busch Brewery, which provided some of the most popular souvenirs from this event. These were colourful enamelled metal bartenders' knives, with Stanhope views of the brewery buildings and its President. A Bavarian brewery had been established in St.Louis in 1852, which was acquired by Eberhard Anheuser in 1860. Adolphus Busch married Lilly Anheuser, and soon became a partner in the brewery. In 1893 the brewery was able to advertise "Anheuser-Busch Brewing Association Highest Score Award, World's Fair". A knife with a Stanhope portrait of the worthy Adolphus Busch is a very desirable collectable, and a dated inscription adds even more to the value of such an item. Busch knives sold during the 1893 World Fair were decorated with the original "A and Eagle" symbol first employed on brewery products in 1872. This included an eagle standing on the American shield, with its wings folded back into the initial "A".

Other Stanhope souvenirs feature images of the "Ferris Wheel", an American carnival ride introduced to entertain the vast crowds flocking to the site. It had been constructed by G.W.G. Ferris of Pittsburgh, and had thirty-six cars each carrying sixty passengers. It made a fortune for its creator, and a handsome profit was also made for the city, for by the time the "1893 Chicago World Fair" closed, the total attendance was more than sixteen million visitors.

Les expositions universelles et les Stanhopes

La plupart des expositions internationales importantes de la fin du dix-neuvième siècle et du début du vingtième siècle furent commémorées dans les souvenirs microphotographiques. Les Expositions Universelles de Paris de 1867, 1878 et 1889 furent très réussies. En 1876 L'Exposition de Philadelphie commémora le centenaire de l'indépendance américaine, et l'Exposition de Chicago en 1893 célébra le 400ème anniversaire de la découverte de l'Amérique par Christophe Colomb. On trouve peu de souvenirs Stanhope de l'Exposition 1900 de Paris sans doute parce que les cartes postales illustrées devenaient à la mode. Cependant, il reste beaucoup d'exemples de Stanhope des foires universelles britanniques et américaines jusqu'en 1939.

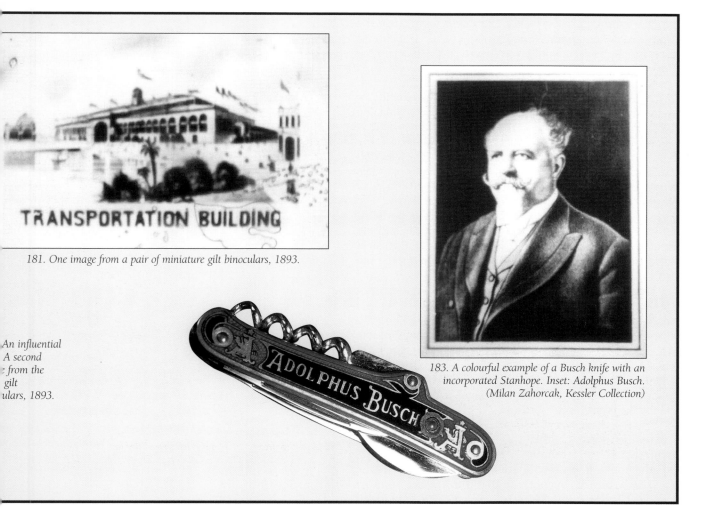

181. One image from a pair of miniature gilt binoculars, 1893.

An influential
A second
e from the
gilt
ulars, 1893.

183. A colourful example of a Busch knife with an incorporated Stanhope. Inset: Adolphus Busch.
(Milan Zahorcak, Kessler Collection)

"World Fair" Stanhopes

The birth of the twentieth century was celebrated in Paris with an exhibition in the style of the great international fairs. The *1900 Exposition Universelle* was larger than ever before, occupying an area of more than three hundred acres. The imposing *Porte Monumentale* was erected on the *Place de la Concorde* as the main entrance, and a popular venue was the *"Palais de l'Électricité et Chateau d'Eaux"*, where fountains and pools were illuminated by electric light.

Many countries erected separate pavilions beside the Seine, along the *Rue des Nations*. The *"Trottoir Roulant"*, a French version of the "Movable Sidewalk", encircled the *Champs de Mars* and the *Esplanade des Invalides*. There were eighty thousand exhibits visited by a record-breaking attendance of more than forty million visitors. Even so, the event made a substantial loss, but the French Government was satisfied that national prestige had been upheld. One can only begin to guess at the amount and variety of souvenirs produced for an event of this size, but the number of Stanhopes found by collectors commemorating the *1900 Exposition Universelle* is small in comparison with those existing from the 1889 event, have some degree of rarity value. A possible reason may have been the recent introduction of the picture postcard. These offered a greater variety of views, could be seen easily and were probably cheaper than Stanhope novelties. They provided the added advantage of postal communication.

The unsettled political situation in Europe had given rise to several well-publicised friendship treaties between various countries. As these became firm and established, dual exhibitions were organised to promote each other's products and industries. France and Russia jointly held the *"1902 Exposition Franco-Russe"* in Paris, while British and French manufacturers united to present the 1908 Franco-British Exhibition in London.

A site of 140 acres was prepared at Shepherd's Bush, and a number of elaborate domed and pillared buildings were erected to house the 13,500 exhibits. Copying the 1893 Chicago Columbian Exhibition, these constructions were covered in white plaster to create a "White City", the name of which remains in the area today. The elevated exhibition halls could be visited on foot, or by gondola along the many canals. They included The Palace of Women's Work, Machinery Hall, The Palace of Music, The Fine Arts Palace, Congress Hall and various large pavilions for exhibits from France, Canada, Australia, India and the great British and French manufacturers. It was the greatest event of the Edwardian era, and was visited by more than eight million people.

The main reason for this exhibition's popularity stemmed from the inclusion of the 1908 Olympic Stadium. The "White City Stadium" was built to house a crowd of 150,000, and was the largest stadium in the world at that time. Stanhope souvenirs from the 1908 Franco-British Exhibition usually include a view of the Olympic Stadium, and the captions were written in both English and French, to stress the dual nationality of the exhibition theme.

The following year the site and buildings of the White City were used for the 1909 "Imperial International Exhibition". A number of Stanhope souvenirs commemorating this event have been found, mostly of the same design. The majority of these are in the form of wooden "bottles" which can be unscrewed and reformed

184. Two views of the 1900 Paris Exposition Universelle, from a bone monocular. (Terence Taylor).

185. An interesting aerial view of the 1908 Franco-British Exhibiti[on] image from a paperknife. (Charles Horton: Lishman Collection.)

186. Detail showing the Olympic Stadium at the 1908 Franco-Briti[sh] Exhibition at White City, London: one image from miniature bone binoc[ular]

187. Bottle-shaped pipes and cigar holders. The Stanhope images are concealed in the metal caps. Actual height: 14cms.

THE BRITISH EMPIRE EXHIBITION WEMBLEY 1924

BIRDS EYE VIEW OF THE EXIBITION

BY COURTESY OF THE BRITISH EMPIRE EXHIBITION 1924 INC

188. General view of the British Empire Exhibition at Wembley, 1924: image from a bone penholder.

NEW YORK WORLD'S FAIR

TRYLON and PERISPHERE

9. The "Trylon" and the isphere", symbols of the 1939 New York World's Fair. (Milan Zahorcak: Kessler Collection)

to make pipes or cigar holders. Although the pipes are inscribed with the name and date of the exhibition on the outside, the Stanhope views rarely show the White City: more often they hold nude views! Unusually, the same design was produced in olive wood and sold with views from the Holy Land.

International enmities engendered by the Great War (1914-1918) made it impossible to arrange world fairs for several years afterwards. The next event of any importance was the British Empire Exhibition at Wembley, in 1924. At this time Britain still governed a large empire, and the occasion was used to show the rest of the world the wealth, resources and above all the unity of those colonies within the realm. King George V, Queen Mary and other members of the Royal Family drove in state to open the exhibition on 23rd April, St. George's Day. The site at Wembley covered 216 acres, composed of lakes, fountains, gardens and a large number of pavilions, each illustrating architectural styles of the country exhibiting there. Forty-two countries were represented from all the continents, and visitors were amazed at the variety of cultures and resources on view.

The most imposing building was the "Empire Stadium" which later became known as Wembley Stadium. It had been built in just three hundred days for the 1923 Football Association Cup Final. It was the setting for the "Pageant of Empire", which took place in the summer months with a cast of fifteen thousand and was a spectacular illustration of the history of the British Empire. The British Empire Exhibition was so popular that it was extended for a second year and had over twenty-six million visitors.

In the U.S.A. the last important world fair before the advent of World War II was the 1939 New York World's Fair, commemorating the 150th anniversary of the inauguration of President George Washington in New York. Its theme was "Building the World of Tomorrow", and with exhibits from sixty-three nations, it had the largest amount of foreign participation of any fair in history. At the centre of the site were two futuristic monuments of impressive size: the Trylon, a soaring three-sided obelisk, and the Perisphere, a massive globe containing some of the many technical and industrial exhibits unveiled at this event. Images of these constructions appeared on most souvenirs from the 1939 World's Fair, including those with Stanhopes. King George VI and Queen Elizabeth, who arrived from Canada by train across the Niagara Suspension Bridge, visited the exhibition; this was the first time that a British sovereign had visited the U.S.A. The New York World's Fair attracted an unprecedented attendance of almost fifty million visitors in less than a year, but the outbreak of World War II was a sad finale to an outstanding exhibition.

World fairs and exhibitions were the main occasions of the late-nineteenth and early-twentieth centuries when millions of people travelled to one venue. Whenever they occurred, souvenir sellers with a plentiful supply of cheap Stanhope novelties were hoping to make their fortunes. In addition to achieving his own financial success, Dagron made it possible for many others in France and elsewhere to do the same.

15 Dagron: the Final Years

Possibly the earliest experiment to produce a variation of Stanhope novelties is preserved in the Dagron family archives. A small box was found to contain a number of Stanhope lenses adhering together in pairs. The double glass lenses were rectangular instead of cylindrical, with the standard ground magnifying lenses at one end. Close inspection reveals an image at the plane end of each rod, which show almost identical views from the magnifying end. By moving the double rods vertically in front of the eye one view comes into focus, to be immediately replaced by a slightly different view of the same scene. The eye sees this as a small flicker of movement in one picture, enhanced by the choice of subject, rather than the reality of two images.

In one example, a young woman sits sewing, with her needle in the fabric, while the second image shows her uplifted arm pulling the needle and thread away from the embroidery. The optical effect produced by moving the lens combination up and down is an illusion of continual sewing. A second pair of lenses shows a young lady picking up a pair of opera glasses and then looking through them. Yet a third example reveals the same model holding a flower and then removing a single petal: "he loves me, he loves me not".

Another pair shows a man slumped over a table, sleeping off the effects of heavy drinking. Beside him stands a companion with his hand on the forgotten bottle. In the second image the companion is stealing a drink, while the drinker awakes and leaps up to retrieve the bottle. Two movements are visible here: the arm as the bottle lifted from the table to the companion's mouth, and the drinker who changes from a sitting to a standing position.

These are all examples of the optical illusion known as "persistence of vision", in which the brain is tricked into perceiving movement where none exists. The little box of paired lenses is further evidence of René Dagron's inventive mind. Each image is captioned *"Kinéscope"*, although it is not known whether or not *"L'inventeur"* actually patented or registered the design. Novelty toys with the same name have been discovered which use pairs of joined lenses. The *"Kinéscope"*, which is marked *"Déposé"* inferring that this item was registered in France,

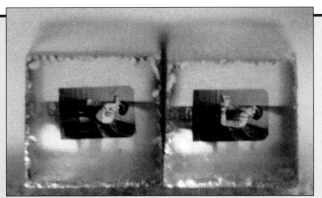

190. A pair of Stanhope lenses with double microphotographic images. Actual size: 2.6 x 5.5mm. (Dagron Family Archives)

192. A similar embroidered and beaded slipper pattern from the same period. Actual length: 30cm.

191. "Sewing Girl": Kinescope images, c.1890. The girl is embroidering a pair of slippers, using a "Berlin Wool Work" design on canvas. (Dagron family Archives)

is shaped like a small round pocket watch made of base metal. It has a hanging loop for the watch chain and a knob at the top. A hole in the centre of one side is the viewing window, and a light source enters from the opposite side. When the knob is pressed a spring mechanism changes the position of the image, revealing a second similar picture. The action is rapid enough to produce an impression of movement, updating Dagron's original static microphotographs to a fleeting moving picture. One attractive example shows a lady moving her hand to and from her lips, seemingly blowing kisses. Another shows a man using continual arm movements as he works at a carpentry task.

Another variation using the double Stanhope lens is the "Cinématographe Bijou", again registered in France. This is a small book-shaped watch fob made of base metal, stamped with a decorative design. The viewing frame is a small round hole on one narrow side, while there is a larger rectangular hole on the opposite side as a light source. At the top is a flattened hanging loop that also activates the movement mechanism. When the loop is pressed, the picture already in view through the round hole moves downward, and a different image flicks into place. The loop is spring-loaded, so that it immediately returns to its original position. No clicks are heard, and the speed of the two moving pictures is as quick as the blink of an eye. If one looks through the rectangular opening with a magnifying glass, two Stanhope lenses with single microphotographic images attached can be seen moving up or down.

Dagron – les dernières années

Vers la fin du dix-neuvième siècle, plusieurs variations des créations de Stanhope furent inventées. René Dagron produisit le Kinéscope, qui était semblable au Cinématographe Bijou. Deux images Stanhope étaient légèrement décalées pour donner une impression de mouvement. D'autres nouveautés utilisèrent des objectifs tournants pour montrer une série d'images, tandis que le Photoscope faisait tourner un disque avec des images devant une lentille simple, avec le même effet.

La maison de Photographie Dagron fut vendue en 1897, après la mort de Madame Caroline Dagron. René Dagron mourut trois ans après (le 13 juin 1900), dans une chute de bicyclette. Ce n'est qu'en 1959 qu'il fut reconnu dans son pays comme l'inventeur du microfilm, et une plaque fut érigée à son lieu de naissance.

195. The Kinescope. Actual diameter: 2.2cm. (Leonard Collection)

193. "He loves me, he loves me not": Kinescope images, c.1890. (Dagron Family Archives)

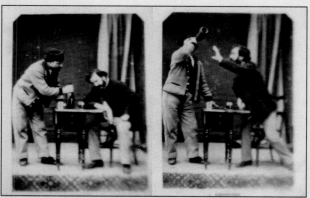

"Drinking partners": Kinescope images, c.1890. (Dagron Family Archives)

196. Two views of the "Cinématographe Bijou". Actual size: 2.0cm x 1.4cm.

Dagron: the Final Years

A rarer version of the Cinématographe or the Kinéscope was mounted under the cap of a plain wooden walking stick and activated by pressing a metal button. The positions of the viewing window and aperture for the light source are on opposite sides of the cane, and covered when the cap is in place. As with most novelties where the Stanhopes were hidden away in inconspicuous locations, the animated images were nearly always "exotic", such as a nude lady putting on her stockings.

A very unusual novelty dating from the same period is a miniature metal ball. When opened it reveals an inner section resembling a toy Gatling gun which holds six Stanhopes. These include a varied selection of images including the British Prince and Princess of Wales, captioned in French and dating from the mid-1860s, when they were first married, and President Abraham Lincoln and his Cabinet.

Twelve Stanhope lenses were used in an imitation pocket-watch novelty multiple viewer. It is stamped "Breveté" and "S.G.D.G." which indicates that it had been granted a French patent, but may not necessarily have been manufactured there. The initials stand for "sans garantie du gouvernement" and are often found on items imported into France. The knob at the top turns an inner wheel, which circulates the large disc holding the lenses. Each lens then appears in the viewing window.

The "Photoscope", patented by E. Lizé at the end of the nineteenth century, also offered a selection of twelve different images, but functioned by a more complicated mechanical system. It was described as "une visionneuse Stanhope", and was again the size and shape of a pocket watch. However, only a single magnifying lens was used, and this was incorporated into the viewing window. It was also longer and almost double the diameter of a standard Stanhope lens.

An interior view reveals a circular disc with twelve microphotographic images arranged around the circumference. This was rotated by a spring and ratchet device, activated when the knob at the top was pressed. The disc turned segment by segment, so that each image passed before the magnifying lens. The pictures were advertised as "bien parisienne", or "typically Parisian". A series of photographs of famous actresses photographed by Reutlinger at the end of the nineteenth century helped to make this novelty a popular souvenir of a trip to Paris during the "Naughty Nineties". Another series showed different views of the *1900 Exposition Universelle* in Paris.

Although these multiple Stanhope "toys" were popular in Europe and North America at the beginning of the twentieth century, novelties with single Stanhopes were beginning to lose their impact. Changes had taken place in the relatively small area of Paris where the industry used to be centred. The former elegant galleries of the Palais Royal area had begun to deteriorate, and the decaying facades no longer attracted the wealthiest customers. Baedeker, in the Paris Handbook for Travellers had already noted this decline in the 1891 edition: "The Palais Royal, long a favourite rendezvous of visitors to Paris, is now becoming gradually more and more deserted. It is superseded by the newer and more elegant quarters farther west, while its unobtrusive entrances, accessible only to foot-passengers, are not calculated to attract strangers". The cramped workshops began to close through lack of work and changed production techniques.

197. Mechanism for movable twin Stanhopes on a walking stick. (Kessler Collection)

198. A novelty with six Stanhope lenses. Actual diameter: 1.7cm. (Kessler Collection)

199 .Two views of a "pocket watch" multiple viewer. Actual diameter: 3.8cm. (Kessler Collection)

200. The "Photoscope", exterior view. (By courtesy of the Musée Nicéphore Niépce, Chalon-sur-Saône, France.)

201. The "Photoscope", interior view. (By courtesy of the Musée Nicéphore Niépce, Chalon-sur-Saône, France.)

202. Famous French actresses, a series photographed by Reutlinger: enlarged microphotographic images from a "Photoscope". By courtesy of the Musée Nicéphore Niépce, Chalon-sur-Saône, France.)

Many Stanhope items were no longer used, due to changes in lifestyle. The decline in intricate needlework techniques meant that bone stilettos, needle cases and other sewing accessories lay idle in the workbox. By Edwardian times even the familiar miniature parasol-shaped container for storing needles was rarely used for this purpose, for needles had long been available in cheap and rust-free packets. Although tape measures were still necessary sewing accessories, more modern examples on spring winders in colourful neat cases were preferred to the old-fashioned bulky hand-wound examples made of vegetable ivory. The style of writing equipment and desk accessories had also changed. Seals became obsolete when adhesive envelopes replaced "sealing wax". "Fountain" pens were used for handwriting, and penholders were mainly to be found in schools, where they were provided for pupils to practise their script.

Dozens of workers, who had previously supplied *Dagron & Cie.* with a vast selection of novelties to suit all pockets, discovered that their specific skills were becoming outmoded. Workers in bone and corozo found less demand for their products. The elaborate turning and carved details were not appreciated in an era when flowing simpler designs were more fashionable. An improvement in tooling machines and techniques replaced the traditional craftsman's skills, and the completed product became devalued by mass-production. Also, the brighter colours and smoother texture of plastic were considered more attractive and modern, and were quicker and cheaper to produce. All these factors gradually began to affect the large-scale manufacture of souvenir novelties in Paris.

Meanwhile, what of the Dagron family business which had played such an important part in establishing the Stanhope souvenir industry in Paris? René Dagron's youngest son Georges managed the business at 34 *boulevard Bonne Nouvelle* for his mother for several years before her death on 16th August 1897. None of the Dagron family wished to continue the photography studio or microphotography business, and two months later it was offered for sale. Leaflets announced the sale of the photography and microphotographic business of the late Mme. Dagron, which consisted of the customer list, all types of negatives held at the premises and the right to the lease of the business premises.

The business was eventually sold to a former employee, Joseph Luzzatto, who bought Dagron's laboratory at the same time, in order to continue trading in microphotographic souvenirs. Business continued as "*Photographie Dagron*", with the addition of "*Luzzatto Succursale*" ("Luzzatto Subsidiary"), and later as "*Dagron-Luzzatto*". René Dagron himself lived to see the dawn of the twentieth century, but died in Paris during the summer of 1900, at the age of eighty-one. He had fallen from his bicycle while taking a daily ride in the Bois de Boulogne. He received a head injury from which he failed to recover and died shortly afterwards on 13th June. The funeral was private, attended by four of his children and seven grandchildren. His obituary in "*L'Illustration*" (23rd June 1900) included the words: "His name will always be connected to that painful period of the siege, because he established the link between the capital and the rest of France which calmed so much anxiety."

Dagron: the Final Years

The Dagron family's direct association with microphotography ceased from this time, although Lucile Dagron was careful to preserve any records, information and artefacts connected with the father-in-law she honoured and respected. French history records René Dagron's momentous efforts to open lines of communication with Paris when the capital was besieged by the Prussians, but this period occupied less than six months of his lifetime. Admittedly, he seemed to achieve little of public interest before he reached the age of forty years, but the second half of his life was filled with photographic endeavours and useful inventions. Microphotography was to become a passion that charted the course of his life and led to a certain amount of fame and fortune. Unfortunately, throughout his life he was hampered by competitors who copied his ideas, colleagues who overshadowed his glory and businesses owned by others who profited from his inventions.

René Dagron was always aware that commercial success depended on widespread publicity, but his methods were not always appreciated. In the field of microphotography he knew what attracted the public, and was not averse to catering for a variety of different tastes in France and abroad. However, this made him vulnerable to criticism not only within his own household but also from those in positions of authority in the country he served so well. His courage and endurance during the siege of Paris were ignored by those who might have awarded him honours, but were swayed by the opinions of upholders of morality.

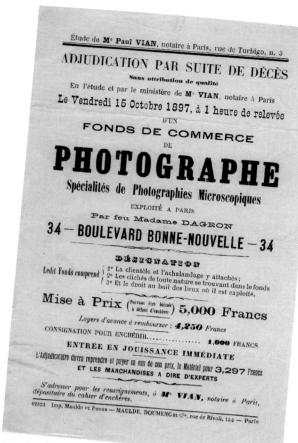

203. An advertisement announcing the sale of the Dagron photographic business: 15th October, 1897. (Dagron Family Archives)

Thirty years after his death the manifold uses of microfilm were becoming evident, and interest in the work of René Dagron revived as new patent applications were made. Although he had failed to patent his process for the "dry collodion" microfilms he produced during the Franco-Prussian War, he came to be universally recognised as its inventor. It was not until the centenary of his first patent application for microphotographic novelties that René Dagron's contributions to the world of photography and microfilm were to be officially recognised. In 1959 the National Microfilm Association of America organised a congress in Washington to celebrate "One Hundred Years of Progress in Microfilm". On this occasion they awarded a posthumous Medal of Merit to René Prudent Patrice Dagron, in recognition for "distinguished service to the art and science of micro documentary reproduction". In addition, a commemorative plaque was dedicated by his grandson René Georges Dagron at his birthplace in the little village of Aillières-Beauvoir, Sarthe.

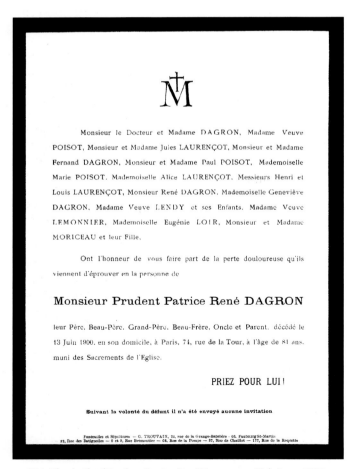

204. The death of Prudent Patrice René Dagron, on 13th June, 1900, is announced by his family. (Dagron Family Archives)

205. A commemorative plaque at the birthplace of René Dagron: Aillières-Beauvoir, Sarthe, France.

16 The Gex Stanhope Lens Industry

Although the Dagron family business had come to an end, Stanhope souvenirs continued to be made and sold by Joseph Luzzatto and his successors for many more decades. There were also several significant competitors, for microphotographic novelties were still considered commercially viable in the twentieth century. Small workshops continued to provide work for a few skilled individuals, each specialising in the manufacture of limited types of souvenir or in some aspect of the optical process. The Stanhope industry became fragmented yet still survived. It was able to continue because, just as it had been in the beginning, each small enterprise was organised by the microphotographer himself.

As the twentieth century progressed, those photographers experienced in the techniques of microphotography no longer needed to follow the entire laborious procedure described by René Dagron in 1864. Cameras had become less cumbersome, and improvements in photographic processes and film made it easier to produce microphotographs. However, the main processes remained the same: a glass plate holding the multiple images still needed to be cut into tiny squares, and each square with one microphotograph was applied by hand to a Stanhope lens. Optical grinding to achieve a cylinder shape from the rod-shaped lens was still the final process. It was specialised work, known and practised by a dwindling number of skilled microphotographers, but they continued to make a reasonable living in this trade. Orders for completed Stanhopes still arrived from several countries where regional souvenir industries included the insertion of microphotographic lenses with local views. There was also a developing market in gaudy jewellery and trick novelties, particularly in the U.S.A. However, one vital component was needed to sustain the Stanhope industry, without which it would cease to exist. This was the Stanhope lens itself, still manufactured and available in the same format as it had been when René and Caroline Dagron set up their own factory in Gex in 1862.

In 1998, when my research had not yet unearthed details of the Dagron Stanhope lens-making enterprise, I made the acquaintance of M. Georges Pérot. I had previously visited the *Musée Français de la Photographie* at Bièvres, France, and had found a small pamphlet by M. Pérot explaining the origin of *"photos microscopiques"*. When we met, he described how he had been interested in Stanhopes for thirty years, and had searched for anyone who might provide him with information about the techniques and processes involved in this discontinued industry. M. Pérot recounted how he had tracked down two elderly men who had been connected with the trade before World War II. One of these had been an unnamed microphotographer working with a small group making Stanhope souvenirs, but he steadfastly refused to divulge any information about the methods used in his part of the production. He had since died, together with his trade secrets.

According to M. Pérot, the other contact was "M. Freymond" (later established to be M. Roger Reymond), who had inherited a family business manufacturing Stanhopes. M. Pérot made notes about their conversation, which concerned the history and production methods of *"Etablissements Luzzatto"*. He wrote that this factory had originally been set up in Paris, but sometime after 1860 it had moved to a new site "near the Swiss border", where economic and working conditions were better. However, the name "Luzzatto" is not mentioned in any Dagron correspondence until 1897, when *Joseph Luzzatto* purchased Mme. Dagron's photographic business in Paris. The Reymond Family archives also mention this name only as a Paris client and successor to the Dagron business at the same time. It is not known whether there had been any connection between Dagron and Luzzatto concerning the Gex factory at an earlier date, but by the early 1880s the business faced bankruptcy. The factory was reprieved when one of the employees, M. Regard, took it over from "the Parisians", who then left the area.

M. Pérot had also made a number of notes about the production of Stanhope lenses, but I was not able to verify these at the time. Neither had I been given the exact location of the Regard factory, knowing only that it was "near the Swiss border". Later, my own research in the Dagron family archives revealed the existence of the Dagron factory at Gex, and I realised that the two factories could be one and the same. The time had come to extend the field of research, and this was instigated by my sister, who fortunately lives a short distance from Gex across the Swiss border in Geneva. She and a friend started the trail with the archivist at Gex Town Hall, where they learned that the oldest and first established factory producing Stanhopes in Gex had been owned in the twentieth century by the Reymond family, although it had been sold shortly before. Through a friend of the family my sister was able to establish the chain of ownership linking the unnamed Parisians, M. Regard and the Reymond family. During my subsequent visit, M. Roland Reymond of Ferney-Voltaire provided much of the source material for the rest of this chapter.

Under the ownership of M. Regard the industry seems to have been more successful and business flourished, particularly after the *1889 Exposition Universelle* in Paris, where he "made a fortune with his Stanhopes". He employed female outworkers, some of whom lived at a considerable distance across the border in Switzerland. The chain of production depended on a cyclist, who travelled around the outworking group every day. He delivered raw materials, inspected the work and collected the completed components. These were returned to the factory for finishing.

The Gex Stanhope Lens Industry

(This system was the opposite of that established by René Dagron in 1862, who had employed up to sixty workers supervised by a foreman in the factory itself. It is probable that economic factors influenced the change to a cheaper arrangement using outworkers.)

Roland Reymond's grandfather, Eugène Reymond (1880-1954), worked at the Stanhope factory from the age of twelve years and was highly regarded by his employer. Later on, he decided to leave the business in order to learn carpentry. Having completed his apprenticeship, he made a *"Tour de France"* honing his skills with various master craftsmen. *"Compagnonnage"* was a method of learning specialist skills that entitled the travelling journeyman to be a master craftsman himself, and the Reymond family are justifiably proud that their ancestor became a *"Compagnon de France"*.

Eventually Eugène Reymond returned to his birthplace, settled down and married. M. Regard was an elderly bachelor with no heirs, and needed someone reliable to carry on the business. He respected Eugène's achievements and persuaded him to take over the Stanhope factory. In 1905, at the age of twenty-five, the young man found himself in charge of an optical business, instead of plying his carpentry skills. Nevertheless, Eugène Reymond proved to be a good businessman, and when M. Regard died about fifteen years later he would have been content to know the factory was in good hands.

Eugène Reymond decided to improve production by modifying some of the current working practices, and made a major change by ending the system of outworking. According to M. Pérot's notes from his conversation with Roger Reymond, there had been a number of problems with the cyclist. The whole chain of production had depended on this one person, who had proved to be untrustworthy. By setting up all processes at the factory Eugène Reymond was able to keep a better check on his business, which had been René Dagron's intention some forty years earlier. Using skills and experience gained from his travels, Eugène also designed and installed some items of semi-automatic equipment. Some of his original drawings for items of machinery are preserved by Roland Reymond, and are evidence of his grandfather's intention to achieve the best methods of production in his workshop. In 1910 he designed a system of four pulleys for driving machinery and despatched the diagrams to *J. Lambercier & Cie.* of Geneva, who had a factory making machine tools and precision instruments.

Eugène Reymond employed twelve people: ten female workers and two men, plus himself and his son Roger. The procedures hardly changed over the years, with optical skills being passed from father to son, and eventually to Eugène's grandson Roland. He wrote the following account, in the knowledge that his grandfather and father employed the same methods and tools, all producing Stanhopes of the same high quality in the same workshop overlooked by the Jura Mountains. Further explanatory notes have been added to the translation.

The glass used was the highest quality clear optical glass. It was purchased in plates about 600mm and 800mm square and 3mm thick. It came from different glass manufacturers, one of which was Goetzenbruck of Alsace-Lorraine.

J. Scory and their successors, of *rue de Chateau-Landon*, Paris, were agents supplying optical glass to the Reymond factory during the first part of the twentieth century. They specialised in optical glass and photographical plates.

Eugène Reymond (1880-1954)

From 1933-1937 Eugène Reymond purchased large amounts of "verre brut" or plain glass from what was then Czechoslovakia, and also from Germany.

Using diamond cutting-tools the plate was cut into smaller squares 90mm x 90mm, and the thickness was reduced from 3mm to 2.6mm by grinding on a cast iron wheel. This measured 600mm in diameter and 30mm in depth, and emery powder and water achieved the grinding process.

J. Lambercier & Cie of *rue Vuache*, Geneva, who had manufactured Eugène's pulley system, also supplied the emery powder, machine oil and other items of small equipment. Things had changed since all the supplies for Dagron's foreman had been sent from Paris.

Again using diamond cutting-tools, the square plates were cut into strips 3mm in width. The resulting 30 rods each measured 90mm x 3mm x 2.6mm. (Diagram A) These rods were glued together with shellac, placing the 3mm sides face to face. This formed another plate 3mm thick, which could also be ground down to 2.6mm by the same method. The resulting plate (90mm x 78mm x 2.6mm) was then composed of 30 rods each measuring 90mm x 2.6mm x 2.6mm. It was scored across at intervals of 8mm by a diamond cutter, and the pieces broken off with pliers. (Diagram B) They were then placed in a bowl of hot water and caustic soda to dissolve the shellac. After rinsing and drying, the basic cuboid shapes (parallelepipeds), each measuring 8mm x 2.6mm x 2.6mm, were used to make the Stanhope lenses.

Shellac is a natural resinous substance produced on the bark of trees by a scale-shaped insect. In order to soften the shellac, it was placed in a linen sheet and soaked in boiling water. When the glue was soft, it was kneaded into sausage-shaped pieces, which were then cut into slices for use. The operation to remove the shellac was known as *"blanchir"*, or "laundering".

Each cuboid was placed in a specially designed grip handmade from *"cytise"* or laburnum wood and attached to a spindle. This rotated the wooden grip in a 6mm wide steel shaft with a concave end, which formed a rounded dome at the end of the glass rod.

The convex lens was originally ground by hand, but Eugène Reymond designed a series of rotating vertical spindles to reduce the labour intensity of the process. The timing of the spindles was controlled so that the female worker had just enough time to change the individual wooden grips. Roland Reymond remembered learning how to make the grips turned from laburnum wood when he was young.

207. A laburnum wood grip holding a rod before grinding. Actual size.

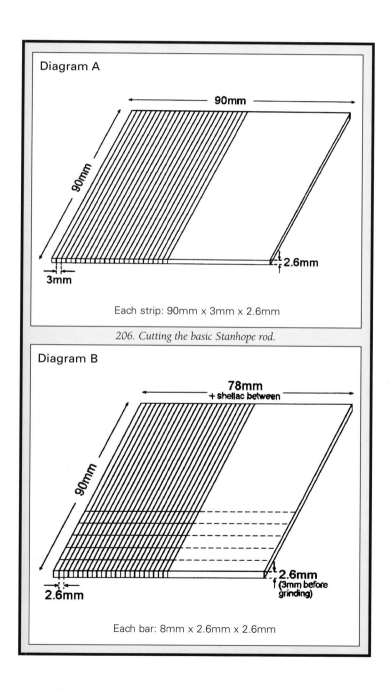

Diagram A

90mm

90mm

2.6mm

3mm

Each strip: 90mm x 3mm x 2.6mm

206. Cutting the basic Stanhope rod.

Diagram B

78mm
+ shellac between

90mm

2.6mm
(3mm before grinding)

2.6mm

Each bar: 8mm x 2.6mm x 2.6mm

L'industrie de la lentille Stanhope à Gex

La production de Stanhopes continua en France pendant de nombreuses décennies suivant la mort de René Dagron. Bien que n'étant plus la propriété de la famille Dagron, l'usine de Gex produisait toujours un grand nombre de lentilles Stanhope. Eugène Reymond acheta l'usine en 1905, et augmenta la production grâce à diverses modifications techniques. Son fils Roger lui succéda après la deuxième guerre mondiale, et continua à fabriquer les Stanhope jusqu'en 1972. Ce chapitre contient une description en français, rédigée par Roland Reymond, des méthodes de fabrication, ce qui perpétue le souvenir de cette petite industrie locale.

The Gex Stanhope Lens Industry

To form "le bombé" (also referred to as "la bosse") or dome, three main steps were involved. At first the dome was ground into a convex shape as it rotated in the steel tool, using carborundum (coarse emery powder) and water. This operation was known as "calbotage". Then the surface of the dome was smoothed by rotation in a second steel tool with fine emery powder and water. Finally it was rotated in a similar tool made of pewter and polished with "tripoli"or rottenstone and water. At the end of this operation each rectangular glass rod would have a finished magnifying dome, and would measure 7mm x 2.6mm x 2.6mm.

Roger Reymond noted in a magazine article that one had to avoid a *"lune"* ("moon"or flattened area) forming on top of the dome, as this would prevent the magnifying properties of the lens.

From 1910 and for many years afterwards, carborundum was supplied by the Paris agents of "The Carborundum Company"of Niagara Falls, U.S.A. It was advertised as "the hardest and sharpest". Rottenstone is obtained from a type of decomposed limestone, and is the finest form of polishing powder. It was also used by early photographers to give a final polish to the silvered surfaces of daguerreotype metal photographic plates.

208. A machine designed by Eugène Reymond to produce the dome on several Stanhopes at the same time. (Emmanuel Reymond)

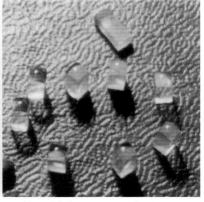

209. Polishing the domes: (left) smoothing with fine emery powder and water, (right) with tripoli and water. (Emmanuel Reymond)

211. *Completed Stanhope lenses.*
Actual sizes: 5mm, 6mm and 7mm.

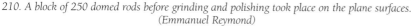

210. A block of 250 domed rods before grinding and polishing took place on the plane surfaces.
(Emmanuel Reymond)

In order to complete the manufacture of a Stanhope lens, the length of the rod had to be reduced at the square (plane) end to the final focal length of 6mm. This was done by fitting about 250 lenses vertically side by side into a square brass jig about 40mm x 40mm. To ensure that all the lenses were in the same plane, they were inserted dome downwards and pressed against a glass plate. Melted resin was poured over them, which hardened as it cooled. This produced a solid block of lenses, which were subjected to the following processes:

On the same type of metal wheel used for grinding the glass plates, the flat blocks of lenses were ground down with emery and water. It was important to ensure that the length of the lenses did not become shorter than 6mm.

Still on a grinding wheel, the flat ends of the lenses received a smoothing process with fine emery powder and water. During this operation the focus of each lens would be frequently checked by eye, looking at the scratches on the flat end through the domed end.

As soon as the focus was judged to be clear and sharp, the blocks of lenses were transferred to a small wheel only 250mm in diameter. This was covered with a 2mm thick pad of felt impregnated with jewellers' rouge and water. After a final check of the polishing, the lenses could be considered finished at the correct focal length of 6mm. The final process was to dissolve the resin around the lenses in a weak solution of caustic soda in warm water, followed by rinsing and drying.

Roger Reymond had his own method of speedily checking for lenses that were too short. He touched the block onto a layer of talcum powder, and then looked to see any clear rods. These would be the extra short examples to be rejected, which he would mark with a spot of Indian ink. He would then put the block on a heated metal plate to soften the resin, and push out any rods with ink marks to be thrown away. The standard length of a Stanhope lens used for the majority of orders was 6mm. Sometimes, however, longer versions of 7mm or shorter

lenses of 5mm were specified, which required adaptations to the focal length.

The final operation at the factory was to count the completed lenses into lots of one gross (144), and put them into packets of 25 gross (3,600) for despatch to customers.

By using the semi-automatic equipment created by Eugène Reymond, each female worker could accomplish about 5,000 operations per day, be it roughing, smoothing or polishing. With 10-12 employees the production attained 19,000 gross per year (about 2.75 million completed Stanhope lenses per year!)

Roger Reymond described how he himself did the most precise work, such as cutting the glass rods or checking the focal lengths of the lenses. He prepared and inspected all the completed work, once the factory had closed for the day.

The Reymond family has preserved the order books and invoices from the time when Eugène Reymond took over the business in 1905, and they provide much interesting information about twentieth century Stanhope production. The customer base was fairly small, but between them the orders were large enough to provide continuous production for the workers at the Gex factory. At the beginning of the twentieth century the biggest orders were placed by *"Dagron-Luzzatto: Successeur"* of *15 rue Turbigo, Paris*. These orders arrived at the rate of 2-4 per month, and totalled more than one million Stanhope lenses per year! The lenses produced at the factory set up by René Dagron continued to supply the microphotography business he had also established, and the connection remained for many more decades. By 1913 the Stanhopes were despatched to *"Luzzatto"*, and from 1919 to *"Mesdames Colas et Roche"*, noted in the Reymond order book as *"Luzzatto-Successeurs"*. From 1922 orders from the same address were placed by *"La Photographie Industrielle"*, which remained the most important customer of Eugène Reymond. The company still purchased more than one million Stanhopes annually, although the amount decreased in the 1930s. After World War II no more orders were received from this address.

Further along *rue Turbigo*, at No.48, was *"Établissements Lizé"*, which had traded as *"E.Lizé et Costil"* in the late nineteenth century. They also needed substantial numbers of Stanhope lenses for their microphotographic and souvenir business, particularly for the export market. In 1914 orders were received from the *"Veuve"* (widow) *Lizé*, who continued in business until 1928. From the *Lizé* documentation at the *Musée Nicéphore Niépce*, old business cards provide the information that Mme. Menard took over the Maison Lizé after this date. From World War II until the 1960s the business was owned by Mme. Prochasson, who purchased her lenses from Roger Reymond, but by 1965 it had been taken over by the "Société Européenne de Décoration" and was no longer in production. The sale to this company included all the apparatus and equipment for microphotography, a Dagron camera and a large number of glass negatives, together with all accessories and documentation. Much of this material is now preserved at the *Musée Nicéphore Niépce*, including the *Lizé* inventory that has proved so useful for Stanhope research.

In 1909 Eugène Reymond received an order from *"E. Legorgeu"* at *13 rue Beranger, Paris*. The invoice revealed that he was the successor to *"P. Adry"*, who had founded a microphotographic business at *7 rue de Malte* in 1866, specialising in *"Articles de Paris, St. Claude et Méru"*.

Microphotographic views on a wide range of subjects were offered, both in France and for export. Certainly this enterprise would have been one of René Dagron's earliest competitors. Few other orders were received from E.Legorgeu, but from 1917 they were received from another microphotographic business next-door, at *15 rue Beranger: "Établissements Lecarpentier"*. This company produced *"Photographies Microscopiques sur Verre"*, with no mention of souvenirs or novelties. It is possible that all business was by mail order, with microphotographic images applied to the lenses to order, and then despatched elsewhere.

Eugène Reymond fulfilled substantial orders for M. Lecarpentier and later for his wife until the outbreak of World War II. In 1941 more personal correspondence took place, when Mme. Lecarpentier wrote to thank the Reymonds for the gift of potato ration coupons. She informed them that in central Paris food distribution was very difficult, and that for over a year they had been unable to do any microphotographic work as all their clients were abroad or in Free France. Later she wrote to warn them that "a foreigner" had come to see her and was very interested in learning the secrets of Stanhope fabrication, and might subsequently arrive in Gex. She hoped M. Reymond would take steps to safeguard the secrets of his industry. Three months later Mme. Lecarpentier began to send orders for substantial orders of Stanhopes: 100 gross of 6mm lenses at fortnightly intervals. Given that the souvenir trade in wartime was

212. Roger Reymond
in his workshop.
(Emmanuel Reymond)

almost non-existent, and also that she had been unable to contact her usual customers, one wonders whether Mme. Lecarpentier was engaged in secret wartime activity. Roger Reymond continued to supply Mme. Lecarpentier after the war, and from the 1950s the business was known as *"Établissements Maurice Lecarpentier"*, possibly owned by her son or another relative.

Between them, Eugène Reymond and his son managed to keep the business going, despite the low demand for Stanhope lenses. Roger Reymond found additional work in the lapidary trade, cutting synthetic jewels for a manufacturer in nearby Mijoux. However, from 1950 onwards the industry entered a new period of importance, and under the management of Roger Reymond the factory began to produce up to fifteen thousand lenses per day. The bulk of the orders came from Maurice Lecarpentier and Mme. Prochasson in Paris, but there were also substantial amounts needed by local companies. The name of *"Établissements A. Grand-Perret et Fils"* of St. Claude figures prominently in the order book, and surprisingly it is also included in the *Lizé* inventory for the 1930s. This indicates that although they previously ordered completed microphotographic lenses, they now had the expertise to apply the images themselves onto the Stanhope lenses. St. Claude, in the Jura Mountains, is at the centre of a region famed for the manufacture of excellent tobacco pipes, many of which have been found with Stanhopes.

From the 1960s onwards, major clients of Roger Reymond gradually ceased trading and the demand for Stanhope lenses decreased. When Roger's son Roland returned to the area, he realised that the Stanhope industry was facing an uncertain future and decided to choose a different occupation in the manufacture of spectacle lenses. Roger Reymond continued to fulfil any remaining orders, but in 1972 finally ceased making Stanhope lenses commercially. The original factory building still exists at *37 ruelle de l'Église, Gex*. For many years Roger Reymond kept it as a small family museum, preserving his workbench, wheels and precision tools. He died in 1998, and ownership of the premises has now passed from the Reymond family. Eugène Reymond's great-grandson Emmanuel has become a professional photographer, perhaps a significant link with the past. Before the workshop was dismantled, Emmanuel made a photographic record of the various processes involved in the manufacture of Stanhopes, a final homage to his disappearing heritage.

Working with equipment and tools they designed and sometimes made themselves, Eugène, Roger and Roland Reymond were all able to produce fine examples of these tiny magnifying lenses, yet the perfection of their work resulted more from their own inherent skills. Roger Reymond described the essential qualities as "meticulous measurement, perfect eyesight, remarkable skill and unfailing patience". To have produced about eighty million Stanhope lenses during a period of sixty-seven years, the Reymond family of Gex must have possessed these qualities in abundance.

213. The former Stanhope Factory at Gex, France: south view. (Emmanuel Reymond)

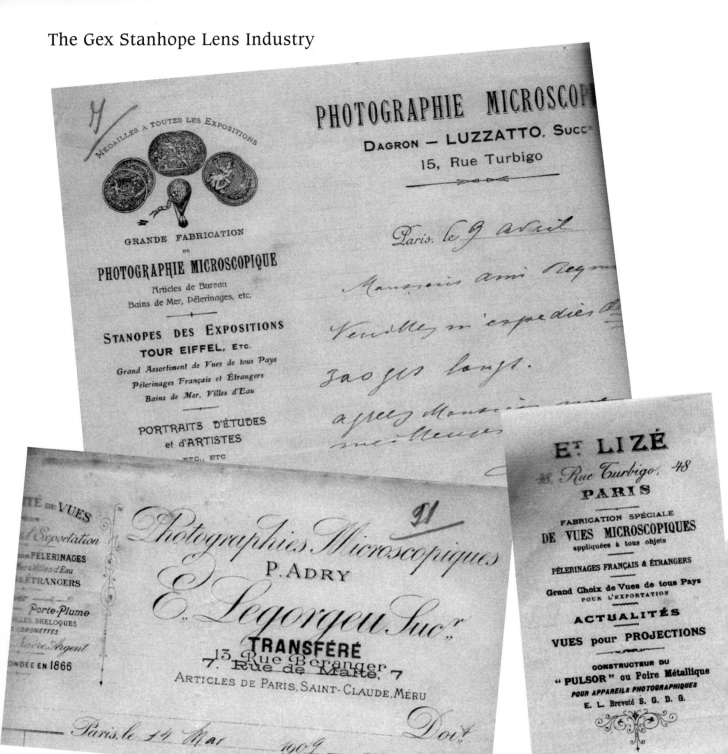

Fabrication des Loupes Stanhope

Selon la technique mise au point par mon grand-père Eugène Reymond (1880-1954) de 1905 à 1939 et perpétuée par mon père Roger Reymond (1909-1998) de 1939 à 1972, date d'arrêt de la fabrication.

1. Achat de verre extra-blanc d'optique en feuilles d'environ 600mm et 800mm, d'épaisseur environ 3mm, à différentes verreries dont les verreries de Goetzenbruck en Lorraine.

2. Découpe au diamant en plaques de 90mm x 90mm, d'épaisseur d'environ 3mm qui est ramenée à 2.6mm par usure sur une meule en fonte de 600mm de diamètre, d'épaisseur 300mm avec l'émeri et de l'eau.

3. Découpe au diamant de ces plaques de 90mm x 90mm en baguettes de 3mm de large (2.6mm d'épaisseur et 90mm de longueur). Ces baguettes sont ensuite collées de champ côte à côte à la gomme laque pour obtenir une plaque de 90mm x 78mm qui est usée à l'émeri sur les 2 faces pour obtenir une épaisseur de 2.6mm.

4. Cette plaque d'environ 90mm x 78mm qui comprend maintenant 30 baguettes de 2.6mm x 2.6mm x 90mm est découpée au diamant en bandes transversales de 8mm qui sont cassées à la pince et mises dans un récipient d'eau et de soude portée à l'ébullition pour dissoudre la gomme laque.

5. Après rinçage et séchage on obtient des parallélépipèdes de 2.6mm x 2.6mm x 8mm appelés "carrés" qui sont la forme brute de la future loupe Stanhope.

6. Chaque "carré" est ensuite placé dans une pince en bois (cytise), pince placée sur un tour qui permet de façonner le bombé (bosse) de la loupe Stanhope par rotation dans une tige d'acier de 6mm dans laquelle une cuvette permet au bombé (bosse) de se former.

1ère passe: Calbotage sur tige d'acier avec carborundum (gros émeri) + eau pour former la bosse.

2ème passe: Doucissage avec émeri fin + eau pour doucir la bosse sur tige d'acier.

3ème passe: Polissage sur tige en étain avec tripoli + eau pour polir la bosse.

On obtient la loupe Stanhope plat brut, bosse terminée de 2.6mm x 2.6mm x 7mm.

7. Pour terminer la fabrication de la loupe Stanhope il faut amener la loupe Stanhope à sa focale définitive de 6mm en usant le plat. Pour cela on procède comme suit. Dans une boucle de laiton de forme carré d'environ 40mm x 40mm qui repose sur une plaque de verre, on place verticalement et côte à côte environ 250 loupes Stanhope, les bosses reposant sur la plaque de verre. Après avoir callé et pressé sur les plats, on colle le tout avec de la résine fondue (genre résine de pin) qui durcit au refroidissement.

8. On obtient un "bloc" de 250 loupes Stanhope dont les plats sont usés de la façon suivante.

1ère passe: Sur une meule identique au poste 2 on use les plats avec émeri + eau tout en surveillant l'épaisseur qui doit toujours être supérieure 6mm.

2ème passe: Sur une meule, opération de doucissage avec émeri fin + eau. Vérification à l'oeil de la netteté suffisante des rayures de douci sur les plats en regardant au travers des bosses.

3ème passe: Dès netteté suffisante, polissage des plats du "bloc" sur une petite meule de 250mm sur laquelle est collé un feutre d'environ 2mm d'épaisseur avec rouge à polir + eau.

9. Après vérification du polissage, on peut considérer les 250 loupes Stanhope du "bloc" comme terminées et à la bonne focale de 6mm.

Après une ultime phase de vérification à l'oeil sur la bonne netteté focale de chaque loupe Stanhope on place chaque bloc de 250 loupes Stanhope dans un récipient chauffé avec eau + un peu de soude (dosage léger) pour dissoudre la résine. Ensuite rinçage et séchage.

La loupe Stanhope est terminée à la bonne focale de 6mm.

10. Opération finale de comptage par grosse (144 pièces) et emballage par paquet de 25 grosses et expédition à des clients fabricants de photos microscopiques sur verre.

N.B. Avec l'outillage crée par mon grand-père Eugène chaque ouvrière pouvait produire par jour soit 5 000 bosses au calbotage, soit 5 000 au douci soit 5 000 au poli.

Avec 10 à 12 personnes la production atteint jusqu'à 19000 grosses par an, soit 2 765 000 pièces par an, soit une moyenne journalière de 11 500 loupes Stanhope.

L'atelier de fabrication était situé au 37 ruelle de l'Église à Gex, 01170 France.

Fait à Ferney-Voltaire, France, le 5 décembre 2001, par Roland Reymond né en 1937 qui a participé dans sa jeunesse à la fabrication des loupes Stanhope.

"Une taille minutieuse, une vue impeccable, une habileté remarquable et une patience à toute épreuve, telles étaient les qualités nécessaires pour travailler à la fabrique des Stanhopes.

Tout passait par mes mains car je préparais et contrôlais tout le travail. Je faisais ça le soir, après la fermeture de l'atelier. C'était vraiment du travail artisanal."

Roger Reymond

17 Twentieth Century Stanhopes

The miniature bone monoculars and binoculars first mentioned in Dagron's earliest patent designs were still produced long after World War I. In the U.S.A. some were marketed as "The Smallest Telescope in the World" and were attached to cards confirming that they were "Made in France". In 1924 they were priced at 15 cents (U.S.) each, or 85 cents per dozen. They could be ordered with a Stanhope image of The Lord's Prayer, but were also available with a microphotograph of an actress or other "attractive lady forms".

The penholder with paperknife handle was another long-term Stanhope souvenir that continued to be manufactured in great quantities in France well into the twentieth century. Coloured plastic was the material of the age, although plain cream or pearlised plastic was often used to simulate the bone or mother-of-pearl items from an earlier time. Local artists painted appropriate scenes on the handles, but later coloured transfer prints were applied to cope with mass production. Views were available for most towns and resorts in France, and Stanhopes were inserted with matching images. There were also attractive pictures designed to appeal to young children for their schoolwork, including scenes from the fables of La Fontaine to illustrate well known proverbs. The colourful transfer labels were mainly printed in Lyons by the firm of *A. Besson*. Plastic Stanhope pen and paperknife combinations may not be greatly valued by collectors, but examples in good condition with appropriate microphotographic images can form an attractive display in a specialist category.

Some early twentieth century Stanhope novelties were designed as an unkind practical joke, and were advertised in various American trick and joke catalogues. In "Heaney's Professional Catalog of Wonders No. 25", published in 1924 by the Heaney Magic Company of Berlin, Wisconsin, trick No.243 is the "Surprise Moving Picture Machine". It is described as "a great novelty, consisting of a small nickled metal tube, 3 inches long, with a lens eyeview which shows a pretty ballet girl or any other scene. Hand it to a friend, who will be delighted with the first picture. Tell him to turn the screw on the side of the instrument to change the picture, when a fine stream of water squirts in his face, much to his surprise. The instrument can be refilled with water in an instant, and this will last for four or five victims." The price in 1924 was 45c each.

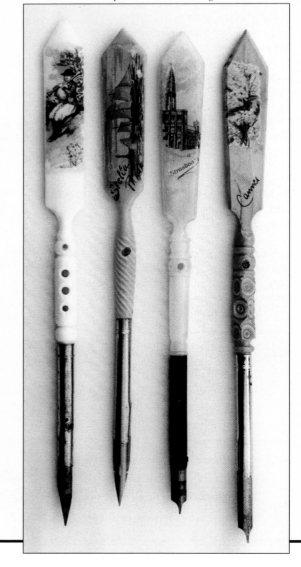

215. Twentieth-century penholder and letter opener combinations in plastic and wood. Length: 21-22cms

214. A French monocular marketed in the U.S.A., c.1924. Actual size.

Johnson Smith and Company of Racine, Wisconsin, included the same article in their catalogues of "Surprising Novelties, Puzzles, Tricks, Joke Goods and Useful Articles". The lens was set in a metal mount across the top of the tube, and the water squirted out from a tiny pinhole just below the viewing lens. The tube was filled with water by removing the top, and a waxed felt plug was inserted to prevent leakage. Another version of this humour-dampening device has the pinhole at the base of the tube, whereby the water dribbles down the sleeve of the innocent victim.

Although the Heaney Magic Company and Johnson Smith and Company were retailers of this trick, it is very unlikely that they were also the manufacturers. The fact that examples have been found with captions in the German language indicates a probable origin in Europe. One collector has discovered a far more dangerous variation. The tube is deceptively decorative in gold-stamped metal. The Stanhope is set into the end of the tube instead of across it, giving the appearance of a miniature telescope. The image is of a smiling buxom barmaid in a peasant blouse, and a pink filter set into the far end heightens her rosy glow. If the side knob is turned when the eye is looking through the viewer, the spring-loaded front of the tube moves backward to give the viewer a sharp poke in the eye. An even more evil version of this was featured in the film "Oklahoma!" The villain aimed to trick the hero into looking through the viewing lens, so that when he turned the knob a spike would be driven into his eye. Fortunately this was not allowed to happen, and the villain got his just deserts.

Inexpensive base metal rings and items of male jewellery with concealed Stanhopes found a ready market until the mid-twentieth century. Again, they were mainly advertised in American novelty catalogues. One advertisement described a "Novelty French Ring With View" as a "Very Great Curiosity". Priced at $1.00, it was made from "imitation platinum set with one of our genuine Alaska Diamonds", which explained its inclusion in a catalogue of jokes and tricks. It was available with "an assortment of pictures that should suit all tastes", including views of places of interest in France, the Panama Canal, the Lord's Prayer, etc., but the catalogue noted: "the kind that seemingly are in greatest demand" were of models or French actresses. Would-be purchasers were assured that "they are interesting without being objectionable".

"Lucky pig" charms with political Stanhopes had made their first appearance in America in the early 1880s, and they were still on sale in 1924, when the price was 25c. They were made of gilt base metal and were advertised as novelties "which always sold enormously, especially during campaign seasons". They could also be purchased "with girl views and actresses".

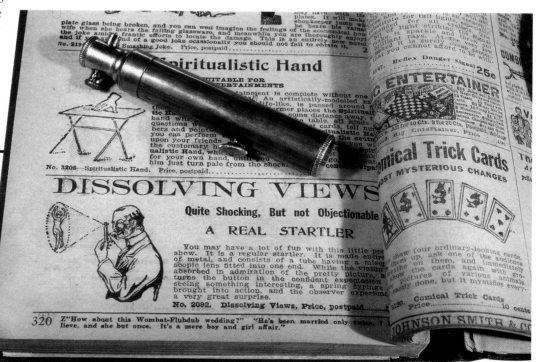

216. "Dissolving views" novelty. Actual length: 9cm. (Kessler Collection)

Twentieth Century Stanhopes

Les Stanhopes du 20ème siècle

Au vingtième siècle un choix plus restreint de créations Stanhope furent produites. Les jumelles miniatures et les porte-plume étaient encore fabriqués en grand nombre, et aux Etats-Unis les bagues bon marché en métal avec des microphotographies de nus furent populaires jusqu'en 1939.

Pendant les années 1950 l'usine de Stanhopes à Gex reçut des commandes importantes de fidèles clients qui fournissaient des fabricants de breloques. Des souvenirs furent produits pour des événements spéciaux, tels que l'Année Sainte (1950) et le couronnement de la Reine Elizabeth II (1953). A partir de la fin des années 60 les commandes diminuèrent progressivement jusqu'en 1972, date à laquelle la production de lentilles Stanhope cessa d'être rentable.

Après la Deuxième Guerre mondiale des ateliers en Extrême-Orient commencèrent à fabriquer des nouveautés avec microphotographies, utilisant une série d'images (souvent des nus) tournant devant une lentille en plastique. Les fabricants allemands et italiens montèrent des souvenirs avec des images transparentes colorées, et depuis, de nombreuses variétés ont vu le jour. Aucune de ces méthodes n'utilise de vraies lentilles Stanhope.

Stanhopes were also inserted in charms and religious jewellery of better quality and more tasteful design, with images to match. Charm bracelets became popular in Europe and America, and many slim wrists were encircled with a tinkling array of love tokens and sentimental commemorative charms.

The fact that Roger Reymond was producing Stanhope lenses in substantial quantities for various customers until 1972 is an indication that Stanhope souvenirs were still being manufactured in France and elsewhere until that date and for some time afterwards while stocks lasted. From the mid-twentieth century onwards, probably the most prolific market continued to be metal charms. The year 1950 had been designated a "Holy Year" by Pope Pius XII, and one enterprising souvenir manufacturer who was a customer of Roger Reymond decided to produce key-shaped charms with religious microphotographs. The key has always been a significant Christian religious image, symbolising St. Peter and the Keys of Rome, and this souvenir became very popular. The Gex factory received several large orders for Stanhope lenses to cope with worldwide demand. Three years later, the coronation of Elizabeth II in Britain provided another opportunity for specially designed microphotographic souvenirs: crown-shaped silver charms containing images of the radiant young Queen.

Stanhope images also began to be influenced by the world of advertising. During the l950s, cheap or give-away items included a range of mechanical or "propelling" pencils produced in the U.S.A. to advertise companies such as the Underwood Coal Co. of Underwood, North Dakota, and Gulf Oil. A single nude image was the preferred secret view in these items. A British company produced an elegant gilt metal mechanical pencil with a Stanhope at the end. The image advertised "Hadfield's Steel Foundry Co. Ltd." of Sheffield, which produced "Good, Sound and Durable Steel Castings".

217. Cheap base metal rings with Stanhopes, c.1920-1940. (Kessler Collection)

In the 1950's cheap sparkling jewellery set with rhinestones and other fake gems became fashionable and enjoyed widespread popularity. The mounts were made of gilt base metal, and many of the items were pendants hanging from neck chains. Crucifixes or crosses within hearts were the most popular motifs, with Stanhope lenses as focal points. Generally the images had a religious theme, usually the text of The Lord's Prayer. Similar versions of this design continued to be produced throughout the remaining decades of the twentieth century: in 1993 a British national newspaper advertised a mail order crucifix with "four diamantés" on a "gold tone chain". Would-be purchasers were urged to "carry the comfort of the Lord's Prayer with you always for only £9.95, plus postage and packing". The words could be viewed through "a magnifying crystal". The same design continues in the twenty-first century, as large numbers of Stanhope crucifixes studded with "real" rhinestones flood Internet auctions. Marienbad and Karlsbad, in what is now the Czech Republic, have a history of manufacturing glassware and cut crystals. They also produce imitation stones to be set in jewellery, similar to the well-known "Austrian crystals". Some rhinestone crucifixes are described by their sellers as "Czech crystals", indicating the probable source of supply. However, a few isolated Stanhope images bear the captions "Made in Czechoslovakia". Given the history of glass cutting and polishing in that region, it is possible that the processes involved in manufacturing Stanhope lenses may have been reproduced there, although no specific manufacturers have yet been identified.

In the latter part of the twentieth century gold and silver charms were manufactured in more delicate designs, usually to supply the fashion for charm bracelets. They were often purchased for a specific occasion, such as a wedding, christening or confirmation. Those with Stanhope images usually revealed a piece of text in memory of the event: the Marriage Lines, the Lord's Prayer or "Bless This House". Many such charms could be opened on a tiny hinge to reveal a miniscule view of the interior of a church or a chalet. A great variety of charms were distributed by Aetna Enterprises (also Aetna Creations Inc.), which ceased trading in the early 1980's. Their stock consisted of mainly sterling silver charms, often with moveable parts and microphotographic views. The charms

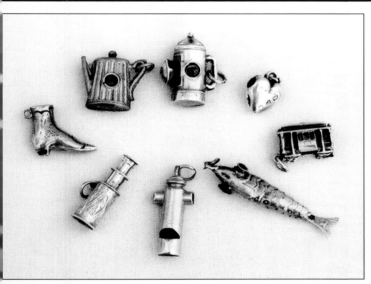

218. Early twentieth-century charms with Stanhopes. Actual size.

220. An advertising image from a metal mechanical pencil, c.1950.

219. Image from a plastic penholder commemorating "Holy Year", 1950.

221. Late twentieth century Stanhope charms. Actual size.

were manufactured by a variety of different small companies, such as the Wells Charm Co., Top Hat Charm Co., J.M. Fisher Charm Co., Beau Charm Co. and the Griffith Charm Co. The majority of these charms were produced within a relatively short period from 1957-1964, but are still available from retailers who bought up the remaining stock. Roger Reymond's main clients added microphotographic views to the large numbers of Stanhope lenses they had ordered from him, and then exported most of the completed units to their own customers abroad. It is probable that manufacturers of charms and other items of jewellery were supplied with the completed Stanhope lenses from the French distributors. Most of these had originated from the little workshop in Gex.

In the latter part of the twentieth century, M. Pérot's interest in the Stanhope industry led him to set up a small souvenir business himself, in the footsteps of René Dagron and his competitors. From dealers in Paris, M. Pérot had managed to find a number of Stanhope lenses complete with microphotographical images. These dated from the late nineteenth century and were mainly topographical views from many resorts and major cities in France. A further supply came from a retailer who still made small tourist souvenirs, such as models of the Eiffel Tower. M. Pérot hoped to make use of this collection of pre-war Stanhopes in a series of souvenirs of traditional design.

M. Pérot located a bone-turner from the Méru area, whose skills enabled him to recreate the original designs of penholders and paperknives. Holes were included to enable M. Pérot to insert his Stanhope lenses. Similar penholders can be purchased at the *Musée de la Nacre et de la Tabletterie* at Méru, and the whiteness of the newly turned bone examples demonstrates how attractive this material can be before it is affected by the dirt and discoloration of the passing years. Unfortunately, the cost of materials and production proved too high for the limited market for this type of handmade souvenir.

Among items in M. Pérot's collection of historical Stanhope artefacts was an original mould for the plastic penholders, together with a large number of pre-war transfer labels in various designs for the letter opener handles. He decided to use the original mould to reproduce a standard penholder/letter opener, using cream-coloured ivorine plastic. Coloured transfers were applied to the handles and matching topographical views were inserted, recreating the plastic Stanhope souvenirs of the early twentieth century. Finally, following the tradition of René Dagron's Stanhope novelties and *"tabletterie"*, M. Pérot created a very small number of unusual and attractive souvenirs. The skills of a *dominotier* produced several complete sets of dominoes, made of cream plastic and ebony wood fastened together with tiny brass rivets. Each of the twenty-eight pieces contained an original early twentieth century Stanhope lens with a topographical image.

Meanwhile novelties with hidden views but alternative and cheaper magnifying methods had already been introduced in different parts of the world, and most of these had very little in common with Dagron's Stanhope process. Unfortunately many such items have been included with sales of antique Stanhope articles, and have often achieved high prices when buyers have been confused as to their origin. In order not to mislead prospective purchasers, their correct classification can only be "twentieth century magnifying novelties". Nevertheless, some of these items are more than fifty years old, and can form a colourful and inexpensive category for many collectors. "Peep views" were well known in most countries, and were often associated with suggestive pictures and secretive viewing. Early post-war "peep" items were cheap, colourful and tawdry, and the majority contained black and white photographs of nudes.

A black and cream plastic toy camera, "Made in Hong Kong", still exists in its original cardboard box, which is decorated innocuously enough with a picture of a little girl with Shirley Temple golden ringlets taking a photograph. However, the images in the viewing lens of the camera were aimed at the adult market. It contains a series of ten circular photographs of bathing beauties and starlets. A small lever at the side of the toy camera can be depressed to change the image, while the internal mechanism to turn the inner cardboard disc is a simpler version of the "Photoscope" with plastic parts.

An adult toy cigarette lighter of the same period was

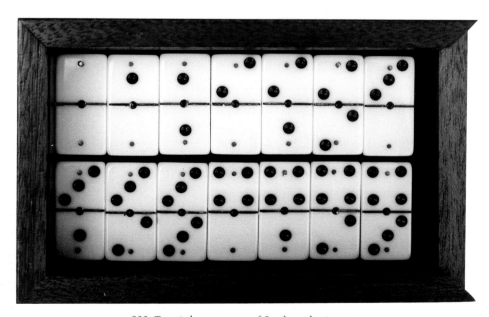

222. Twentieth century sets of Stanhope dominoes.

probably manufactured in Hong Kong, as it is marked "Empire Made". This time the knob on top is pressed to reveal twelve images of young ladies, and although only upper views are shown, the pictures are quite explicit. A British viewer of the same period took the form of an early movie camera, and was made in virulent pink plastic by "Selcol". It contains eight images of full frontal nudes, and when the large knob on the camera is turned in either direction, the images are screened from side to side, instead of in a circular direction. The movement is continuous, as a loop of miniature film moves around small rollers to provide the parade of unclothed lovelies. This item is definitely an adult toy.

A strange and ugly magnifying novelty appeared in Britain for a short period in the mid-twentieth century. A popular pastime of the early 1950's was making decorative models by setting plaster-of-Paris in rubber moulds, and then painting and varnishing the results. A number of plaster shoe-shaped souvenirs have been found, all for the right foot and usually with the name of some British West Country holiday resort inscribed inside. They are painted in the same colour scheme in a fairly amateur fashion. Each has a lens inserted through the centre of the bow, with quite a large magnifying lens and a fairly crude coloured transparency image. An even less attractive version is the bust of a pirate, complete with tricorn hat, patch over his eye and a barrel of smuggled brandy over his shoulder. The lens is found in the centre of the barrel, but is only half the length of the available hole. All these features point to the product of a small cottage industry,

223. Plastic novelty magnifying viewers from Hong Kong and the Far East, c. 1950

224. Ugly plaster novelties with magnifying viewers. British, c.1950. Height of pirate: 8.5cm; length of shoe: 10.0cm.

225. German novelty "transparency" viewers, c.1960-1970.

Twentieth Century Stanhopes

with a number of plaster models produced cheaply and quickly. The link between this type of souvenir and the Stanhope novelties of earlier times is tenuous, but the intention of a secret magnified image is the same.

The 1960's and 1970's saw the popularity of cheap package holidays and the advent of colour television, in Europe. The two were combined in a series of plastic souvenirs available at most European tourist resorts, in the form of miniature television sets with magnified topographical views. Most of them were "Made in Western Germany", often of the "Plastiskop" brand. The images are in colour, and collectors refer to them as "transparencies", their only connection with Stanhope novelties being the magnification of a small photograph. Other "transparencies" include the popular Swiss chalets, which were "Made in Western Germany" in the 1970's. In most examples the chimney is pressed downwards to move the views in a circular direction, and there are usually no more than eight views of resorts in Switzerland or Germany.

"C.V.M." was an Italian company that specialised in elaborate cream-coloured plastic souvenirs in the 1970's, mostly including coloured transparency topographical views. An enormous tasselled key is another example of this important symbol in Italy, although the images are not always of religious significance; topographical views from many Italian regions can be found in this type of souvenir. Would-be purchasers of similar items on Internet auctions should ensure that both sides of the object are pictured. From the front it can appear that this plastic novelty may incorporate a glass Stanhope lens. However, the presence of a small lever at the back to move the views shows that it is a "twentieth century magnifying novelty", and a later glance through the viewer will confirm that it is indeed a "transparency" souvenir.

Some "transparencies" still copy the novelties of long ago, and can be quite attractive. Dainty plastic binoculars hanging from a brooch have two different images of "St. Blasien im Schwarzwald", a German Black Forest resort. The transparencies are magnified by plastic lenses in the binoculars and do not move. They are probably the most closely related of modern souvenirs to René Dagron's conception of inexpensive novelties which enabled most tourists to return home with pictures from their travels.

With the arrival of the twenty-first century one would imagine that new versions of magnifying novelties would make little impact in a world of sophisticated and ever-changing technology. However, the famous Harry Potter's influence on the "muggle" world is far-reaching, and an antique toy has been updated as a source of wonderment for today's children. Made in China, the "Story Scope" is found in a series of clip-on "jewels" made of coloured but transparent geometric chunks of plastic. Purchasers are invited to "take a peek inside the Scope", and a small viewing window in the jewel reveals a circular transparency of a character from J. K. Rowling's popular books. Unlike past magnifying novelties, the complete "scope" unit is visible through the plastic jewel, ensuring that the modern child is quite aware of the process that reveals the picture. However, the power of Harry Potter's magic is strong enough to conceal the commercial irony: surely no worse than the gimmicks of two centuries ago!

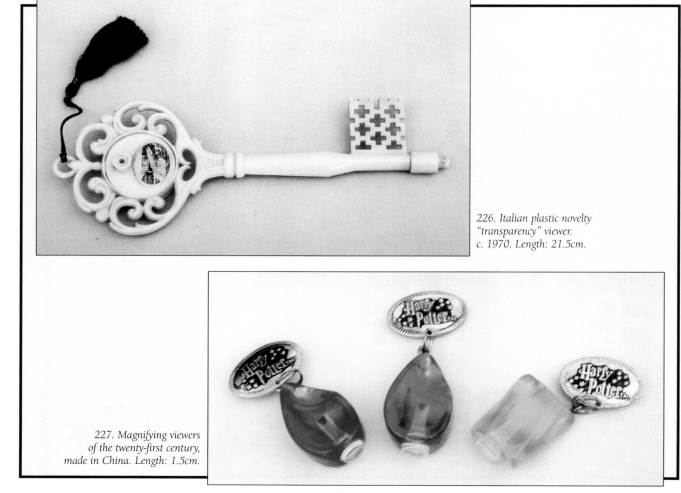

226. Italian plastic novelty "transparency" viewer. c. 1970. Length: 21.5cm.

227. Magnifying viewers of the twenty-first century, made in China. Length: 1.5cm.

18 The Stanhope Image

As with all enthusiasts, collectors of Stanhopes are influenced by personal preferences when deciding which piece to purchase. Some may be attracted by the sheer variety of microphotographic novelties, aiming to find all known examples, as well as the hitherto undiscovered treasure. Others may restrict themselves only to those items suitable for inclusion in a specialist collection of similar objects with identical functions. All purchasers of Stanhopes prefer that the lens is in place and the image, with a legible caption, can be identified. However, while some collectors consider that the novelty itself is of primary importance, a good proportion is primarily interested in the quality and subject matter of the microphotographic image. Many would be unconcerned if their collection included several examples of the same object, provided the images displayed different dated, commemorative or other specialist views.

The survival and remarkably good condition of many early microphotographic images is a tribute to the quality of J.B. Dancer's process and Dagron's adaptation. In fact, despite the inevitable deterioration around the edges of images caused by the intrusion of dirt, damp or the breakdown of the original Canada balsam adhesive, many of the earliest Stanhope views are clearer than some mid-twentieth century efforts. A few collectors are fortunate to own dated pieces made almost 140 years ago, yet these would have been considered cheap "toys" with a short lifetime even then. Most examples have suffered more than a century of careless handling or neglect, so it is amazing that any Stanhope image should survive to be studied in the twenty-first century. Fortunately, there are many superb examples in collections around the world, and many more awaiting recognition and discovery. They offer a wealth of useful and fascinating information about places, events and lifestyles of Victorian and Edwardian times, and careful research is rewarding and personally satisfying. Those who ignore such an opportunity overlook the main reason why a particular Stanhope novelty was produced in the first place.

Microphotographs exist in a variety of shapes and arrangements, from one picture to adventurous composite groups. Maximum impact is gained from a single image, and this style was used for commemorative portraits of royalty, national heroes and personalities of the day. Several man-made constructions of impressive proportions were also depicted within a single frame, often including considerable amounts of explanatory text and precise dimensions. The Statue of Liberty predates the Eiffel Tower on a Stanhope microphotograph. The French government planned to present Frédéric-Auguste Bartholdi's immense memorial representing liberty and freedom to the American people in 1876, the centennial year of American Independence. Unfortunately, funds and the construction were not sufficiently advanced to meet this deadline, although the

228. Image from a bone monocular, c.1886. (Dagron Family Archives).

L'image Stanhope

Il y a une grande variété de taille, de forme et de nombre d'images microphotographiques. Des portraits des membres des familles royales et impériales, des personnalités importantes, des grands monuments et des femmes nues, ont été reproduits en images simples mais frappantes.

Les images multiples démontrent la qualité de la microphotographie du dix-neuvième siècle. Quelques images topographiques contiennent jusqu'à seize vues différentes du même endroit. Des portraits des dix-huit premiers présidents des Etats-Unis ont été également trouvés sur une seule microphotographie Stanhope. Le plus grand nombre connu jusqu'à nos jours, présente vingt-huit portraits de dirigeants indiens (c.1890) avec leur nom et devient ainsi la plus grande série historique trouvée sur une lentille Stanhope.

Il existe même des images sur fond colorié où le verre supportant l'image a été teinté en rose, mais elles demeurent assez rares.

upraised arm bearing the torch was completed in time to be displayed at the 1876 Centennial Exhibition in Philadelphia. The components of the entire monument were finally transported across the Atlantic, and on 28th October 1886 the Statue of Liberty on her vast pedestal was dedicated by President Grover Cleveland. At that time it was the tallest construction in New York, at a height of 305 feet.

Nude and erotic images are another specialist category in which the picture is viewed to the best advantage in a single frame. Attractive examples are much sought-after, and can be found in unobtrusive but essential accessories of a Victorian or Edwardian gentleman's attire, such as watch keys and fobs, tie pins, small mechanical pencils or smoking requisites. These Stanhope images would only be displayed at the owner's choice of time and companion. Nubile young ladies in a variety of provocative poses displayed their charms to a selective audience, and occasionally two women posed together, or made a very rare threesome. Erotic microphotography was one of the longer-lasting aspects of the novelty trade, and much can be learned from a selective study of this category.

Nineteenth century painters and sculptors frequently portrayed nudity in their work, and early photographers followed their artistic style. Nevertheless, all were guided by certain unwritten rules that ensured the results were regarded as tastefully classical rather than obviously indecent. Subjects were mainly drawn from Biblical dramas or the legends of Ancient Greece. Statuesque models veiled in clinging draperies left little to the imagination, but provided the pose and accessories suggested a recognisable classical reference, the photograph was seen to portray purity rather than pornography. The model held an indirect or lowered gaze, so that neither she nor the observer was considered compromised by any hint of a relationship.

"Le Grenier" was one of the earliest erotic images produced by *Dagron & Cie*, dating from about 1860. The name means "an attic" or "garret" and the image depicts a young servant girl being seduced in her attic room. Although French attitudes were more permissive than those in Victorian England at that time, this image would have been considered fairly scandalous.

Given Dagron's commercial expertise, it is probable that this lucrative sector of the market formed a significant part of his business. There are several signed examples of nude studies in the coloured glass "jewels" preserved in the Dagron Family Archives. The compositions of lightly draped groups of nudes are elegant and delicate, depicting famous classical statues and paintings. They are no more scandalous than the works of art on display in the Louvre a few streets from the Dagron workshops, from where the photographer probably gained his inspiration. One example is entitled *"Andromède"* and is an interpretation of "Chained Andromeda", a work of art which had caused a great furore at the 1851 Great Exhibition in London when it was first displayed. Others are arrangements of up to five nude figures, which would have been regarded in Victorian Britain as orgiastic rather than purely classical!

In the late nineteenth century any suggestion of movement in the pose of the model was considered indecent. "Persistence of vision" novelties, such as the Cinématographe and the Kinéscope, produced a flicker of movement in the image from dual Stanhope lenses. If a nude picture appeared to move, the subject became pornographic rather than attractively erotic. The young lady illustrated is an example of this attitude. The individual pictures show that she is putting on her stocking, but by introducing movement, the changing images also illustrate the more shocking suggestion that she is removing the last item of her clothing.

Towards the end of the nineteenth century photographers abandoned elaborately staged classical themes and began to use fewer accessories. Photographers posed their

229. "Le Grenier": erotic image produced by Dagron & Cie in a gold watch charm, c. 1861. (Jull Collection.)

230. "Le Lever": Dagron nude study from a green glass "jewel", c. 1861. (Dagron Family Archives)

respectable and fully clothed clients against the artistic folds of a draped curtain, a curved chaise longue or a leafy palm, creating an illusion of careless wealth and opulence. A similar style was used in nude studies, but now the body of the model was clearly revealed. Nude photographs no longer masqueraded as "classical art", but were produced specifically for titillation. At a time when elegant hats and carefully-styled hair completed the costume of all well-dressed women in Europe and America, a fall of casual curls resting on a bare shoulder was a more shocking indication of the model's abandoned behaviour than the ample proportions so freely on display. From the early twentieth century onwards, photographers realised that the background arrangement mattered less to the observer than the visible charms of the nude model, and she looked boldly into the camera lens with the seductive smile of a temptress.

Apart from the model herself, there are few other clues available to date the image. Changes in dress and hairstyle give some indication of the body shape fashionable during a particular era, and nudes of the 1920's are recognised by short sculptured hair, large shadowed eyes and flatter chests, occasionally draped with a feather boa. Fun props,

such as a large crescent moon, copied the scenery ideas from the dance troupes shown in many films from the following decade.

Nude models were often referred to as "actresses". As the majority of microphotographic images were captioned "Made in France", it is probable that many of the nude models and their photographers were French also, doing much to enhance the racy reputation of Paris. Cheap base metal rings usually conceal the image of an attractive but scantily clad "actress", and date from the early twentieth century. The large size of most metal rings with Stanhope nudes would seem to limit them to male wearers, while their general lack of refinement in style and stone would not have enhanced the delicacy of feminine fingers. In fact, nude images are very rarely seen in items used by women, and purchasers should view with extreme caution items such as a "needle case with a naughty nude". Given the climate of prudery disguised as respectability prevalent in both Europe and the U.S.A. for many decades from the mid-nineteenth century onwards, it is unlikely that any woman would wish to appear "fast" by keeping in her workbox a sewing tool with such a risqué image. She would certainly never accept such an item from a member of the opposite sex, for fear of compromising her reputation.

These single Stanhope images of models in erotic and exotic poses form a specialist collectors' category that is gaining in popularity. Whatever the subject, all single Stanhope images are prized by collectors for their clarity, interesting topics and informative captions. Multiple images also suggest many opportunities for research, and exist in several combinations. Independent surveys by two different collectors, produced almost identical results when tabulating varying numbers of views in Stanhope images. Groups of six views were found to be most prolific, due to

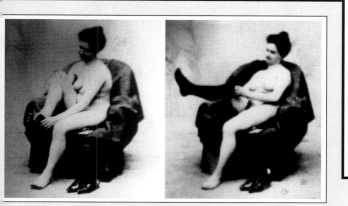

231. Dual nude images for a "persistence of vision" mechanism in a walking stick, c. 1880. (Milan Zahorcak: Kessler Collection)

Salon des Beaux-Arts

BOULARD

La Femme au Bilboquet. par A. Chantron

232. Early twentieth century nude images from (left) a metal ring, c. 1900 and (right) a vesta case, c.1920. (Milan Zahorcak, Kessler Collection).

233. Nude image from an ivory manicure set, c. 1930. (Milan Zahorcak: London Collection)

the abundance of six-view topographical Stanhopes. *Cartes de visite* showing different views of important cities were forerunners of the picture postcard, and their size made them ideal for reproduction by Dagron's microphotographic camera. This became a favoured arrangement with many distributors. A rectangular glass plate was made up of six individual aspects of a resort, which was then reduced to microphotographic size by the usual method. McKee of Dublin usually grouped six views around a central title, and other photographers preferred a rectangular block of pictures with a caption above or below the frame. Several different arrangements exist of the same six views of Niagara Falls.

Four views on one image are also common, with the pictures grouped in a regular rectangular frame. Many early twentieth-century Stanhopes were arranged in this style, particularly views of French resorts. There are also many examples within four separate oval frames, which produces a very attractive image. A considerable number of these are of Scottish places, and they date from the late Victorian era.

Multiple images in other number combinations are rarer, and a 1993 survey recorded no examples of microphotographs with 3, 8, 9, 10, 11, 12 or 15 views. Since then additional groupings have been recorded, and now every variation from a single image to eighteen views has been claimed in various collections. Bournemouth in Dorset is unique in that examples have been found with images of twelve, thirteen, fourteen and even sixteen topographical views. Baedeker pronounced it "a fashionable watering-place and winter resort" which owed "much of its salubrity to the luxurious pinewoods in which it is embosomed". Multiple views of Bournemouth always include "The Invalids' Walk", a path through the pinewoods close to the sea, where convalescents were given a daily outing in a wheeled basket chair. The smell of pines and the ozone were purported to have health-giving properties. The remarkable microphotographic image with sixteen views is captioned "Made in France", but surprisingly the names of the retailer J.E.Beale and "The Fancy Fair" are missing from this souvenir.

Multiple portraits are particularly interesting, both in subject matter and arrangement. To be able to recognise personalities and distinguish names when the individual pictures are so small demonstrates the excellence of the nineteenth century microphotographers' skill. Two American group photographs, although undated, give clear clues as to when they were produced. Nine oval portraits of the "President and Cabinet" reveal the familiar features of President Abraham Lincoln, surrounded by eight leading members of the American government. The sixteenth president of the United States held office from 1861 to 1865, which was the year of his assassination; this microphotographic image can most likely be dated within that period of five years.

A collection of eighteen oval presidential portraits also provides an approximate date of between 1869 and 1877, being the term of office of the eighteenth president commemorated in this microphotograph.

235. Nine portraits in one image from a ball-shaped novelty, c. 1861-1865. (Milan Zahorcak: Kessler Collection)

234. Sixteen topographical views in one image, from a bone and vegetable ivory needlecase and measure combination, c. 1920. (Private collection.)

236. Eigh... portraits... image, fro... fist-shape... cravat-pi... c. 1869-1... (Jull Colle...

A monocular from the Dagron Family Archives shows the portraits of no less than twenty-eight "National Leaders" of India, each clearly numbered and with their names listed beneath. This remarkable image not only qualifies as the largest existing arrangement of individual portraits, but also as the microphotograph with the longest caption.

In the late nineteenth century India was still part of the British Empire, but in 1885 the Indian National Congress was founded by prominent Indians who hoped to achieve a larger role in the making of British policy in India. However, the inclusion of certain names indicates a later period for this microphotograph. For example, Mahatma Gandhi would have been only sixteen years of age in 1885. He left India in 1888 to study law in England, but returned in 1891, so it is more likely that the image dates from the early 1890's. This rare multiple Stanhope image is a superb feat of nineteenth century microphotography. It may also have been one of the last microphotographs designed by René Dagron towards the end of his life.

Although the majority of microphotographic images are rectangular in shape, variations do occur, as oval and very occasionally circular frames can be found. A final note about Stanhope images concerns coloured versions. These do not resemble coloured photographs, but were produced by tinting the collodion film on the glass plate from which the tiny squares holding the images were cut. Examples of seaside resorts in pink, lilac or blue have been found, and also a number of somewhat garish and inappropriate pink images of the Church of the Holy Sepulchre in Jerusalem. These coloured images are probably late nineteenth century attempts to enliven Stanhope souvenirs when the initial wonder of microphotography had diminished.

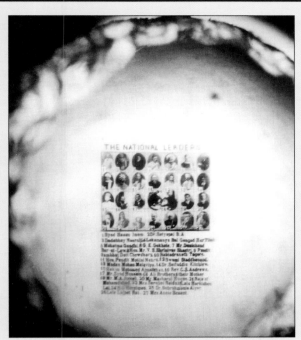

237. A rare multiple image from a bone monocular, c. 1890. This view shows the entire microphotograph on the Stanhope lens. (Dagron Family Archives).

239. An attractive image from a bone letter opener, c.1890.

238. Enlarged image of the same microphotograph, showing all twenty-eight portraits and a full list of names on the caption. (Dagron Family Archives)

240. A pink-tinted microphotograph from a vegetable ivory tape measure, c. 1900.

⟨19⟩ Collectors' Categories

Although there is a growing number of specialist collectors of Stanhope novelties, representative groups of Stanhopes are often included in other categories of collectables, such as sewing accessories, smokers' requisites, reading and writing equipment, religious artefacts, jewellery and World Fair souvenirs. As a result of such "cross-over" interest, Stanhope novelties are becoming well known among most collectors of small antiques, and this popularity is reflected in their rising prices.

It has been estimated that at least 25% of Stanhope items in collections today are needlework accessories. Common examples have been featured in other sections of this book, but many more unusual items also found a home in the Victorian workbox. It would be possible to furnish an entire workbox with sewing tools containing Stanhopes, as examples exist among needle cases, tape measures, thimbles and thimble cases, pin cushions, scissors, thread barrels, knitting needle guards, stilettos and crochet hooks.

Stanhope containers of sewing equipment were the most practical, but those items that were actually used for a needlework activity often suffered a dislodged lens. Crochet hooks and stilettos are both tools in which a firm grip and frequent hand movements are involved, so that those with Stanhopes still in place in the handle are rarely found.

Unusual pairs of scissors featuring many other functions apart from their use in needlework may be found to contain a Stanhope. The "Universal" scissors were of German design and manufacture, and the earliest known pair has a dated Stanhope from the *1889 Paris Exposition Universelle*. If the scissors were first introduced at this event, this may account for the choice "Universal" as the trade name. American versions are usually inscribed "Patent Feb.12 1901". The specification information revealed that

242. "Universal" multi-function scissors with an appropriate advertisement, 1890-1930. Actual length: 11.6cm. (Kessler Collection)

241. An instruction sheet included with "Universal" scissors. (Taylor Collection)

Friedrich Wilhelm Klever Jr. filed his U.S. patent application on 14th September 1899 (No. 667,914) in New York, and it was granted on February 12th 1901. It stated that he was "a subject of the Emperor of Germany, and a resident of Solingen", which is a town as famous for the manufacture of scissors in Germany as Sheffield is in England. Klever had invented "certain new and useful improvements" to his "Tool-Scissors": a wrench, buttonhole cutter, cigar-cutter and wire-cutter. This implies that an earlier version of these scissors existed with fewer functions, but the final number was eighteen. Scissors of this kind can be found complete with a protective leather sheath and a page of instructions, sometimes in four languages: German, French, English and Spanish. The Stanhope was included in the list of functions, entitled "Stereoscope".

Klever's scissors were obviously invaluable for cutting,

pattern-marking, filing the nails, hammering and even breaking glass, but the functions of cutting gas pipes and extracting cartridges may have a limited use in today's society. One blade was marked as a measure, and versions exist in either centimetres or inches. Some Stanhopes have been noted in "Universal" scissors with German views, and others show London, Paris and Washington. A similar pair of multi-function scissors was patented as "Multiplex", and these have been found with Belgian views. Although most views are topographical, occasionally a nude microphotograph is found.

It is surprising that so many Stanhope scissors still retain the lens, given the robust nature of their usage. In the 1920's, Johnson Smith & Co. catalogues of novelties advertised these multi-function scissors at a price of $1.50, and the Stanhope lens was correctly entitled "microscopic view".

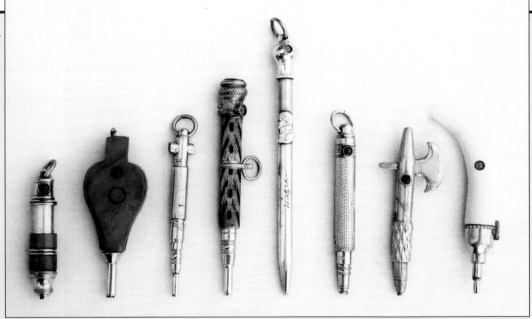

243. A selection of mechanical pencils: 1880-1920. Actual size.

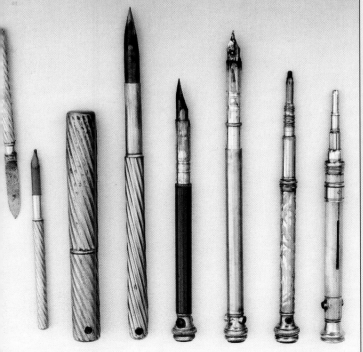

244. A selection of metal writing accessories (left to right): container with matching pencil and pencil sharpening knife, three reversible penholders, a reversible pencil and a sliding mechanical pencil. c. 1890-1930. Actual lengths: 8-16 cms.

Les collections Stanhope

On peut trouver des Stanhopes dans toutes sortes de petits objets de collection, tels que les accessoires de couture, le matériel d'écriture, les articles de fumeurs, les bijoux, les objets religieux, etc. Des genres moins fréquents tels que des cannes, des chopes de bière et des cartes postales ont été également réalisées. Parmi les plus rares, on trouve les poupées Stanhope de Rochard. Elles furent fabriquées juste avant le siège de Paris et quelques-unes seulement ont survécu dans les musées et les collections privées. Les lentilles étaient encastrées dans la porcelaine du décolleté, pour simuler un collier merveilleux d'images cachées.

Collectors' Categories

Stanhope articles feature prominently in collections of reading and writing equipment. Penholders, letter openers and combinations of both have been illustrated already, but many other useful "articles de bureau" were available at a time when some handwriting chore was a necessary part of most people's daily routine. Small size and gadgetry made writing equipment more appealing. Metal mechanical pencils were produced in many designs, and versions with loops to suspend them from watch chains were made in very small sizes. The section holding the lead was usually retractable, and the Stanhope lens was incorporated in a metal tube across the end of the pencil. Reversible penholders were also popular, but were larger in size and kept in the pocket.

Letter openers became shorter and more decorative, and examples made in pearlised plastic and gilt metal were particularly attractive. They were manufactured in France, and the Stanhopes are well hidden in the design. Plastic letter openers became cheap and colourful souvenirs throughout most of the twentieth century.

Writing equipment from a bygone age included a range of seal ciphers. They were used to imprint a design on melted wax securing folded documents. If the wax seal was cracked, the recipient knew the document had been tampered with. Rudimentary seals can be found on the ends of early bone penholders, but others were specifically designed with initials or crests. They were still sold as novelty souvenirs at the beginning of the twentieth century, long after the introduction of envelopes had made the use of seals obsolete.

Bookmarks with Stanhope views are delightful small collectables. They can be found in a range of styles and

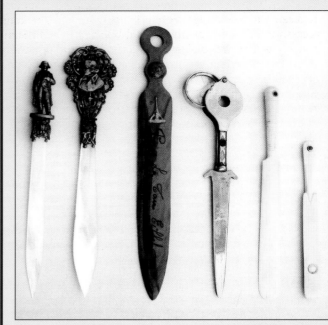

245. A selection of letter openers in (left to right): mother-of-pearl with gilt metal, bakelite, metal, combined with a magnifying glass and bone. 1900-1930. Length: 10.2cm – 17.5cm.

246. A selection of seals: 1870-1920. Length: 4.0cm – 7.5cm.

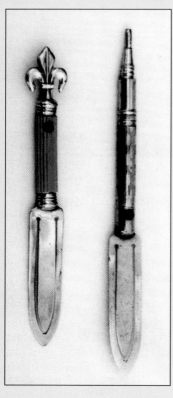

247. Metal bookmarks with Stanhopes, one of which is extended for use as a mechanical pencil. 1900-1930. Length: 11.3cm.

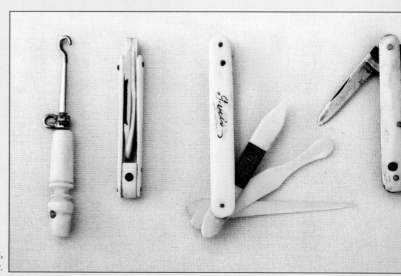

248. Late nineteenth century grooming aids, 1870-1910. Actual size.

materials, and are easily framed and displayed. Wooden Tyrolean ware examples are particularly attractive reading accessories. A series of small metal bookmarks with Stanhopes was made in England, and dates from the beginning of the twentieth century.

Small personal grooming sets had been made in the bone-carving Méru area of France some time before the introduction of Stanhopes. They invariably consisted of three bone items: *"cure-dents"*, *"cure-oreilles"* and *"cure-ongles"* (toothpicks, ear-spoons and nail cleaners with a file). The tools were held within a protective holder in a similar way to multi-tool penknives, and could be pushed out or retracted as needed. Together with bone combs from the same region, these little sets were essential aids to

grooming for both sexes throughout the nineteenth and early twentieth centuries. To accommodate the addition of a Stanhope lens, a small block of bone was added at one end, pivoting on a metal rivet. The design was also reproduced in plastic until the mid-twentieth century, often with an applied souvenir motif. Similar accessories included buttonhooks to facilitate the fastening of glove, boot and shoe buttons, and miniature penknives.

Smokers' requisites from the past are surprisingly popular collectables. Those with Stanhopes are keenly sought after, due to the fact that the microphotographic subject is often a nude! Stanhopes were inserted into tobacco pipes soon after their introduction. An extremely decorative meerschaum and bone pipe with a carved stag on the bowl has the additional highly prized caption: *"Rep. Dagron & Cie Btés Paris."* This indicates a probable date before 1862, the year when René Dagron lost his patent rights. The image is of an elegant bearded gentleman seated in formal pose, with the annotation "Rieger". Despite considerable research by a noted collector of tobacco pipes, no link has yet been found with a pipe manufacturer of this name. It is possible that this Stanhope image was privately commissioned by a pipe-smoking customer of René Dagron in the early years.

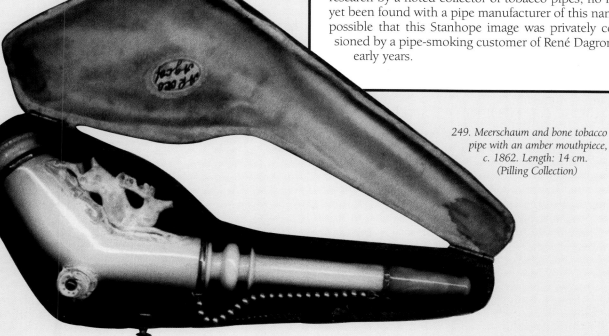

249. Meerschaum and bone tobacco pipe with an amber mouthpiece, c. 1862. Length: 14 cm. (Pilling Collection)

250. Clay and wooden tobacco pipes of British manufacture, 1900-1920. Length: 12.5cm.

251. The container of these combined cigarette and cigar holders has two Stanhope lenses. c. 1910. Length of container: 11.7cm.

Collectors' Categories

The tobacco pipe industry of St. Claude in the Jura Mountains of France was well established by the time the Stanhope lens factory was set up in nearby Gex by René Dagron. Pipe manufacturers became aware of the commercial possibilities and a few decided to make adjustments to their designs to incorporate Stanhope lenses. Stanhopes have also been found in tobacco pipes of Native American workmanship and less decorative but more practical examples were of British manufacture. The lenses were usually inserted in small knobs situated below the bowl of the pipe.

In addition to the familiar bottle-shaped wooden pipe souvenirs from the early twentieth century, other interesting Stanhope novelties can be transformed into smoking accessories by reassembling the different components. A mouthpiece can be joined to one or two tubes of different diameters to form a cigarette or cigar holder. The rolling-pin shaped container illustrated on P.117 has a Stanhope lens at both ends, but the subjects of the images are quite different: the Virgin Mary and a dancer.

Ladies' versions of this type of novelty were more elegant, and the dainty containers for telescopic cigarette holders took up little space in a handbag. The metal acorn-shaped novelty dates from the early twentieth century, and can be found in different designs. In some the Stanhope is inserted in the base, and in others it is situated through a knob attached to the lid.

"Vesta" cases, or match holders, are rare Stanhope novelties, and command high prices among specialist collectors in their own right. Smokers needed to carry a means of igniting the tobacco when outdoors. Matches were sold cheaply from the early nineteenth century but they were unreliable and dangerous. Decorative containers with hinged lids were introduced in Europe from the 1830s, to prevent accidental ignition of the matches in the pocket. These were known as "match safes", but are usually termed "vestas" by today's collectors. The designs were probably not adapted to incorporate Stanhopes until the 1880s.

In some collectors' categories a small number of items incorporating microphotographic lenses are known to exist, but further examples are extremely difficult to find. They include walking sticks, parasol handles, hatpins, beer steins, buttons and postcards. Unique novelties with Stanhopes may exist, but usually someone, somewhere, has managed to find another like it! By including a "miscellaneous" category, some item unrelated to any other Stanhope collecting groups may be termed "in a class of its own". Such an item is an adjustable brass "telescope", which is really a desk thermometer. The mercury tube is missing, but the temperature scale is inscribed in degrees Centigrade and Fahrenheit along the barrel of the telescope. The object is 15cm tall and conceals two Stanhope lenses. One is in the main part of the telescope, with a good image of the *"Hotel de Ville à Paris"*. The other is found in the telescope sight, and is a female nude in art deco style.

The most beautiful and unobtainable of all is the fabled Stanhope Doll, of which just a few surviving examples are to be found in museums and private doll collections scattered around the world. Stanhope collectors count themselves fortunate just to find themselves in the right place to be able to view one of these superb antique dolls. Their rarity is caused by the number of microphotographic lenses embedded in the bisque porcelain of the doll's

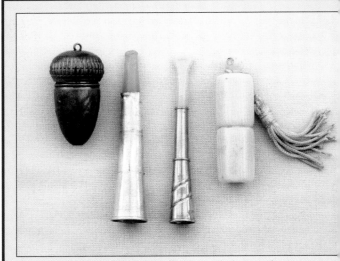

252. *Two telescopic cigarette holders with their novelty containers: 1910-1930. Actual size. ("Acorn" from the Jull Collection)*

253. *A selection of late nineteenth century vesta cases. Height: 4.4cm*

254. *A selection of walking sticks with Stanhopes. (Kessler Collect*

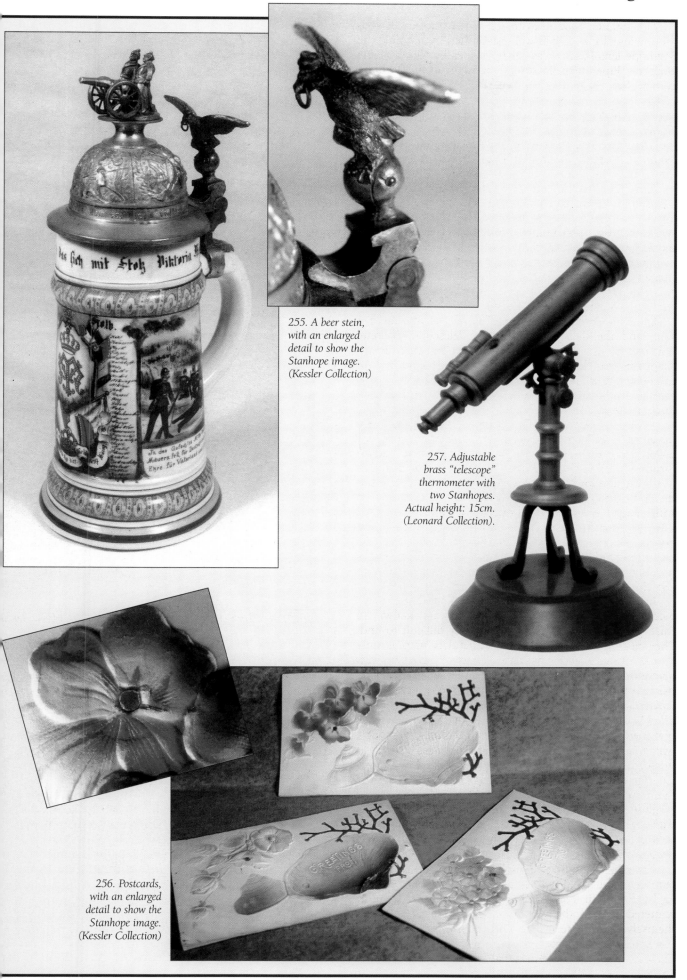

255. A beer stein, with an enlarged detail to show the Stanhope image. (Kessler Collection)

257. Adjustable brass "telescope" thermometer with two Stanhopes. Actual height: 15cm. (Leonard Collection).

256. Postcards, with an enlarged detail to show the Stanhope image. (Kessler Collection)

shoulder plate. They were arranged like the jewels of a festoon necklace, and completed the elegant ensemble of a French fashion doll, which could never have been a child's plaything.

The existence of seven Stanhope dolls is known to collectors, although it is probable that more are preserved in private collections. The name inscribed on the shoulder plates of these examples is "Ed. Rochard", but it has yet to be established that he was actually the doll maker. Antoine Edmond Rochard applied for a patent in France for dolls and other toys incorporating Stanhopes and kaleidoscopes (No. 75762, 27th March 1867). The patent drawing is headed *"Rochard Jouets"* ("Rochard Toys"), which indicates that he was either a toy retailer or possibly a toy manufacturer. Certainly each doll's unique design points to his personal involvement at each stage of the production.

All the dolls are dressed in adult gowns, with a deep décolletage to allow the necklace to be clearly displayed. This was a style favoured by the Empress Eugénie, who was still a fashion leader in France during this period just before the Franco-Prussian War. The necklace and earring combination was known as a *demi-parure*, and the series of delicate chains linked by large gems reflected a jewellery style of the same era. Often a prominent cross is added to the festoon necklace, which includes more Stanhope "jewels". On Rochard dolls the design of chains and jewel mounts was directly applied to the porcelain torso in gilt paint.

The lenses set into the bisque are usually larger than standard microphotographic lenses which measure only 2.6mm in diameter. On some Stanhope dolls the jewels measure 4mm, 5mm and even 7mm in diameter,

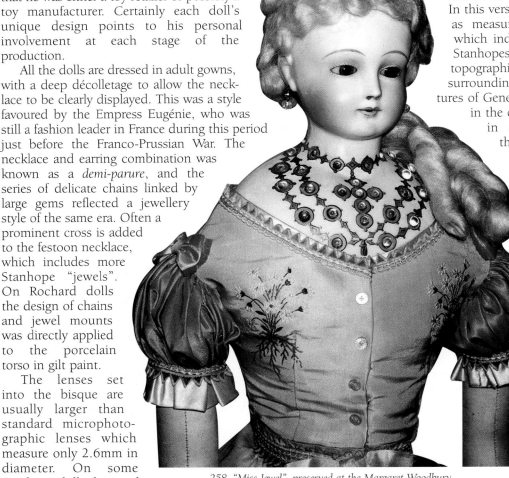

258. *"Miss Jewel", preserved at the Margaret Woodbury Strong Museum, Rochester, NY. (Ralph London)*

with a pronounced curvature on the lenses to compensate for the different focal lengths. (In the collection of Stanhope artefacts preserved at George Eastman House there are loose examples of these larger lenses, with a diameter of 5mm and a length of 10mm.) All Stanhopes need a light source opposite the viewing end, and an oval aperture was made in the bisque torso to provide the necessary illumination to perceive the images. The pictures were usually an unrelated compilation of topographical and religious images, with some portraits.

One fine example of a Stanhope doll is "Miss Jewel", on view at the Margaret Woodbury Strong Museum in Rochester, NY. She is 66cm high, and like other Rochard

dolls, consists of a bisque bust attached to a hand-sewn kid body. Her necklace is designed to incorporate thirty Stanhope lenses, many of them in the larger sizes. The other known dolls are all slightly different in height, facial features and the design of the jewellery. Rochard dolls usually have slightly parted lips, through which the kaleidoscope could be viewed. This was inserted through an opening in the bisque head, concealed by the wig.

Another well-known Rochard doll is exhibited at the National Museum of Monaco. She is dressed in a deep pink gown trimmed with antique lace, in the style of the Second Empire. Her necklace consists of two strands and a crucifix, and is formed of twenty-two linked medallions each encircling a Stanhope. In this version the lenses are recorded as measuring 2-3mm in diameter, which indicates the use of standard Stanhopes. The majority of images are topographical views of Paris and the surrounding area, but also include pictures of Geneva and Venice. The images in the crucifix are mainly religious in content. It used to be thought that the lenses were tinted pink, but it has been proved that the colour is a reflection of the rose-pink gown as it covers the opening in the shoulder plate. The Monaco Rochard doll is complete with a kaleidoscope inserted in the head.

The Rosalie Whyel Museum of Doll Art in Bellevue, Washington, possesses a Rochard doll with an amazing total of forty-four lenses embedded in the shoulder plate, but unfortunately none of them has an image intact. It is improbable that the lenses would have been originally inserted without microphotographs, for in the late nineteenth century unmounted but complete microphotographic lenses could be obtained easily and cheaply from several sources in Paris. Sadly, it is more likely that the images were obliterated during an unsuitable cleaning operation during some period of the doll's unknown history.

Each one of these dolls is a superb example of a Stanhope novelty, yet even in the nineteenth century the price of such a doll would have set it apart from other microphotographic "toys" and novelties. Today such a treasure is beyond the means of most Stanhope collectors, even if they were to discover a hitherto unrecorded example.

20 Reproductions – and Others!

When considering reproduction collectables, it should be remembered that copying has always been the sincerest form of flattery. The workmanship of others, whether in the past or present time, is often admired and reproduced, in an attempt to achieve the same degree of quality. Art, fashion, architecture and many other aspects of design are copied, adapted and sometimes improved. Those who make sincere reproductions of antique items are not afraid to display their names, or add dates and other codes to identify their work as a modern copy.

Among collectors of Stanhopes, souvenirs produced by Woodsetton Designworks are well known and appreciated as excellent reproductions of microphotographic novelties, and are becoming collectables in their own right. In 1983 this small British company was set up by David and Gillian Bates to produce their own versions of what they termed "Woodsetton Peep Curios" or "secret picture curios". Each item is individually boxed, and an accompanying leaflet states that the novelties are "based on the original 'Stanhope Peeper' made between 1860 and 1939. Woodsetton 'Peeps' feature an improved, patented lens which is much easier to look through. Each pin-head sized picture is individually cut out and mounted in its lens, which magnifies the image about 100 times. The 'Secret Pictures'

cover many subjects: tourist views, period fashion, historical and current events, advertising, commemorative, Royalty and special pictures commissioned by retail and business houses."

Woodsetton lenses are quite different from antique glass Stanhope lenses, being made of Perspex (acrylic) and much larger in size. They are 5.5mm in diameter and 10-11mm in length, compared with 2.6mm and 8mm of the standard Stanhope lens. The views are microphotographed on to transparent black and white film, and each individual image is cut out by hand. They are then placed at the hollow end of the acrylic cylinder, and held in place with a tiny plastic plug. This is intricate work, and is usually carried out by ladies with deft fingers. Certainly this part of the operation follows the tradition of the female workers employed in René Dagron's workshops to apply by hand the tiny glass squares holding a microphotograph to the end of Stanhope lenses. The magnifying lens is surrounded by a black disc for easy location. If the Woodsetton lens is mounted in a pewter item, it is possible to push it out from the soft metal for examination and comparison with a loose antique lens.

Over the years Woodsetton Peep Curios have included novelties such as letter openers, needlecases, lace bobbins, thimbles and ornamental spoons. Materials include wood,

259. A comparison of Woodsetton and antique Stanhope lenses: actual size, and greatly enlarged.

260. Woodsetton and antique brass thimbles: side view.

261. Woodsetton and antique brass thimbles: apex view.

Reproductions – and Others!

china, pewter and other metals. The most popular item has proved to be thimbles, which are now exported worldwide. The original thimbles were made of pewter, but brass, copper, enamelled and inscribed metal, china and even a few silver examples have been made since then. One series of thimbles was made of brass, and like the antique Pursall thimbles, were plain in design. Side by side they are similar in size, although the antique version has the indented surface of a proper working thimble. However, when viewed from above the difference is clearly visible, the black disc immediately identifying the modern reproduction.

Woodsetton Designworks have therefore made it easy for collectors to recognise their own "peep" souvenirs immediately, avoiding confusion and the much higher prices of antique examples. Also, the larger lens size makes it impossible to insert a Woodsetton lens in an antique novelty with a missing lens. Finally, unlike the brass antique thimbles with Stanhopes from the late nineteenth century, Woodsetton thimbles with 'peeps' also exist in several other materials.

Woodsetton Peep Curios are made in small exclusive batches and Limited Editions, and are fairly inexpensive to buy. Unfortunately, once sold they can become separated from their boxes, either accidentally or deliberately, and it is in the second-hand market when misrepresentations can and do occur. Nevertheless, the informed collector will know that the name "Woodsetton" is visible beside each of their images, establishing that they could not have been made before 1983. Every transparency is numbered, and often titled and dated.

Collectors themselves may reproduce another prized Stanhope novelty: the Rochard fashion doll! Seeley's, an American company specialising in moulds and patterns for makers of porcelain dolls, has made it possible to make the head and shoulders of such a doll in nineteenth century style. Artificial "gems" 10mm in diameter may be used to simulate the lenses forming the necklace. It is unlikely that

Les reproductions – et autres !

Le travail artistique a souvent été copié, dans le but de reproduire la même qualité. Depuis 1983 Woodsetton Designworks a produit une petite gamme de dés à coudre et autres articles contenant des images microphotographiques. Ils ne peuvent cependant pas être confondus avec les authentiques objets Stanhope, car ils sont numérotés et les lentilles sont plus grandes et faites de matière plastique.

Malheureusement le prix croissant des Stanhope anciens a encouragé la contrefaçon. Différentes méthodes ont été utilisées pour produire de faux articles Stanhope en forant des trous pour loger des lentilles dans des objets récents, ou en insérant des lentilles modernes dans des objets anciens. Quelques objets truqués de cette manière ont été vendus aux enchères sur Internet. La meilleure protection pour les collectionneurs d'aujourd'hui est la prudence. Autant que possible les collectionneurs doivent acheter seulement les articles qu'ils peuvent examiner personnellement, ou ceux qui proviennent de sources offrant des garanties sérieuses.

262. A selection of Woodsetton "peep" thimbles. Top row (left to right): silver, pewter, china, brass. Bottom row (left to right): enamel and inscribed metal.

122

a modern copy of a Rochard doll could be made with enough skill to fool antiques experts, although when prices of the genuine article are so high, there are always those who might be tempted. However, some personal satisfaction may be gained by a creative collector who otherwise has no hope of finding a real Rochard doll.

Stanhope MicroWorks is a recently established American manufacturer of "picture lenses" that offers to reproduce customers' own choice of image on 2mm and 3mm diameter lenses. These lenses were originally devised for insertion in modern interpretations of the nineteenth century violin bows made by J. P. Vuillaume. This Parisian craftsman supplied violin bows to some of the greatest violinists of the era. He arranged for Stanhope lenses to be made bearing his own portrait image, so that he could insert them as a pictorial signature into the frogs of the bows he had made. Vuillaume was said to have incorporated lenses with different portraits in other examples of his work, but few have survived. A. E. Prager, a twentieth century German bowmaker, revived the idea of "picture bows" with a self-portrait, and Stanhope MicroWorks continues the tradition in the twenty-first century. This company has developed further commercial applications of their products by suggesting their use in personalised private and corporate commissions. The lenses can also be supplied in metal tubes of different lengths, made of aluminium, copper, brass, sterling silver or even 18ct. gold. In addition, the Stanhope MicroWorks website offers antique American Civil war bullets incorporating their own modern lenses. Restoration of antique Stanhope collectables is undertaken, and an explanation of all work performed is provided.

M. Georges Pérot of France produced bone and plastic penholders and sets of dominoes in the late twentieth century, but it is difficult to decide whether or not to class them as reproductions. The Stanhopes themselves are genuine glass lenses with microphotographs dating from the beginning of the twentieth century and were produced by the traditional method. They have been "married" with novelties made in modern times, although using moulds and materials from an earlier era. Leaflets prepared by M. Pérot explained their origin, and described his efforts in reviving an industry that had all but disappeared in France.

All collectors of antique items, whatever the category, know that it is in their own interests to be aware of modern reproductions and to note the differences between them and similar antique versions. Unfortunately, Stanhope collectors are often assailed with doubts concerning the authenticity of a novelty, because of the very nature of the product. The original method of inserting a Stanhope lens in an item is the same today as it always was: a hole was made in the object of a suitable length and diameter, with adhesive to hold the lens in position. When the lens and the novelty become separated, certain moral dilemmas are presented, which must be considered by collectors individually and collectively.

It would be a rare collector who failed to use modern adhesive to replace a lens that had become dislodged from its long-time position in some novelty. Replacing a missing lens with a different lens is more debatable. Occasionally a few loose lenses can be discovered which may be kept for this purpose. Provided the microphotographic image is suited to the age and style of the item, there seems little point in failing to unite the two. However, rarer and therefore more expensive novelties with missing lenses can introduce a hint of temptation, particularly when no substitute loose lenses are available. Is a "transplant" an acceptable practice among the majority of collectors? If a lens with an unusual or spectacular image is found in a dirt-encrusted bone monocular, would it be more appreciated transplanted into a prized novelty? Some collectors would agree, provided the novelty stayed to enhance a collection. If, however, the refurbished item is destined for resale, the undoubtedly antique but alien lens will have substantially increased the value of the Stanhope novelty, and the seller will make a good profit. Can a true collector perform such an operation with a good conscience?

"Marriages" occur in most categories of collectables, but somewhere between these and fakes are the "metamorphic" items. These usually have missing components or have suffered some damage, but undergo amazing transformations to become completely different articles! Beware the pierced bone reversible penholders with missing nib sections which are reborn as "highly decorative needle cases". A little thought should remind the would-be purchaser that needles cannot fail to drop through the open gaps, and that the original bone carvers would never have offered such an impractical design to the needlewomen of Victorian times. I learned another painful lesson financially when I bought a beautiful mother-of-pearl and gilt filigree Stanhope paperknife, without considering why it was considerably shorter than normal. A more careful examination at home revealed that a previously broken blade had been carefully reshaped.

Outright forgery is regarded with universal abhorrence, but many Stanhope collectors have begun to notice or even experience certain malpractices. A loose lens with a good

263. Example of a Woodsetton image with
its identifying caption and issue number.

Reproductions – and Others!

image becomes available, either from a damaged piece or a very cheap item, but no special souvenir with an empty hole awaits a transplant. Collectors are then offered a "very rare" nineteenth or early twentieth century Stanhope collectable, which, of course, will be very costly. Such items are subsequently discovered to have been drilled with a hole to accommodate the antique lens. Unfortunately such forgeries can be difficult to prove, particularly as there are many examples of nineteenth century souvenirs which genuinely exist both with and without Stanhopes. e.g. Tyrolean thimble and needle cases.

Another type of forgery exists because it has been possible to reproduce microviewers of similar size to those of Dagron, using modern materials and film. When such lenses have been inserted into antique items to replace missing Stanhope lenses, it can be difficult to distinguish the fake from a genuine collectable. To achieve a similar degree of microphotographic expertise as that of René Dagron is indeed a great accomplishment, but to reproduce copies and pass them off as genuine antique articles for financial gain is to devalue his life's work. Fortunately for collectors, most reproduction microviews are very clear, with no sign of the deterioration usually seen on most genuine old microphotographs. Also, by using a hand viewer to observe the circumference of the plane surface of the Stanhope lens, one should be able to distinguish the roughly ground edges of the genuine image glass. A modern lens inserted in an old novelty is a fake, as is a hole deliberately drilled in an object to accommodate an old lens. Both are deliberate attempts to achieve a higher price among unwary collectors, and are practices denounced by Stanhope collectors as a group.

International auctions on the Internet have become very popular, and many collectors use them to purchase Stanhope items. Fake or forged Stanhope novelties have been included in sales of genuine articles, with misleading descriptions that imply age and rarity but never actually state antiquity. The temptation to sell a dubious item that cannot be handled or shown from every angle has overtaken many. Novice and even experienced collectors may be fooled into paying inflated prices for articles designed to deceive. The result is disillusionment for many, and a reluctance to purchase from this source. In the end, who has gained?

The collector may avoid becoming a victim of fraud in several ways. Protection comes from a thorough knowledge of the subject, gained from good research. Background reading and all available sources should be explored, including libraries, the Internet, patent enquiries, etc. Collectors' clubs and societies promote and share the latest information and discoveries, and answer queries in regular newsletters. Catalogue lists are prepared by pooling details among members and become useful reference sources. Articles in collectors' magazines often concern newly discovered items and requests for further help in identification. Subsequent information from collectors around the world can reassure the enquirer with details of similar examples, or issue warnings of possible "improvements". It is also wise to become familiar with as many Stanhope items as possible, by viewing and handling the collections of those who share your interest, and by being equally generous in offering the same facility. Fellow collectors can usually be trusted to handle the treasures of others with the same delicacy as they do with their own collections.

The best protection of all is caution. Whenever possible, purchase items in person from a dealer you know well. You will become a valued customer, and you may benefit from choice items retained specially for your eyes only. Having discovered a possible addition to your collection, examine it carefully from all angles, using a good magnifying lens. The Stanhope image should be viewed in the best possible light, paying particular attention to the clarity of the caption. Look for those with interesting subjects and opportunities for research. When considering an Internet purchase, study the description carefully: you may learn more about the item and the seller from what is NOT mentioned. If you are puzzled, worried or mystified about some item, use the chance to question the seller via email. Those who neglect to reply should be regarded with caution. Even if you do not buy a specific item, print out the description and file it with a note of the final price achieved for future reference. No matter how many views are shown during Internet auctions, disappointment can occur when reality arrives in the post. However, you may also receive an item you have longed to add to your collection, in perfect condition and at a reasonable price! In the end, you alone make the final decision to "click the mouse". Just remember that with Stanhopes, as with any collectable, "you get what you pay for"!

(21) Caring for your Collection

Great care should be taken when handling and storing Stanhope collectables, for one must always consider the fragile structure of the microphotographic lens. It is, after all, just a tiny cylinder of glass, to which another smaller fragment was attached with Canada balsam many decades ago. The latter holds the all-important image, and once this component is dislodged or damaged, the main attraction of the novelty disappears, together with a large proportion of its value.

Handling

When examining a Stanhope souvenir, it is wise to avoid holding the item over a hard surface to view the image. Accidents can and do happen, and if dropped the impact can cause damage to either the novelty or the lens, or both. If the lens is shot out of its hole, it is occasionally possible to find it again, and provided it has survived the shock intact, it can be replaced. Unfortunately, in most instances the impact shatters the adhesive bond between the lens and the image glass, which is usually irretrievably lost because of its minute size. Should a Stanhope novelty be accidentally dropped, but the object and the lens appear unharmed, always check that the image glass is also securely in place, for otherwise its loss can remain unnoticed for some time. The soft surface of a carpet may cushion a fall, but a Stanhope lens lost in long pile is a disaster. If a number of items are being examined at one time, a plain padded cloth on the table and a sheet over the floor may provide additional insurance.

Cleaning

A large proportion of Stanhope articles are made of bone, which often becomes discoloured and appears to be in need of a good clean. Bone is a natural substance that yellows with age, and its tubular composition enables specks of dirt to become ingrained on the surface. Do not be tempted; once again the presence of the delicate lens must take priority. NEVER immerse a Stanhope novelty in water or some other cleaning fluid: even if the Canada balsam does not soften and set free the image glass, liquid can seep between it and the lens and ruin the microphotographic image. Enthusiastic rubbing to polish up some item should also be avoided, as a careless slip of the fingers can dislodge a lens. Gentle brushing with a fine soft brush can remove most dust from the cracks and fissures of the novelty.

The crazed and bubbled effect that spoils many images cannot be rectified easily, for it is due to the deterioration of the Canada balsam itself. Apparently it is possible to separate the image glass from the Stanhope lens and re-cement them together with a fresh application of Canada balsam, but few collectors possess the expertise necessary to carry out this intricate operation. However, a clearer image can be achieved simply by removing the dust of decades that

has collected on and around the lens at both ends. Stanhope collectors have their preferred methods for doing this, but that employed by Douglas Jull, Chairman of the Stanhope Collectors' Club, does produce a noticeable improvement. He advocates using a one-inch square of soft tissue, rolled tightly into a cylinder. This should be torn in half, and the torn end of one part moistened with the tip of the tongue. This can be used to brush both ends of the lens, and the process may be repeated if necessary with the second half of the tissue cylinder. Energetic rubbing or strong pressure should be avoided at all costs during this operation, particularly at the plane end of the lens, where the image glass could be dislodged.

Repair

Should a Stanhope lens become dislodged from some novelty, and you have been lucky enough to find it before it became irretrievably lost, it is possible to replace the lens successfully. A tube of strong clear liquid glue is needed, but not an extremely quick-setting "superglue". You will also need a round wooden cocktail stick and a soft cloth pad.

Do not squeeze out the glue, but dip the pointed end of the cocktail stick down into the nozzle of the tube until it reaches the glue. Rotate it until it is coated with a thin layer of glue: there should be no droplets of glue on the stick, but just a thin sticky coating. Now rotate the stick in the empty hole for the Stanhope, so that it touches against the sides of the hole and leaves a thin coating of adhesive.

Place the soft cloth pad beneath the article, so that the hole for the lens is resting against it, and gently push the lens into the hole, with the rounded magnifying end first. The cloth pad will hold the lens in place until it sticks firmly to the sides of the hole. Should there be any residue of glue left around the magnifying end of the lens, wait until it has dried just enough to be peeled away with the end of another clean cocktail stick. (Anything sharp and metal may scratch the glass.) During the entire operation, be careful never to exert any undue pressure on the cover glass at the flat end of the lens.

Storage

Do not store your Stanhope collection near a source of heat or in strong sunlight, for this may soften the Canada balsam and loosen the image glass. Stanhope novelties should not be stored loosely together, enabling them to roll around and knock against each other. The objects themselves can suffer chips and cracks, while sudden sharp taps can loosen a lens. Often the convex magnifying lens or the flat image glass can protrude slightly from the hole, and become susceptible to scratches on the glass. Both circumstances affect the clarity of the image, and a crazed cover glass, while revealing a clear image through the magnifying lens, makes photography using a microscope impossible.

Caring for Your Collection

Ideal storage for a large collection of Stanhope novelties is a cabinet of shallow drawers, felt lined and partitioned in sections of suitable sizes. In this way, each article can be seen and identified at a glance, while avoiding unnecessary handling. However, not every enthusiast has been able to amass an extensive collection, although each piece is prized and treasured. Any small sturdy container may be used for their storage, provided each item is individually protected and labelled, using soft tissue and slide-fastening plastic bags of suitable sizes. Whatever the size of the collection or the method of storage, it should permit a minimum of unwrapping and handling.

Sometimes smaller collections are arranged in purpose-made glass-topped tables. Provided the pieces rest on a padded surface and cannot roll around, this is safe and attractive storage. Dedicated collectors should be aware that this type of display invites attention from those who may not understand the fragility of prized Stanhopes!

Comment soigner une collection.

Une collection d'articles Stanhope a besoin de soins particuliers en raison de la fragilité de la lentille. Les objets ne doivent jamais être immergés dans un liquide destiné au nettoyage ou placés près d'une source de chaleur, car l'adhésif entre la lentille et le verre de l'image risque de ramollir. Ils ne doivent pas être stockés les uns à côté des autres afin d'éviter de les entrechoquer.

Chaque objet doit être étiqueté et identifié pour éviter des manipulations inutiles. Les informations concernant chaque objet doivent être soigneusement notées, notamment le prix payé, le matériau de fabrication, les dimensions et la description des vues microphotographiques. Il est recommandé de prendre des photographies des objets, pour la constitution de références et pour des raisons d'assurance. Quelques collectionneurs réussissent à prendre des photos des microvues Stanhope en utilisant un appareil photo fixé à un microscope.

Les collectionneurs d'aujourd'hui, qui savent être les heureux propriétaires des articles Stanhope doivent s'assurer que ces objets demeurent en bon état pour que les générations futures puissent apprécier le miracle des photographies miniatures du passé.

Identification

Every Stanhope novelty should bear an individual identification of its image. This is particularly important if your collection includes half a dozen bone parasol-shaped needle cases or innumerable pairs of miniature binoculars. Without adequate identification, a lot of unnecessary handling may take place when attempting to pick out the one containing a specific image. One idea is to use a small card label attached to a thread loop, such as those used as price tags on small collectables at antique fairs. The identification of the novelty can be written on one side of the label, and the image description on the other. The loop can be passed around the handle, loop or knob on the article, and can easily be removed when necessary.

Never use adhesive labels, which might damage the surface of the novelty or leave traces behind after removal. Further damage can occur if rubbing hard when trying to eliminate the sticky deposits left by the adhesive. Such labels are particularly injurious to leather or paper-covered items, rarely failing to lift off a surface layer from these materials when they are removed. As with all collectables, if offered a Stanhope item for sale bearing an adhesive label it is wise to request that the vendor should remove the label before completing the purchase.

Cataloguing

Cataloguing a collection of Stanhope novelties is even more important than with other collectables, for it will avoid undue handling of the items, while providing information and pleasure during "look and tell" sessions with fellow collectors. The following information could be recorded for every article, as and when it is purchased:

- code number of article
- type of article
- venue and date when purchased
- price
- material
- measurements
- number of views
- category of views
- description and special features of views

Those who have computers can tabulate their information however they wish, and print out an up-to-date catalogue at any time. Those who prefer to depend on traditional methods of cataloguing by hand can still find great pleasure in a clearly written card index file. Whatever the system, accurate information about one's collection should always be at hand. The worst scenario is theft, and by circulating the relevant information one can alert friends and dealers to the details of particular pieces. It is of course an invaluable record for insurance purposes.

The main record consists of a numbered list of Stanhope items in order of purchase, but this information can then be resorted and used to categorise a collection. As it grows, it will reveal interesting aspects about your own preferences, and if you wish, will be an indication of where and how to specialise. The list can be regrouped as "types of novelty" and "types of image". It has been illustrated that Stanhope novelties are represented in nearly all categories of small collectable, providing suggestions for a variety of subdivisions. Microphotographic images are mainly topographical or historical in content, but in each of these main categories there is plenty of scope for more groupings. Topographical images can include views of seaside resorts, spas, cities, battleground sites, religious shrines and any other specific tourist attractions. Historical images include portraits of royalty and those of political, heroic, theatrical or clerical personalities, monuments, cathedrals and other notable architecture, exhibitions and world fairs, shipwrecks and any newsworthy events. Nude images should probably be catalogued in a class of their own!

Most collectors try to keep abreast of current prices for items in their collections, as it is always wise to have some idea of their value. Those who use computers and the Internet to keep abreast of items sold by international auction can print out pictures of similar items and note their prices. The informed seller is more likely to ask a realistic amount for the novelty, and to achieve its proper value from the purchaser.

Photography

A photographic record of your collection is a practical idea, and many Stanhope collectors carry with them a small album to meetings or antique fairs, for immediate referral or comparison. A computer scanner and printer are even more useful, for your items can be scanned from both sides in a short time, and can also be arranged with similar novelties to illustrate different categories. With a few adjustments it is possible to scan the largest Stanhope novelties.

Photographing the microphotographic image itself is a more complicated operation, requiring considerable patience and dedication, and one must be prepared for many disappointments. Few collectors have access to the necessary specialist equipment, but nevertheless some have been fortunate enough to achieve superb reproductions of images from Stanhope items. Even so, there are some microphotographs that resist all attempts at photography, and are destined to remain viewed by the traditional method only: the naked eye.

The microphotographs produced by J.B.Dancer and his contemporaries were mounted on glass slides, which being thin and flat, can be photographed with a camera mounted on a powerful microscope with little difficulty. However, the images from Stanhope novelties are mounted at the end of a glass cylinder 6-8mm in height, and opposite a magnifying lens. These circumstances produce several complications. The magnifying lens distorts the image through the microscope, so the glass cylinder must be inverted to enable the microphotograph to be viewed at the plane surface, i.e. back to front. When the film from the camera is developed, the negative must be reversed to reveal the positive image. There is no such problem with transparencies, of course, as the slides are simply reversed in the carousel.

Damage to either end of the Stanhope lens produces an inferior photograph, but the worst results occur if the outer surface of the image glass is crazed. Viewing by eye from the magnifying end can reveal a clear undamaged picture because it has an unimpeded view. Unfortunately, to view the image in reverse under the microscope, the damaged cover glass blocks a clear view of the microphotograph. On several occasions, after vainly trying to focus the image, a check with a hand magnifier on the plane surface revealed examples of badly scratched and crazed cover glasses.

In many instances the tiny squares holding the microphotographs were cut with less than mathematical precision, so that the images were set off-centre. Occasionally the image glasses were carelessly glued to the Stanhope lenses, so that they slipped to one side and part

of the glass cylinder can be seen at the edge. Both of these situations make it very difficult to focus the microscope on the entire image.

Sometimes the Stanhope lenses themselves were inserted into their holes at a slight angle, a circumstance often found in regional souvenirs. Holes were drilled for the imported French lenses without regard for the correct diameter or length of the glass cylinders, and if these were a little smaller, the adhesive allowed them to settle at a slant. Viewed through the microscope, it can be extremely difficult to achieve the entire microphotograph in focus at the same time: it may mean a choice between a clear image and a clear caption, or between the left and right sides. A camera mounted on a microscope with two-way adjustment requires infinite patience to achieve any sort of result, but microscopes permitting complex adjustments in any direction can solve this problem.

The Stanhope article itself can prevent successful photography of the image. Dark materials, such as bog oak, olive wood or "Tyrolean" carved wood, absorb much of the microscope light directed up through the reversed Stanhope lens. Other lenses are too deep-seated, such as those in granite barrels or jet book-shaped charms, and it is rarely possible to achieve a good reproduction of the microphotographic image from such items. In some cases, it is impossible to manoeuvre the object into a suitable position to enable the microscope lens to focus on the glass cyclinder. A Stanhope lens mounted across a small knob on top of a bulky sandshaker resisted all attempts to photograph the excellent image of an ancient olive tree from the Garden of Gethsemane. Fortunately, some of the easiest items to photograph via the microscope are the ubiquitous monoculars or binoculars. They were so cleanly and skilfully turned that even now all parts can be easily unscrewed. The eyepiece containing the lens presents the flat surface held at the correct angle, while the lenses have kept very clean inside these tiny containers. As many of the most interesting images are to be found in this type of novelty, photography of miniature binoculars using a microscope has proved rewarding in many cases.

Even if a collector has no intention of parting with any item, his collection should be carefully preserved. Some of the earliest Stanhope articles are well over one hundred years old, and being relatively inexpensive novelties at the time of original purchase, they were not expected to last undamaged for any considerable length of time. They may not have been handled roughly, but several types would have been in continual use, especially penholders and paper knives. It is due to the expertise of the lens manufacturers, the clarity of the early microphotography and the final grinding of the optical workers that such a number is still in existence today. Nevertheless, many now show signs of age, particularly in the deterioration of the Canada balsam holding the image and cover glass to the rod lens. Having lasted this long, Stanhope novelties must now be gently handled and treated with care, to enable them to survive long enough for another generation to appreciate these "windows of the past".

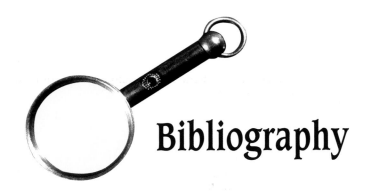

Bibliography

BOOKS

Alsford, Denis B., **Match Holders, 100 Years of Ingenuity**, Schiffer Books for Collectors

Althorp, Jean; Pollard, Nick; Pollard, Sue; Ward, Pat, **Lost Houses of Sunbury and Shepperton**, Sunbury and Shepperton Local History Society,

Baedeker, K., **Great Britain**, Karl Baedeker, Leipzig, 1910

Baedeker, K., **La Suisse**, Karl Baedeker, Leipzig, 1878

Baedeker, K. **Le Nord-Ouest de la France**, Karl Baedeker, Leipzig, 1913

Baedeker, K., **Palestine and Syria**, Karl Baedeker, Leipzig, 1898

Baedeker, K., **Paris and Its Environs**, Karl Baedeker, Leipzig, 1891, 1894

Bonnet, Laurence, **La Nacre, La Tabletterie, Le Bouton, L'Éventail**, Édition District des Sablons, 1998

Bracegirdle, Brian and McCormick, James B., **The Microscopic Photographs of J.B. Dancer**, Science Heritage Limited, Chicago, IL., U.S.A., 1993

Collins Robert, **French-English, English-French Dictionary**, London, Paris, 1990

Cruickshank, Graeme, **The Edinburgh International Exhibition of 1886 and Its Souvenir Mauchline Ware**. Mauchline Ware Collectors' Club, October 2000

Dagron, René Prudent Patrice, **Cylindres photomicroscopiques montés et non-montés sur bijoux, brevetés en France et à l'étranger**, Dagron & Cie, Paris, 1862

Dagron, René Prudent Patrice, **Traité de photographie microscopique**, Dagron & Cie, Paris, 1864

Dagron, René Prudent Patrice, **La Poste par Pigeons Voyageurs: Souvenir du Siège de Paris**, Dagron & Cie, Paris, 1871

Darrah, William C., **Cartes de Visite in Nineteenth Century Photography**, Darrah, Gettysburg, U.S.A. 1981

Druitt, Silvia, **Antique Personal Possessions**, Blandford Press, Dorset, England, 1980

Erickson, Carolly, **Her Little Majesty: the Life of Queen Victoria**, Simon and Schuster, 1997

Evans, Joan, **A History of Jewellery, 1100-1870**, Dover Publications, Inc. NY. 1989

Farrell, Jeremy, **Umbrellas and Parasols**, B .T. Batsford, Ltd., London, 1985

Field, June, **Collecting Georgian and Victorian Crafts**, Heinemann, London, 1973

Figuier, Louis, **Les Merveilles de la Science ou description populaire des inventions modernes**, Furnes, Jouvet & Cie, Paris, 1869

Garrad, Larch S., **A Present from...... Holiday Souvenirs of the British Isles**, David and Charles, Newton Abbot, Devon, England, 1976

Gaussen, Elaine, **Miller's Sewing Accessories A Collector's Guide**, Miller's, Octopus Publishing Group Ltd., 2001

Groves, Sylvia, **The History of Needlework Tools and Accessories**, Hamlyn Publishing Group, London, 1968

Hadrill, John, **Rails to the Sea**, Atlantic Publishers, 1999

Hannavy, John, **Victorian Photographers at Work**, Shire Publications, 1997

Hayhurst, J. D., **The Pigeon Post Into Paris, 1870-1871**, Hayhurst, 1970

Hickey, Kieran, **The Light of Other Days, Irish Life at the Turn of the Century in the Photographs of Robert French**, Allen Lane, 1973

Holmes, Edwin F., **Thimbles**, Gill and Macmillan Ltd., Dublin, 1976

Holmes, Edwin F., **A History of Thimbles**, Cornwall Books, London, 1985

Hough, Richard, **Victoria and Albert**, St. Martin's Press, NY. 1996

Jull, Douglas, **Collecting Stanhopes**, D.S. Publications, England, 1988 and 1997

Lothrup, Eaton S., Jr., **A Century of Cameras. From the Collection of the International Museum of Photography at George Eastman House**, Morgan & Morgan, Inc., Dobbs Ferry, NY. 1982

Luther, Frédéric, **Microfilm: A History from 1839-1900**, Barre Publishing Co., Annapolis, U.S.A., 1959

Mell, George, **Writing Antiques**, Shire Publications, England, 1980

Moore, Simon, **Penknives and Other Folding Knives**, Shire Publications, England, 1988

Muller, Helen, **Jet Jewellery and Ornaments**, Shire Publications, England, 1980

Pinto, Edward H., **Treen and Other Wooden Bygones**, G. Bell & Sons, London, 1969

Proctor, Molly, **Needlework Tools and Accessories**, B. T. Batsford Ltd., London, 1990

Rogers, Gay Ann, **An Illustrated History of Needlework Tools**, John Murray Ltd., London, 1983

Rubenstein, Bernard, **Souvenirs des bords de la mer**, Éditions Gallimard, France, 1999

Shadel Spillman, Jane, **Glass From World's Fairs, 1851-1904**, Corning Museum of Glass, Corning, NY 1986

Taunton, Nerylla, **Antique Needlework Tools and Embroideries**, Antique Collectors' Club, England, 1997

Tissandier, Gaston, **A History and Handbook of Photography**, Edited by J. Thomson, London,1876

Vatelot, Étienne, Sabatier, Françoise, **Métiers D'Art: La Tabletterie**, Société d'Encouragement aux Métiers d'Art France, 1994

Whalley, Joyce Irene, **Writing Implements and Accessories**, David and Charles, Newton Abbot, U.K. 1975

Wichard, Robin and Carol, **Victorian Cartes-de-visite**, Shire Publications, England, 1999

Zalkin, Estelle, **Thimbles and Sewing Implements**, Warman Publishing Co., Inc., Pennsylvania, U.S.A. 1988

ARTICLES

Blakeney, Anne, **Victorian Peep-shows**, Antique Collecting, U.K., March, 1974

Chauveau, Elizabeth, **The Rochard Doll of the National Museum of Monaco**, Doll Reader, November 1992

Hallett, Michael, **John Benjamin Dancer: 1812-1887**. The British Journal of Photography, April, 1989

Johnson, Mary, **Stanhopes; A Real (and rare) Button Curiosity**. National Button Bulletin, May, 1993

Kirlin, Raymond H., **Stanhopes**, Antique Trader, U.S.A., January, 1986

Kirlin, Raymond H., **Stanhopes: "Bijoux Photographica" (Photographic Jewels)**, Internet, 2001

Lee Pratt, H., **Stanhopes: Miniature Peep-eye Viewers**, The Antiques Journal, U.S.A., April, 1980

Lefebvre, Bernard, **Quel matériel utilisa Dagron pour réaliser les "dépêches" du siège de Paris en 1870?**, Photo-Club Rouennais, June, 1969

Lishman, Michael, **Paper Knives**. Journal of the Writing Equipment Society, No. 40, 1994

London, Bobbi, Zahorcak, Milan, **Images in Stanhopes**. Photographica, October, 1992

London, Bobbi, **A Visit With a Stanhope Doll**, The Photographist, Winter 1994/5

Luther, Frédéric, **René Dagron and the Siege of Paris**, American Documentation, October, 1950

Luther, Frédéric, **The Earliest Experiments in Microphotography**, Isis, Official Quarterly Journal of the History of Science Society, December, 1950

NicKenzie Lawson, Ellen, **The Brothers Langenheim (Fathers of Modern Photography)**, Pennsylvania Heritage, Quarterly of the Pennsylvania Historical and Museum Commission, Fall, 1987

Rouyer, Philippe, **L'Âge d'or du Microfilm**, Université de Paris III, 1999

Scott, Jean, **A Stanhope Survey**, The Dorset Thimble Society, May, 1993

Scott, Jean, **Stanhopes: A Closer View**, Bulletins, Thimble Collectors International, October 1993, January 1994.

Winsby, Roy, **The Microphotograph Slides of John B .Dancer and Richard Suter**, Manchester Microscopical Society Newsletter, No. 26, August, 1993

"The Peeper": Magazine of the Stanhope Collectors' Club

SOURCES

FRANCE

Musée de la Nacre et de la Tabletterie, 47, rue Salengo, 60110, Méru (l'Oise)

Musée Nicéphore Niépce, 28, quai des Messageries, 71100 Chalon-sur-Saône.

Musée Français de la Photographie, 78, rue de Paris, 91570 Bièvres.

Bibliothèque Nationale de France, Paris

Institut National de la Propriété Industrielle, 26 bis, rue de Saint-Pétersbourg, 75800 Paris.

MONACO

The National Museum of Monaco, 17, Princess Grace Avenue, Monte Carlo,

UNITED STATES OF AMERICA

International Museum of Photography and Film, George Eastman House, 900 East Avenue, Rochester, NY 14607-2298

Margaret Woodbury Strong Museum, Rochester, NY.

Rosalye Whyel Museum of Doll Art, 116-108th Avenue NE, Bellevue, WA 98004

UNITED KINGDOM

National Portrait Gallery, St. Martin's Place, London, WC2H 0HE

The National Museum of Photography, Film and Television, Pictureville, Bradford, West Yorkshire, BD1 1NQ

Distributors and Retailers of Stanhope Souvenirs

DISTRIBUTORS

*Dagron & Cie
66 rue Neuve des Petits-Champs, Paris;
34 boulevard Bonne Nouvelle, Paris

Dagron-Luzzatto;
Luzzatto; Luzzatto-Successeurs; La Photographie Industrielle
15 rue Turbigo, Paris

E. Lizé et Costil;
Établissements Lizé;
Maison Lizé
48 rue Turbigo, Paris

Maison Arnoult-Lépine;
Établissements Lecarpentier;
Établissements Maurice Lecarpentier:
15 rue Beranger, Paris

P. Adry; L.Legorgeu-Successeur
13 rue Beranger, Paris

Maison Deruaz;
F. Roussarie-Successeur:
13-15 rue du Pont-aux-Choux, Paris

Bernard: 14 boulevard de Belleville, Paris

Établissements
A. Grand-Perret et Fils
St. Claude, Jura

*W. C. McKee: 5 Sackville Street Lower, Dublin

*I. B. & M. Co., Dublin

*C. R. & Co., London

*C. T. & R.

*H. S. & Co

S.W. & Co., Dublin

John H. Morrow
New York City, U.S.A.

* Denotes distributors named on captions of Stanhopes. All others have been recorded from invoices and other evidence.

RETAILERS

UNITED KINGDOM

Barnby & Co:
New Arcade, Birmingham

J. E. Beale, The Fancy Fair (sometimes "Novelty Stores"): Bournemouth

W. M. Bell, Penny Bazaar:
Broadwater Church, Worthing

W. J. Blacket, Bookseller, Stationer & Printer:
34 Northbrook Street, Newbury

C. Belsher: 19 Seaside Road, Eastbourne

T. W. Brand, Bookseller:
Wooler

W. Brooker: Terminus Road, Eastbourne

W. C. Cobb: Fancy Bazaar, Wisbeck

G. K. Cottman,
The S.P.Q.R. Shop:
74 St. Mary St., Weymouth

W. Coupe: Eastbourne

F. Dabell: Arcade, Sandown, Isle of Wight

F. Davies: Dawlish

Dowsett: Southend

J. E. Drew, Serpentine Works: Penzance

J. Dunster: Minster Gate & Lendal Bridge, York

Dyke: Frome

Findlow, Microphoto:
Warwick, Isle of Man

E. Gardner:
28 George St., Hastings

F. Herrmann's Toy & Fancy Warehouses:
46 Queens's Rd. & 57 George Street, Hastings

Hills Department Store:
Blackpool Bazaar

F. C. Hodder:
Sunningdale

Idiens the Bazaar:
Broadstairs

W. Lawrence: Dublin

J. Levy: London

W. C. Lyon Fancy Repository: Olney

Masons Art Repository:
The Lake District

John MacDonald, Cabinet maker:
Fort Augustus, Caledonian Canal

McRoss: Dublin

E. Moor: Hastings

Mowll Fancy Bazaar:
Folkestone

J. Oliver: 8 London Road, St. Leonards

Palmers Plaza:
High St., Hythe

J. Parkinson:
Newell St., Southport

The Misses Parsonsons Bazaar: Sudbury

W. J. Pettit, The Agricultural Institute:
Dover

Philpots Fancy Bazaar:
Herne Bay

J. Pulsford: Eastbourne

A Savage: Oxford

Scotchers Fancy Repository: Holywell

W. Bury Shaw:
206 & 208 Western Rd., Brighton

H. Snelling: Chain Pier Bazaar, Brighton

Stephen & Co., Toy and Fancy Dealers:
Arcade, Cardiff

W. Swaysland:
West Pier, Brighton

W. F. Taylor:
13 High Street, Windsor

J. Theobald & Co:
Queen Victoria Jubilee

J. Thompson,
Post Office & Library:
Church St., Malvern

Twiss Bros: Ilfracombe

Philip Uptons Fancy Bazaar: Folkestone

Walford Arcade:
Folkestone

William Walker & Sons: Kirkgate

G. Ward, Booksellers:
11 Broad Gate, Coventry

Wearing Bazaar:
The Lake District

Webb Lounge: Strand St., Douglas, Isle of Man

A. White:
S. Margate Bazaar

S. Whiteman: 1 York Buildings, Hastings

FRANCE

Emile Pulleys: Calais

H. Sevestre,
Au Gagne-Petit; Cabourg

Soulard:
122 Grand Rue, Dieppe

ELSEWHERE

J. W. Soper: Soper's Curios, Victoria Falls

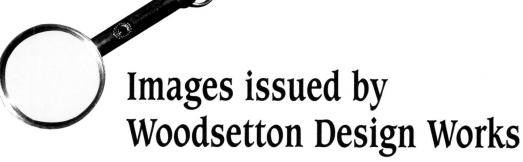

Appendix II

Images issued by Woodsetton Design Works

10. S.S. Great Britain (1983)	62. England Cricket	111. Four Generations: Queen Victoria
11. St. Chads Coseley 1884-1984	63. Alton Towers	112. Edward VIII and George VI
12. Greenwich Meridian Centenary	64. Elizabeth	113. Ruby Wedding 1987
13. Guernsey	65. Alton Towers	114. Princess Royal 1987
14. Lindau am Bodensee	66. Avebury and Silbury Hill	115. Princess Royal 1987
15. Amsterdam Rijksmuseum	67. West Indies Test 1986	116. Charles and Diana
16. Legislative Buildings Victoria B.C.	68. Lincoln Cathedral 1072	117. Andrew and Sarah
17. Empress Hotel Victoria BC	69. Coventry Cathedral	118. The Queen and Prince Philip
18. Fable Cottage Victoria BC	70. Osborne House	119. Wendy Flies Away: Peter Pan
19. Wax Museum, Victoria BC	71. Curiosity Corner	120. Robert Burns
20. Birmingham International 1984	72. The Puppy in the Garden	121. Bob Geldof
21. Royal London Wax Museum	73. The Red Queen	122. Scottish Highlands
22. Sky Ride Vancouver B.C.	74. The Mad Hatter's Tea Party	123. Titanic
23. Pope John Paul II	75. Lace Pillow	124. Honeybee
24. Capilan Bridge	76. Lichfield	125. Australia Bi-Centenary 1988
25. Prince Henry	77. Padstow	126. Margaret Thatcher 1987
26. Prince Henry	78. Prins Claus 1986	127. Page 3 Nude
27. Harrods	79. Brighton	128. Statue of Liberty
28. Macys	80. Andrew and Sarah: Engagement	129. Kennedy
29. Statue of Liberty	81. Andrew and Sarah: Wedding	130. U.S.S. Constitution 1797
30. Charles : Royal Family	82. Andrew and Sarah: Wedding	131. Dusseldorf
31. New Lanark	83. Andrew and Sarah: Wedding	132. Dusseldorf
32. Christmas 1984	84. Royal Baby 1988	133. Lacemaker: frivolité
33. Pope John Paul II	85. - - - - -	134. Bet and Alec: Coronation Street
34. Charles II	86. - - - - -	135. Christmas 1987
35. John O'Groats	87. The Glass House Cone	136. Bing Crosby: White Christmas
36. John F. Kennedy	88. Morwellham Quay	137. Monty
37. Johann S. Bach	89. The Barbican Plymouth	138. Gorbachev and Reagan 1987
38. Yeovil	90. Thermos Gas Barbecues	139. Eamonn Andrews
39. Exeter	91. Margaret Thatcher	140. Elvis
40. - - - - -	92. H.M.S. Warrior	141. The Windmill
41. The Mad Hatter's Tea Party	93. Christmas 1986	142. Dutch Winter
42. The Walrus and the Carpenter	94. Cinderella	143. Dutch Costume
43. Jabberwocky	95. Derby Cathedral	144. Koningin Beatrix
44. Christmas 1985	96. Connemara	145. Prins Claus
45. Ian Botham: John O'Groats	97. The Lord's Prayer	146. Duchess of Windsor
46. Drayton Manor	98. Mt. Rushmore	147. Charles and Diana: Australia 1988
47. Drayton Manor: Sir Robert Peel	99. Virgin Atlantic Flyer	148. The Ten Commandments
48. Spilsby	100. Queen Elizabeth II,. Prince Philip	149. Peter Pan
49. St. Mawes Cornwall	101. Prince and Princess of Wales	150. Coronation Street
50. Cheltenham	102. Victoria	151. The Lord's Prayer
51. Sidmouth	103. Victoria	152. Marriage Vows
52. Lyme Regis	104. Prince and Princess of Wales and Prince William	153. Baptism Prayer
53. Combe Martin	105. Royal Princes 1984	154. Armistice 70th Anniversary 1988
54. Ilfracombe	106. Duke of York and Queen Elizabeth II	155. Wales 1988
55. Colyton	107. Queen Elizabeth II	156. French Revolution
56. Dunster	108. Prince and Princess of Wales and the Royal Princes	157. Bush and Reagan
57. Heights of Abraham: Matlock	109. Prince Charles and his Family	158. Olympics 1988
58. Boston Lincs.	110. The Queen in China	159. William and Mary
59. Rembrandt		160. Your Pub Needs You
60. Wombourne		161. Birmingham: Old Crown
61. Sail '85		162. Birmingham: Town Hall

131

Images issued by Woodsetton Design Works

163. - - - - -
164. - - - - -
165. - - - - -
166. - - - - -
167. Rosemary
168. Sir Francis Drake
169. Claudette
170. Before the Ball
171. Les Girls
172. Ladies : Arts Nouveau
173. - - - - -
174. Boris Becker
175. Stourbridge Warehouse
176. Statue of Liberty Centenary (1985)
177. Cutty Sark
178. Wolverhampton Millenium
179. Great Western Railway
180. The Bruhemsmack Provident
181. Humber Cars
182. The Mayflower
183. H.M.S. Victory
184. Morris Minor
185. Anyone for tennis?
186. The Flower Girl
187. Golf: Fashion for Sportsmen
188. Fashions for 1926
189. Daimler 3?
190. Bedford Cars 1910
191. Wallis's 1927
192. Derry and Toms 1927
193. Hats for 1910
194. Fashion and the Corset 1910
195. Cars Veteran and Vintage
196. English Bobbin Lace
197. Victorian Steam Launches
198. Canals: Boating for Pleasure
199. Canals: Working Narrow Boats
200. - - - - -
201. City of Bath
202. York Minster
203. Cotswolds: Blenheim and Bourton
204. Cotswold Villages: Bourton, Slaughter, Woodstock,
205. Cotswolds: Bourton and Slaughter
206. - - - - -
207. Wiltshire: Laycock, Bidderstone, Badminton, Castle Combe
208. Wiltshire: Corsham, Laycock
209. Wiltshire: Castle Combe
210. City of Chester
211. City of Chester
212. Oxford
213. Constable Country
214. Tewkesbury
215. Worcester
216. Windsor Castle
217. Leeds Castle Kent
218. Oxfordshire: Blenheim, Woodstock
219. Warwick
220. Stratford-upon-Avon
221. Shakespeare Family Houses

222. Shakespeare
223. Ironbridge
224. Wightwick Manor
225. Wolverhampton G.S.
226. Tettenhall
227. Black Country Museum
228. Earl of Dudley
229. Dudley Town
230. London: Houses of Parliament, St. Pauls, Buckingham Palace
231. London: Tower, Westminster Abbey, Old Curiosity Shop
232. London: St. Pauls, Trafalgar Square, Bank
233. London: Tower Bridge, Greenwich Maritime Museum, Observatory
234. London: Tower, British Museum, Kensington Palace
235. London: Westminster Abbey, Tower, Tower Bridge
236. London: Greenwich Museum, Cutty Sark, Observatory
237. Keswick
238. Leeds Castle
239. - - - - -
240. City of York
241. Harrogate & Knaresborough
242. Wright Refractories
243. Steffi Graf
244. Stefan Edberg
245. Secrets
246. WRNS
247. Beccles
248. Stone Mountain Georgia
249. Christmas Day 1990
250. Royal Baby: Eugenie 1990
251. Caramel Peaches
252. French Onion Soup
253. Crunchy Salad
254. Smoked Mackerel Paté
255. Fudge and Walnut Ice Cream
256. Le Louvre
257. Margaret Thatcher 10 years at No.10
258. Gorbachev Meets the Queen
259. George Washington
260. Irma la Douce 1988
261. Fox-Talbot
262. Irma la Douce
263. Irma la Douce
264. Moon Landing
265. Harewood House
266. The Thimblemakers
267. Austin Mini
268. War Declaration 1939
269. Wimbledon 1989
270. Sir Laurence Olivier
271. Stourbridge 1912 (1989)
272. Brandenburg Gate
273. The Seamstress (1991)
274. Busy Fingers (1990)
275. The Queen Mother is 90!
276. Scottish Champions 1990

277. Princess Royal in Russia
278. Princess Royal 40th Birthday
279. Home Guard 1940
280. Battle of Britain 1940
281. The Queen 1926
282. The Queen 1933
283. Coronation 1937
284. War ATS 1944
285. Royal Wedding 1947
286. Royal Baby - Charles 1948
287. Royal Baby - Anne 1950
288. Coronation 1953
289. Andrew and Edward
290. Silver Jubilee 1977
291. Ruby Wedding
292. The Queen 1990
293. Kernewek Lowender (Australia)
294. Indy Car Race Australia
295. Lindau Bodensee
296. Deutschland
297. Graham Gooch
298. John Lennon
299. Channel Tunnel Breakthrough Dec.1990
300. Margaret Thatcher 1979-1990
301. Bugs Bunny
302. Daffy Duck
303. Sylvester
304. Tweety Pie
305. Porky Pig
306. Road Runner
307. Elmer Fudd
308. Yosemite Sam
309. Surfers' Paradise
310. Fishermans Wharf
311. Gulf War
312. Dedham
313. Beatrix-Claus
314. Queen Elizabeth II: 65
315. Prince Philip: 70
316. Diana: 30
317. Charles and Diana: 10th anniversary
318. Andrew Jackson 1829
319. Dedham Church
320. Windsor Castle
321. Columbus (1991)
322. Lavenham Suffolk (1991)
323. President Lincoln (1992)
324. Queen for 40 Years (1992)
325. Fingerhut Museum Creglingen
326. Dedham Church
327. Civil War (1992)
328. President Thomas Jefferson (1992)
329. Alnwick Castle
330. Marilyn Monroe
331. Gloucester Cathedral (1993)
332. - - - - -
333. - - - - -
334. Queen Mother: 101 (2001)
335. Time is
336. Cliff Richard
337. Queen: Jubilee (2002)

Index

Italic numbers indicate Illustrated Plates

Index